THE SILENCE OF JESUS:
THE AUTHENTIC VOICE
OF THE HISTORICAL MAN

JAMES   BREECH

THE SILENCE OF
JESUS

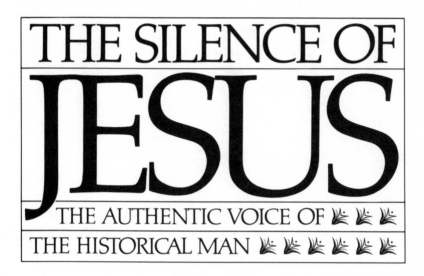

THE AUTHENTIC VOICE OF
THE HISTORICAL MAN

FORTRESS PRESS   PHILADELPHIA

First Fortress Press Edition 1983
Designed by John Zehethofer

Library of Congress Cataloging in Publication Data

Breech, James.
  The silence of Jesus.

  Includes index.
  1. Jesus Christ — Parables.   2. Jesus Christ —
Words.   3. Jesus Christ — Character.   4. Bible. N.T.
Gospels — Criticism, interpretation, etc. I. Title.
BT375.2.B73   1983   226′.806   82-71825
ISBN 0-8006-0691-4 (U.S.)

9609182   Manufactured in Canada   1-691

For Tricia

Contents

Acknowledgements

I would like to acknowledge my debt of gratitude to those from whose learning I have benefited during the course of my quest for the elusive reality of Jesus. These include my teachers: Professor Amos Wilder (Harvard University), who also offered helpful suggestions on the composition of this book; Professors Arthur McGill, Helmut Koester, George MacRae, and Krister Stendahl (all of Harvard University); Professor Franklin Young (then at Princeton University, now at Duke University); and Professors David Belyea and Marshall McLuhan (University of Toronto).

There are a number of scholars whose work has entered into my thinking about the historical Jesus, but since I have decided to keep footnotes to a minimum, I would like to indicate my indebtedness to their work at this point: Amos Wilder, Robert Funk, Rudolf Bultmann, Dan Via, C.H. Dodd, Joachim Jeremias, Norman Perrin, and John Dominic Crossan.

This book might never have been published were it not for the editorial encouragement and gracious assistance of Jonathan Lovat Dickson of Doubleday. I would also like to thank Mr. Norman Hjelm of Fortress Press for his editorial advice.

I began writing this book while holding a Leave Fellowship from the Social Sciences and Humanities Research Council of Canada, which also funded my research project, *Sourcebook on Parabolic Narrative*. While the results of this project are not yet published, comparative analysis of the parables of Jesus with those of other ancient storytellers was an important ingredient in the development of my thinking about the parables, and I am grateful to the SSHRCC for their generous financial support.

Excerpts from "East Coker" and "Little Gidding" by T.S. Eliot are reprinted from his volume *Four Quartets* by permission of Harcourt Brace Jovanovich, Inc. and of Faber and Faber Publishers; copyright 1943 by T.S. Eliot; copyright renewed 1971 by Esme Valerie Eliot.

Passages from the Constance Garnett translation of *The Brothers Karamazov* by Fyodor Dostoyevsky are used with the permission of Random House, Inc.

Excerpts from "As Kingfishers Catch Fire . . ." and "Pied Beauty" by Gerard Manley Hopkins, now available in a fourth edition (1967) of *The Poems of Gerard Manley Hopkins* edited by W.H. Gardner and H.H. MacKenzie, published by Oxford University Press for the

Society of Jesus, are used with the permission of Oxford University Press.

Passages quoted from *Madame Bovary* by Gustave Flaubert, translated by Lowell Blair, are used with the permission of Bantam Books, Inc.

Lines quoted from *Surfacing,* by Margaret Atwood, are used with the permission of McClelland and Stewart Limited.

Quotations from Charles Baudelaire's "On the Essence of Laughter," translated by Jonathan Mayne, are used with the permission of Phaidon Press Limited.

The excerpt from *In Cold Blood*, by Truman Capote, is reprinted with the permission of Random House, Inc.

Quotations from *The Anti-Christ* by Friedrich Nietzsche are taken from *Twilight of the Idols/The Anti-Christ,* translated by R.J. Hollingdale, and used with the permission of Penguin Books, Ltd.

The passage quoted from *Being and Nothingness,* by Jean-Paul Sartre, translated by Hazel E. Barnes, is used with the permission of Philosophical Library, Inc.

Passages quoted from *Ressentiment,* by Max Scheler, translated by William W. Holdheim, are used with the permission of Francke Verlag.

Sayings from "The Gospel of Thomas," translated by Thomas O. Lambdin, are taken from *The Nag Hammadi Library in English,* edited by James M. Robinson, and are used with the permission of E.J. Brill.

Translations of the sayings and parables from the original Greek are the author's own, but, in accordance with good scholarly practice, do follow as closely as possible those of the Revised Standard Version of the Bible, copyrights 1946, 1952, (c) 1971, 1973 by the Division of Christian Education of the Churches of Christ in the U.S.A., and are used by permission.

The quotation from David Magarshack's "Introduction" to *The Brothers Karamazov* is used with the permission of Penguin Books Ltd.

Introduction

The elusive reality of the historical Jesus

In beginning this book about the parables and sayings of Jesus, I find myself in somewhat of a quandary. No doubt prospective readers will have a number of questions that they would like to have answered at the outset. After all, it has become customary these days before taking a trip to work out a fairly detailed itinerary, and there are some travellers who even go so far as to read every book available about the place they will be visiting so that they will know what to expect and what to look for when they arrive at their destination. I prefer to read them when I return home.

My dilemma regarding an introduction is caused partly because I am someone who thinks of writing, like travelling, as exploration — I find the process of discovery exciting. That applies to other things as well. I do not like to read movie reviews before seeing a film, even though my interest in techniques of narration has led me to spend a lot of time in recent years at the cinema. So I am hesitant to say anything at this point that would interfere with my readers' opportunity to make discoveries of their own. I am also reticent about making things easy. Clarity is an ideal, but simplification is something I avoid because "simple" happens to be a word that I find personally distasteful. To me, it suggests the trivial, the commonplace, the uncomplicated, the unintelligent, all that is unelaborate and hence lacking in refinement. I will at all times attempt to be clear, but will never knowingly avoid the complex. Hence, I have written for a literate, presumably college-educated reader who, I

1

hope, will share my preference for the complex, and my liking for discovery. Therefore, although *The Silence of Jesus* utilizes the whole range of historical-critical methods employed by New Testament scholars involved in the quest for the historical Jesus, this book is not written primarily for my colleagues in the field. The sorts of methodological argumentation, engagement with past and current scholarly theories, and the extensive documentation that characterize New Testament scholarship are better left to the appropriate scholarly media. However, in addition to the methods of biblical scholarship, I have employed philosophy, phenomenology, hermeneutics, literary analysis, psychology and theology; but at the same time I have written for the reader who does not necessarily have a knowledge of these specialized intellectual disciplines. Thoughtfulness, intelligence, and curiosity can carry the reader through these pages. Indeed, the reader for whom I have written is one who might be found on any given afternoon in a good bookstore, browsing. Let us agree on a preview of the route we will be taking. What, then, of my introduction; what belongs to it?

Given the nature of the subject matter, the questions which I foresee being asked are as such: "Isn't everything there is to know about Jesus contained in the gospels? Anyway, did he not use pictures from our familiar, everyday world to illustrate ideas that are so simple and clear that even a child could understand them? Why then should I spend time and energy reading a book about things that are by now commonplace?"

Why, indeed, would anyone devote time and effort to learning what everyone already knows? I, too, used to think that nothing new could possibly be said about Jesus, certainly nothing very interesting. That was, until I encountered an image of Jesus which was utterly unlike any other conception of him—even more dissimilar than, for example, Salvador Dali's "Last Supper" is from Leonardo da Vinci's, or Georges Rouault's faces of Christ are from the Byzantine frescoes of the imperial Christ. Usually Jesus is represented as an object of worship, an authority figure, or a teacher, but Dostoyevsky portrays Jesus in *The Brothers Karamazov* (a book I read twenty years ago as a young man) as someone who fully understood the human heart, who therefore remained silent when condemned for refusing to resolve mankind's problems.

This cryptic figure so intrigued my young mind that I set out on a long journey, the purpose of which was to prepare for the opportune moment when Jesus might break his silence and speak openly of what he knew. During the course of my journey, I have learned the languages and methods of New Testament scholarship in order to engage in historical Jesus research, and have continued to read extensively in all the humanistic fields. I felt that if Jesus were indeed so exceptional and original, then I would have to do everything possible to prepare myself for discovering the un-expected. This might seem a contradiction in terms, but in fact learning how to apprehend what is strange and unfamiliar is the most difficult discipline of all.

I would like to clarify immediately that my interest in the figure of Jesus was not originally academic or denominational at all, and that I therefore had no vested interest in the outcome. I was so concerned, in fact, not to develop any stake in the outcome that I did a doctorate of philosophy at Harvard University. If Jesus turned out to be nothing more than an itinerant first-century miracle-working rabbi who used homely metaphors to illustrate his simple ideas about God, man, and religion, then nothing was lost because I could always turn my attention to many other interesting intellec-tual problems.

I have been sustained in my efforts by the piquant possibility that Jesus might be more complex and original than commonly supposed. What if the earliest Christians turned out to be right in holding that his parables were not at all so simple and clear, but were in fact extraordinarily difficult to penetrate?

It was not until recently, after two decades of intense preoccupa-tion with questions connected with historical Jesus research, on the one hand, and with efforts to understand better the heart of man, on the other, that Jesus' parables and sayings began to break their silence. As it happened, this began to occur quite recently, during long walks on the beach at Kailua, as I pondered the parables which I had committed to memory. The more I puzzled over them, the more curious they seemed—unusual, exceptional, and singular. The more I lived with them, the stranger they became. And as that occurred, the muffling mute of familiarity started to fall away.

During those visits to Hawaii to lecture, my students came not only from the mainland, but from Tonga, the Philippines, China, Japan and Korea. They ranged in background from the Dean of the Anglican cathedral to a Samoan minister with a grade school education, a student who already had a doctorate from Claremont and another who had written his doctoral dissertation on the most influential New Testament scholar and theologian of the twentieth century, Rudolf Bultmann. The atmosphere was congenial to the asking of new questions, and necessitated listening closely to unfamiliar voices. In retrospect, I think, this meeting of East and West provided the occasion for breaking free from the presuppositions which control the predominantly Western quest for the historical Jesus.

Those readers with some knowledge of antiquity will realize that first-century Galilee and Judea belonged culturally to the Ancient Near East, not to the West, even though the area had been thoroughly influenced by Hellenism, and at the time was under Roman sovereignty. The possibility that there was something in Jesus' parables and sayings that remains foreign to our Western habits of thought could easily go unnoticed because his words have been transmitted to us in gospel narratives composed by Greek-speaking Christians.

Both the Christ of the Western churches and the Jesus pursued by contemporary scholarship are the products of specifically Western conceptions. But what if, for example, it should turn out that Jesus did not dispose his reality in such a way that he would constitute what we would think of as a "personage" in the Western sense? What if our historical-critical methods were capable only of reconstructing a "Jesus of history", but missed his elusive reality? This is the possibility that presented itself to me as I walked and thought on the beach.

Once, while I was at Princeton, I went to hear W.H. Auden read some of his latest poetry. The lecture hall was jammed with hundreds of people, all of whom were very animated with expectation. Auden read in a voice so still that almost at once people began trying to repeat to each other what they thought he had said, and in almost no time it was impossible for those at any distance from the podium to hear any but intermediary voices. In a completely quite room the speaker could have been heard, but the general hubbub rendered his voice inaudible.

If we want to hear what a speaker is saying while others are talking, even though they are trying to be helpful, their voices distract our attention and interfere with our listening. In order for the speaker's own voice to be heard, the go-betweens must be silent.

Who but a boor would raise his voice in order to force an audience to listen? Those who really have something significant to say are usually best able to keep silence. Jesus does not impose himself, does not raise his voice, but is keeping silent until the audience is prepared to listen. For those who are willing to pay attention, I hope the voice which originally uttered these parables and sayings will be heard once again, revealing its elusive reality.

Early Christianity and the earthly, human Jesus

What does the literature of the early Christian movement tell us about Jesus? Scholars involved in the scientific quest for the historical Jesus fall basically into two groups, those holding that Jesus was the founder of Christianity, and those asserting that Christianity began only with the resurrection experiences. In spite of their differences on this point, virtually all New Testament scholars would distinguish between the Jesus of history and the Christ believed in by Christians, and would insist, often to the dismay of theologians and pastors, that the faithful should be willing to expose their beliefs to the historical Jesus reconstructed by scholarship, because only in that way can they avoid worshipping an image made in their own likeness.

I would like to state at the outset that my interest in Jesus does not derive from a concern with inter-Christian debate concerning the distinction between the Jesus of history and the Christ of faith, even though I must, in so far as I function as a New Testament scholar, deal with this.

During the last hundred and fifty years, scholarship has made tremendous progress in producing new knowledge about the history and literature of the early Christian movement.[1] This progress has been facilitated in part by discoveries of new materials (such as the Dead Sea Scrolls at Qumran and the Coptic Gnostic library at Nag Hammadi in Egypt), and partly by the development and refinement of critical methods used in the analysis of previously known sources. However, no new sources have appeared for knowledge about the historical Jesus, except the so-called Gospel of Thomas, which I shall discuss in Chapter Six. For the

1. For a state of the art presentation of the materials and issues, the reader is advised to consult Helmut Koester's epochal *Introduction to the New Testament* (Philadelphia: Fortress Press, 1982).

most part, we remain dependent now, as we have for almost two thousand years, on the canonical gospel narratives.

The difficulty that arises in using these sources historiographically is that they were produced by people who believed in Jesus as the Christ, as the source for their own teachings, and as the model for their own religious practices. Yet the early Christian gospels are not historical biographies of Jesus, and they do not provide the information necessary for reconstructing a "life" of Jesus. They are "gospels," that is, they *proclaim* a religious *message* about Jesus in narrative form. They express the significance which the early Christians found in Jesus. To be sure, they are written in a genre which appeals to historical truth, but they are not *history* in the scientific sense. Rather, they express an understanding of what happened in the experience of people living in the first century; and for them, what occurred was the revelation of the divine. In short, the gospels are primarily valuable for what they tell us about what the early Christians *believed* about Jesus.

Since our only access to the historical Jesus is through the literature produced by those who believed in him and who propagated a religious movement in his name, we must employ the analytical techniques used by New Testament scholars in order to discriminate between the words of Jesus and the words of his worshippers. Along the way, we will need to learn something of the history of the early Christian movement and of the structure and dynamics of his worshippers' faith, for only then can we hope to disentangle the reality of Jesus from the Christ of faith.

The historical-critical methods of biblical scholarship have been very successful in reconstructing the diversity of early Christian belief in Jesus as the Christ, and in outlining the development of Christian traditions concerning him. The origins and history of the early Christian movement can be traced with a relatively high degree of certainty.

It was not until thirty-five years after the death of Jesus that the first gospel, Mark, was composed (about A.D. 65). Between the death of Jesus and the composition of the first gospel, Christian missionaries and preachers told stories about Jesus in order to communicate to their listeners the significance they saw in him. Christian teachers also interpreted and explained his sayings and parables, sometimes paraphrasing them, sometimes adding to them by way of clarification, and sometimes employing popular proverbs and maxims for illustration (for example: "No one sews a piece of unshrunk cloth on an old garment," or "No one puts new wine into old wineskins," or "Those who are well have no need of a physician").

But the earliest Christian communities were not dependent solely on memories and interpretations of the words of the earthly Jesus, because they enjoyed the experience of his continuing presence with them. They lived out of the awareness that he had been raised from the dead. Consequently, the risen Lord Jesus could speak, when necessary, through the mouth of one of the community's prophets, just as Yahweh had spoken to his people through the prophets of Israel. For example, the apostle Paul, writing 1 Corinthians in the mid-50's A.D., before any of the extant gospels, repeatedly distinguishes between pronouncements of his own on questions regarding proper ethical behaviour and words of the risen Lord Jesus which had been delivered to the community through the mouth of a prophet (cf., 1 Cor. 7:10, 12, 25). As late as the end of the first century, a Christian prophet named John had a revelation from the risen Lord Jesus, who appeared to him and dictated letters to seven Christian communities (the Book of Revelation).

Since the early Christians did not distinguish between the risen Lord Jesus and the earthly Jesus—in their experience he was one and the same person—they also did not distinguish between the words of the risen Lord and the sayings of the earthly Jesus. Nor, for that matter, did they distinguish between the sayings of the earthly Jesus and the explanations, interpretations, and illustrations of them offered by their inspired teachers. Thus the sayings of the earthly Jesus, along with early Christian interpretations of them, various popular proverbial sayings and maxims, and the words of the risen Lord Jesus, were all collected together and eventually written down. The primary collection of these sayings was a source which scholars designate Q (from the German for "source," "Quelle"). All of these materials entered into the gospel tradition at various stages, and are extremely useful in reconstructing the history and theology of the early Christian movement. However, in this book my concern is not with the earliest Christians' understanding of Jesus, nor with words of the risen Lord Jesus, but with the parables and sayings of the earthly, human Jesus. When we question, then, the authenticity of a saying or parable, we are really asking whether it was uttered by the *earthly* Jesus. Whether the saying or parable in question may have been spoken to the community through one of its prophets or inspired teachers is another matter entirely.

The authors of the gospels were actually anonymous, but we use the traditional names (Mark, Matthew, Luke, and John) for convenience's sake. We call the first three gospels (Matthew, Mark, and Luke) the synoptic gospels because they share common souces and can be analyzed comparatively (syn-optically).

The author of Mark composed his narrative using stories about Jesus produced during the first three decades of the Christian movement in order to express his understanding of Jesus as the Christ. He either did not know, or did not choose to utilize, Q. But ten years later, the author of Matthew expanded Mark's gospel using Q and other traditional materials. About five or ten years later still, the author of Luke-Acts (a two-volume work produced by the same person) also published a revised and expanded version of Mark, using Q, additional traditions about Jesus, and stories dealing with the spread of the Christian communities (actually, the term "Christianity" was used for the first time to designate the movement in the latter part of the first century, but, again, I use the term for convenience).

Although our knowledge of the history and traditions of earliest Christianity is reasonably secure, research has not been so successful in achieving a consensus regarding the historical Jesus, and hence the reality of Jesus has proved to be very elusive indeed. Part of the reason for this, I believe, is that the usual procedure in historical Jesus research is to start by building a hypothetical picture of the historical context through analysis of the synoptic traditions, and then to interpret Jesus' parables and sayings in the light of that reconstructed framework. Since all meaning is established with reference to the context of utterances, this procedure has a certain logic to it. However, the methodological difficulty with this means of approach is that a hypothesis (i.e., that which is relatively *un*certain) controls the interpretation of what we do know (i.e., that which is relatively more certain).

My procedure will be to begin with the parables and sayings themselves, and to admit as certain only those elements of the historical situation to which *Jesus himself refers*. This will allow us to start with what is relatively more secure and only then to proceed to what is relatively less secure rather than vice versa, as has been customary in historical research. This strategy involves keeping assumptions and hypotheses to a minimum, and requires that we listen closely to Jesus' own words in order to learn about the historical speaker. It will sometimes be difficult to block out and to suspend preconceptions we might have derived about the historical situation from the gospel narratives, but it will be remembered that the sayings of Jesus originally circulated without any historical or interpretive context, and that these were provided later by the Christian teachers and preachers, and then by the evangelists. In other words, the picture of Jesus and of his ministry that we receive from the synoptic tradition is one that was created during the thirty-five to fifty years during which the Christian movement burgeoned, when the various groups who collected, transmitted, and glossed the sayings of Jesus were eager to demonstrate that his sayings and practice provided the basis for their own teachings. In our interpretation and analysis of Jesus' parables and sayings we cannot, therefore, be guided by the contexts created by the early Christians. We must attend only to his own words. What material, then, will we consider?

The core material

The Silence of Jesus will deal with a selection of eight sayings and twelve parables. Virtually all scholars working in the field would agree that *at least* these sayings and parables are authentic. I therefore designate these sayings and parables as the core material, because anyone interested in the figure of the earthly Jesus must come to terms with it.

This approach has two purposes. In the first place, it avoids the controversy surrounding the question of the criteria which are valid for determining authentic material. Rather than debating which sayings are authentic and which are not, which are the products of early Christianity or borrowed from the contemporary world and attributed to Jesus, I propose to begin with the core material; its authenticity is as far beyond reasonable doubt as is possible in historical research.

In the second place, this material, as we shall see, is remarkably free of the language and concepts of the early Christian movement and also remarkably free of the language known to us from the contemporary literature of the period. In other words, the core material is the least derivative, the most singular in the New Testament. There is, of course, a certain danger in this approach, because it is hypothetically possible that Jesus did sometimes repeat the language and ideas of his contemporaries, and it is also hypothetically possible that he used language which subsequently became current in the Christian movement. I believe that we will never have any sure basis for testing either hypothesis until we fully comprehend the meaning and significance of the core material. If Jesus did share much in common with his contemporaries and worshippers, then the core material will provide many points of smooth transition to other sayings and parables attributed to him. But we will never know whether or not this is the case unless we begin at a relatively secure starting point, that is, with the core material. Once this material has been analyzed and interpreted, it would be legitimate to head gradually outward from the core towards the periphery, testing centrifugal material for its coherence with the core as one moves along.

Interpreting the core material

The prevailing view of the historical Jesus held by a consensus of New Testament scholars today is that he preached a message which in its essentials reflects an understanding of reality congruent with that of his first-century contemporaries. Based on this view, the task of interpretation is taken to involve, to put it simply, first determining what his words meant in a first-century Palestinian context and then asking what they might mean when translated into the twentieth century. According to this view of interpretation —this hermeneutic—interpretation means translation of a past into a present meaning.

My own view is somewhat different. I have come to believe that in Jesus' sayings and parables he disclosed dimensions of reality that are not historically determined *in toto*, dimensions that have also been grasped, in part, however fragmentarily and obscurely, by others—novelists, poets, and philosophers, in subsequent periods and different cultures.

Therefore in order to illuminate these special phenomena which are not ordinarily stressed, I have throughout this book drawn also on the works of those who have been capable of pointing to this or that aspect of the same realities. In other words, I do not conceive of

10

the task of understanding Jesus' sayings and parables as requiring us to learn to think like first-century people, but rather of requiring us to learn to perceive those special areas of human experience toward which Jesus' words direct our attention. To be sure, during the last two thousand years these novelists, poets, and philosophers have functioned within a tradition of construing reality which was inaugurated by Jesus himself. But then if these others have seen in part that which Jesus has seen in whole, their perceptions can be of assistance to us in our effort to understand the core material.

If the reality of Jesus is elusive, perhaps that is because that to which he referred normally escapes our grasp. This is a fundamental tenet of my interpretation.

How do we get to where we are not from where we are?[2] The journey, if it is to be one of discovery, will entail a certain amount of dispossession, that is, of a readiness to re-examine and perhaps to abandon the assumptions which inform our customary modes of questioning. The questions we ask will always determine more or less the kind of answers we receive. In order to prepare ourselves to see that which is unfamiliar, and to hear that which is strange to our ears, we will have to question our questions. Anyone preparing to search for the elusive reality of Jesus must be prepared to re-examine those assumptions which govern the ways of construing reality to which we have become accustomed.

For example, let us look at one very central assumption. We feel certain that Jesus taught the value of love, for Christianity is the religion of love. But what is love? There is an almost endless variety of types of love—charity, pity, love of humanity, love of neighbour, love of God, love as a virtue, love as a duty, love as a value, parental love, romantic love, love of others like oneself, love as union, as desire, etc. Each of these types of love carries with it, as we shall see, a very different understanding of reality as well as diverse assumptions concerning what it means to be human. Since, in the Western world, Jesus is ordinarily associated with love, it will be incumbent upon us to reconsider its meaning, especially as a world-attitude.

In Chapter One, by way of explicating the issues that will guide our inquiry, I will discuss the views of some philosophers and novelists who have been seriously concerned with these questions.

2. See T.S. Eliot, "East Coker," III, in *The Complete Poems and Plays 1909-1950* (New York: Harcourt Brace & World, Inc., 1952), p. 127.

CHAPTER ONE

Jesus and the actual other

The four principal types of response towards others which today are commonly confused with Christ-like love are: feeling sorry for others (pity), love of mankind (humanitarianism), self-denial (altruism), and wanting to be in union with others (sentimentalism). From reading and teaching, I have learned that the thinkers who are of most assistance in clarifying conceptually the human problems connected with these orientations toward others are the philosophers Nietzsche and Scheler, and the novelists Dostoyevsky and Salinger. For those readers who are not familiar with their works, I will provide a review of the basic issues.

In *The Anti-Christ*, Nietzsche has carried out an analysis of so-called Christian love understood as "pity" or "charity"—feeling sorry for others. He bases his analysis on a distinction between two fundamental world-attitudes, which he usually identifies by the terms "will to power" and *ressentiment*. Each is characterized by an unconscious instinct and by an unconscious mood. The will to power is the instinct which distinguishes a reality-affirming attitude, and its attendant mood is joy. Nihilism, or the will to nothingness, is the instinct which marks an attitude that negates the world, and its attendant mood is *ressentiment*—a repressed, unconscious hostility against life.

According to Nietzsche, it is always out of one's fundamental mood and instinct that situations are assessed and intentions are formed. He claims that in all cases one's conscious intentions, however moral or noble they may be, are merely masks for the forces that really drive one's activity and thought. It is from this perspective that a reader should assess Nietzsche's professed anti-moral stance. He stands opposed to those viewpoints which evaluate human behaviour from a moral perspective, because they render thought incapable of judging the instincts that are covered over by human intentions.

Nietzsche takes the position that Christian "pity" generates *ressentiment*. He believes that love as feeling sorry for others has a vested interest in preventing people from being vitally alive, because only when people suffer can pity be active. This type of "love" distracts people from the actual suffering which holds them in its grip, by creating illusory suffering by the use of such other-worldly and anti-worldly concepts as "hell," "sin," "judgment," and so on. These concepts falsify people's consciousness of reality, teaching them to see things as they are not, and to believe that things are not as they are. This illusion-creating force makes people believe that they are beyond the very worst that life can do to them, by creating in them the conviction that they can tolerate any horror. From Nietzsche's perspective, pity is a mimicry of the will to power exercised by those who themselves are not truly vital and who attain a perverse sense of their own position by undermining others. In short, pity is parasitical, is a subterranean strategy of domination, and is rooted in a covert hatred of the world and of others.

A serious effort to come to grips with the question of the causes and sources of mankind's discontent with the actual has also been exerted by Scheler, a German philosopher of the first half of the twentieth century, in his book *Ressentiment*. Scheler asserts:

> Among the scanty discoveries which have been made in recent times about the origin of moral judgments, Friedrich Nietzsche's discovery that *ressentiment* can be the source of such value judgments is the most profound. This remains true even if his characterization of Christian love as the most delicate 'flower of *ressentiment*' should turn out to be mistaken.[1]

Scheler agrees with Nietzsche's observation that *ressentiment* has been a formative factor in Western morality, but argues that Nietzsche made two basic mistakes in his analysis of Christian love.

1. Max Scheler, *Ressentiment*, edited and with an introduction by Lewis A. Coser, translated by William W. Holdheim (New York: Schocken Books, 1972), p. 43.

In the first place, Nietzsche made an error regarding the essence of "true" Christian love, as Scheler understands it. He thinks Nietzsche made the common but fatal mistake of treating Christian love as an ethical idea, and so judged it without considering its religious basis, by which Scheler means its rootedness in the power of the kingdom of God.

In the second place, Scheler observes that Nietzsche failed to distinguish between Christian love and other moralities which have, in the West, entered into complex alliances with Christian moral ideas, when they have been torn loose from their religious basis. These complex alliances have become so familiar to us that we do not notice any more the difference between, for example, Christian love and humanitarianism, altruism, or the doctrine of equality.

Scheler provides a more fully developed analysis of the origins of *ressentiment*. When various human impulses such as revenge, envy, and hatred are not overcome (because one is not strong enough) or are not acted upon (because the sociological situation renders one impotent to do so), but are driven underground, they lose their attachment to definite objects and are transformed into malice, spite, and the impulse to detract, all of which seek satisfaction from indeterminate objects. When repression of these impulses is complete, they breed *ressentiment*, and then a hidden hostility towards life governs all of one's experience.

Scheler diagnoses *ressentiment* as a kind of psychological disease which is extremely contagious and which plays a major role in forming perceptions, generating value judgments, limiting memory, and determining expectations. In other words, it is a fixed pattern of experience that selects only those aspects of reality which nourish it. Scheler notes three primary features of *ressentiment*:

(1) It falsifies one's world-view, so that life is experienced as something meagre, unworthy, and even detestable.
(2) It compels those afflicted with the disease to see only what is objectionable in other people; if others seem to find life more enjoyable than one does, then one feels compelled to undermine them and to find reasons to despise them.
(3) It results in value delusion.

Scheler makes a very acute psychological observation: "We have a tendency to overcome any strong tension between desire and impotence by depreciating or denying the value of the desired object. At times, indeed, we go so far as to extol another object which is somehow opposed to the first. It is the old story of the fox and the sour grapes."[2] *Ressentiment* unconsciously deceives itself into believing that those values which it cannot share are not worthwhile anyway. Scheler calls this "organic mendacity,"[3] for "He who is 'mendacious,' who is self-deceived, has no need to lie!"[4]

There are two ethical ideas, according to Scheler, which are commonly confused with Christian love: humanitarianism and altruism. Humanitarianism (love of mankind) displays the formal structure of *ressentiment*:

> A is affirmed, valued, and praised not for its own intrinsic quality, but with the unverbalized intention of denying, devaluating, and denigrating B.[5]

Humanitarianism is oriented to suffering mankind. Why? Because it has the hidden intention of denying all actual others—the neighbour, one's family, one's community, one's country—and of calling into doubt "God's 'wise and benevolent rule.'"[6] Humanitarianism thus functions on the basis of value delusion. It puts utility values above all other values, acclaiming love as an instrument for the attainment of the general welfare. Moreover, humanitarianism is directed at man's weakness because it wants to deny the higher possibilities of human existence. It does this by selecting the lowest aspects of human nature as the criteria for being human: to be human for the humanitarian means to be *only* human—"to err is human," "we are all human," etc. The doctrine of the equality of all men, meaning their equality from the point of view of the lowest common denominator, their inadequacy, develops from this same organic mendacity. (As an aside, I might note that welfare economists, whose discipline is rooted in utilitarianism, usually take equality to be a self-evident good when evaluating various policy alternatives.)

One of the most significant aspects of Dostoyevsky's novel, *The Brothers Karamazov*, is his effort to distinguish between two types of

2. Scheler, *Ressentiment*, p. 73.
3. Scheler, *Ressentiment*, p. 77.
4. Scheler, *Ressentiment*, p. 78
5. Scheler, *Ressentiment*, p. 68.
6. Scheler, *Ressentiment*, p. 123.

love that have been associated with Jesus: love of mankind and love of neighbour. As I see it, the central issue in his chapter on "The Grand Inquisitor" has not so much to do with the uses made of miracle, mystery, and authority by established religion in the name of Jesus, but rather with the profound difference between these two types of love and their underlying attitudes toward human beings.

Here, the Grand Inquisitor represents the modern humanitarian, that is, someone who loves the abstraction "mankind," and who wishes to satisfy mankind's most urgent religious needs because he believes that loving means wanting to make others happy. The Grand Inquisitor accuses Jesus of not having loved mankind. Why? Because Jesus resisted the three temptations of the devil. The Grand Inquisitor argues that if Jesus had loved mankind, he would have turned stones into bread in order to feed the hungry, he would have come down from the cross in order to captivate mankind's conscience and set it forever at rest, and he would have organized everyone into a single, unanimous and harmonious ant-heap so that mankind would have been relieved of its loneliness. The Grand Inquisitor's secret, of course, is that he harbours a secret contempt for human nature and for mankind's possibilities. He loves mankind in general because he hates the concrete neighbour.

Jesus does not defend himself against these accusations, and *the silence of Jesus* indicates that he represents something quite different than love of mankind—love of neighbour. Dostoyevsky devotes large portions of his novel to demonstrating just how severe and terrifying is love of the actual other, a love beyond the capacity of most people because it requires hard work, tenacity, and almost heroic sacrifice. In other words, it presupposes a much richer sense of man's possibilities than love of mankind does.

If humanitarianism really does affirm an abstraction in order to deny the concrete other, then what about altruism? Is not altruism what it means to love the actual other? According to Scheler, altruism displays the former structure of *ressentiment* because the altruist affirms the other in order to escape from himself. Altruism is a form of self-hatred posing as its opposite—love. Indeed, the stratagems and dissimulations of *ressentiment* are so successful that usually the observer cannot tell the difference between love and hatred posing as love.

Ivan Karamazov, however, is very perceptive in this regard. As he says:

"I could never understand how one can love one's neighbours. It's just one's neighbours, to my mind, that one cannot love, though one might love those at a distance. I once read somewhere of John the Merciful, a saint, that when a hungry, frozen beggar came to him, he took him into his bed, held him in his arms, and began breathing into his mouth, which was putrid and loathsome from some awful disease. I am convinced that he did that from 'self-laceration,' from the self-laceration of falsity, for the sake of the charity imposed by duty, as a penance laid on him. For any one to love a man, he must be hidden, for as soon as he shows his face, love is gone."[7]

The question is, can one affirm the actual other without in some sense hating the self?

If love of neighbour must be distinguished from humanitarianism and from altruism, then does love of neighbour mean feeling oneself in union with the other? In *The Anti-Christ*, Nietzsche argues that this is in fact the type of love that Jesus inaugurated.[8] He bases his analysis of this type of love on two sayings attributed to Jesus in the gospels: "Resist not evil" and "The kingdom of God is within you."

Nietzsche regards the injunction not to resist evil as the profoundest saying in the gospels. It means that blessedness can be experienced by no longer resisting anyone or anything. One does not judge, one does not censure, one does not get angry. To resist either evil or the evil-doer would be felt as an unbearable displeasure, the opposite to feeling oneself in love. According to Nietzsche, Jesus died as he lived, by not resisting.

The assertion that the kingdom of God is *within* you (the King James Version) shows that blessedness is to be found by not recognizing any other, by withdrawing to the inner world. Nietzsche claims that Jesus knew instinctively how one ought to live in order to feel oneself in heaven. One must abolish all distance between oneself and God, between oneself and others. This is the gospel, the good news, the glad tidings.

7. Fyodor Dostoyevsky, *The Brothers Karamazov*, translated by Constance Garnett (New York: Random House, Inc., n.d.), p. 245.
8. Nietzsche based his understanding of Jesus in part on Dostoyevsky's novel, *The Idiot*, and in part on Ernst Renan's famous life of Jesus, which was brilliantly burlesqued by Albert Schweitzer in *The Quest for the Historical Jesus* (New York: Macmillan, 1950).

I believe that Nietzsche erred fundamentally in attributing this understanding of love to Jesus, but he nevertheless provides an extremely perceptive analysis of the mentality associated with the sweet theology of love, one very common today. According to Nietzsche, the retreat to pure inwardness represents a return to childishness in the spiritual domain, "the occurrence of retarded puberty undeveloped in the organism as a consequence of degeneration . . . ."[9] The mentality that is appropriate for the pubescent is, in the adult, retardation, a sign of degeneration because it is rooted in the fear of pain. This love leads to the denial of all otherness and of all reality outside oneself. Why? Because any difference, opposition, or distance is felt as displeasure. The fear of pain leads to the notion that there should be neither conflicts nor alienations in human life, and so love is construed as feeling oneself in union with others; in other words, it is a form of hedonism.

In contemporary literature, J.D. Salinger has provided an example of this understanding of love in his novel, *Franny and Zooey*. Franny Glass cannot bear it that she feels so critical of everyone around her, and so she begins reciting the Jesus prayer ("Lord Jesus Christ, have mercy on me") as a method of achieving Christ-consciousness, which to her means the feeling of being in union with everyone and everything. Her efforts bring her to the verge of a nervous breakdown, because she is incorrigibly intelligent, and she comes home from college to collapse on the living room sofa of her family's Manhattan apartment. Her older brother, Zooey, chides her for wanting Jesus to be an extremely poetic and lovable mountain, lake, and field preacher—a sort of Buddhaesque figure who is St. Francis of Assisi, Heidi's grandfather, and her eldest brother Seymour all rolled up into one. Zooey reminds her of an incident from her childhood which he believes indicated that she didn't understand Jesus then and that she still doesn't. When she was ten, she decided that she didn't like Jesus any more because she "didn't approve of his going into the synagogue and throwing all the tables and idols all over the place. That was very rude, very Unnecessary." And she didn't approve of Jesus' discriminating against all those nice fowls of the air when he said "Are ye not much better than they?" According to Zooey, Jesus was not some-

9. Friedrich Nietzsche, *Twilight of the Idols/The Anti-Christ*, translated, with an introduction and commentary by R.J. Hollingdale (Harmondsworth: Penguin Books, Ltd., 1968), p. 144.

one with St. Francis' consistently winning personality, but rather "the best, the smartest, the most loving, the least sentimental, the most un*im*itative master"[10] God could have picked for the job in the New Testament.

I have examined pity, humanitarianism, altruism, and sentimentalism in some detail and elaborated the basic issues that arise in connection with these types of love, because they are the ones ordinarily attributed to Jesus. Whether that attribution is correct remains to be decided. Whatever be the outcome of our inquiry, however, the central question should by now be clear: *what was Jesus' attitude toward the actual other?*

Each of the four types of love already discussed is an expression, albeit of diverse kinds, of offence at the actual other. But other types of love are not exempt from this charge. I will not analyze them in detail, because they do not concern us specifically in our investigation, but will be content with some general observations. Romantic love, for example, often affirms one person in order to deny other potential mates, or one's family. Desire (Eros, as described in Plato's *Symposium*) is the urge to possess that which can satisfy man completely, and involves a progressive devaluation of the sensible world, which never provides the perpetual possession of a good nor the possession of a perpetual good. Love of others like oneself (for example, one's own race or people) usually is cultivated on the basis of hatred of all outsiders. And so on.

As T.S. Eliot has observed, "... human kind/Cannot bear very much reality."[11] Is it possible to conceive of a mode of being human that is not an expression of discontent with the actual but could affirm the concrete world and real human beings in their otherness without taking refuge in other-worldliness, self-hatred, or inwardness? Is discriminating awareness of particular individuals compatible with unsentimental love? What then would love be—a passion for the actual? These are the questions that will guide our inquiry into the meaning of Jesus' parables and sayings.

10. J.D. Salinger, *Franny and Zooey* (Boston: Little, Brown and Company, 1961) pp. 163, 170-71.

11. T.S. Eliot, "Burnt Norton," I, in *The Complete Poems and Plays*, p. 118.

PART ONE

Jesus came eating and drinking

CHAPTER TWO

Jesus, John the Baptist, and the resentful children

Children playing games

The most informative saying of Jesus historically is the following, recorded by both Matthew and Luke from their source, Q (each evangelist has used the saying in a different context in his own narrative):

> But to what shall I compare this generation?
> It is like children sitting in the market places
> and calling to their playmates,
> "We piped to you, and you did not dance;
> we wailed, and you did not mourn."
> For John came neither eating nor drinking,
> and they say, "He has a demon";
> [I] came eating and drinking,
> and they say, "Behold, a glutton and a drunkard,
> a friend of tax collectors and sinners!"
> (Matt 11:16-19; Luke 7:31-34)

Using the criterion of embarrassment

Why do New Testament scholars feel so certain that this is an authentic saying of the earthly Jesus? Certainty in scholarship is like certainty in any other area—relative. However, when someone reveals to us something that is not in his best interest, or is embarrassing to him, we usually feel rather confident that he is telling us the truth. For example, if I want to hear a concert by the Beaux Arts Trio and I telephone the box office to inquire whether there are any tickets still available, and if the ticket agent tells me that all the tickets have been sold, I will not go down to the concert, since I assume he is telling me the truth because it is in his interest to sell tickets. This criterion of embarrassment is our basic critical tool in arriving at relatively certain conclusions.

In this saying, there are three pieces of information which it would have been contrary to the interests of the earliest Christians to have reported to us. The saying informs us that by his enemies Jesus was called "a glutton and a drunkard." It is virtually impossible to imagine anyone in the Christian tradition fabricating a saying that pictures Jesus in this way; hence, with the highest degree of probability, we can accept the saying as authentic.

There are two other indications that the saying was originally uttered by Jesus himself. We know from the synoptic tradition and from the Gospel of John that the followers of Jesus were engaged in rather intense competition with the followers of John the Baptist right down to the end of the first century. The tendency of the Christian tradition was always to ensure that when John the Baptist was mentioned, he was subordinated to Jesus. Thus, for example, Mark presents John the Baptist as a messenger sent to prepare the way for Jesus (Mark 1:2-3), and has John say, using early Christian terminology: "After me comes he who is mightier than I, the thong of whose sandals I am not worthy to stoop down and untie. I have baptized you with water; but he will baptize you with the Holy Spirit" (Mark 1:7-8).

Matthew expands this section, but follows Mark more or less, with one important difference. Mark states quite forthrightly that "In those days Jesus came from Nazareth of Galilee and was baptized by John in the Jordan" (Mark 1:9). The baptism of Jesus by John is a historical occurrence about which we can be as certain as possible. John preached that God's judgment was fast approaching, and that therefore it was necessary to repent and to be sealed with baptism as a sign of repentance (presumably so that the angels of judgment would know who had repented and would spare them). Why, then, did Jesus undergo baptism by John? The fact that Jesus *had* been baptized by John was embarrassing to the earliest Christians, and so they reinterpreted John the Baptist's mission as a prelude to that of Jesus.

During the course of the first century, we can see that the Chrisian interpreters downplayed John the Baptist's role further and further. Matthew suppresses the direct statement that Jesus was baptized by John and inserts beforehand the following dialogue between John and Jesus: "John would have prevented him [from being baptized by him], saying, 'I need to be baptized by you, and do you come to me?' But Jesus answered him, 'Let it be so now; for thus it is fitting for us to fulfill all righteousness.' Then he consented" (Matt 3:14-15). It is clear that here Matthew is at pains to address the question of why Jesus would have submitted to baptism by John. He answers the question by creating this scene in which John protests, and Jesus overcomes John's reluctance by saying that they will go through with this "to fulfill all righteousness."

Luke goes even one step further. Not only does he introduce a long account of the relationship between Martha and Mary to illustrate John's subordination to Jesus, but he even has John shut up in prison (Luke 3:18-20) before Jesus' baptism which, as Luke narrates it, is not directly said to have been by John: "Now when all the people were baptized, and when Jesus also had been baptized [note the passive with the agent not expressed] and was praying, the heaven was opened, and the Holy Spirit descended upon him in bodily form, as a dove, and a voice came from heaven, 'Thou art my beloved Son; with thee I am well pleased'" (Luke 3:21-22). Luke's version of the baptism thus completely eliminates the potentially embarrassing fact that Jesus was baptized by John.

The Gospel of John, which was written at the end of the first century, also suppresses the information that Jesus was baptized by John the Baptist and, instead, represents John the Baptist as bearing witness to Jesus and as denying any messianic claims for himself. John the Baptist says, "I am not the Christ," not Elijah nor the prophet, but one who prepares the way for Jesus, in comparison to whom he is totally unworthy, for Jesus is "the Lamb of God," the one on whom John the Baptist saw the Spirit descend, "the Son of God" (John 1:20-34). The Gospel of John ensures that the subordination of John the Baptist is complete!

The stages of development from Mark, through Matthew and Luke, to John, show that the tendency of the Christian tradition was progressively to subordinate John the Baptist to Jesus, progressively to eliminate the problem raised by Jesus being baptized by John the Baptist, and, finally, even to make John the Baptist a witness for the developed Christological titles used by Christians to designate Jesus ("Son of God," "Lamb of God").

24

When we approach Jesus' saying about the children in the market places, the difference in attitude toward John the Baptist is startling. There is no effort to subordinate John; on the contrary, Jesus treats him as no less than an equal to himself. This coheres with our knowledge that Jesus respected John the Baptist sufficiently to undergo a baptism of repentance at his hands!

There is a third aspect to the saying which marks it as authentic. It provides us with the information that Jesus did not fast, unlike John the Baptist, who was an ascetic and "came neither eating nor drinking." Indeed, Jesus "came eating and drinking." We know that the early Christian communities did observe such normal religious practices as fasting, and that they were aware that their practice differed from that of the earthly Jesus (see, for example, Mark 2:18-20 and parallels). Authority for their observance of normal religious practice such as fasting could not be established by appealing to the practice of Jesus. Therefore, the information provided by this saying that Jesus himself did not fast is another solid indication that it was originally uttered by the earthly Jesus.

The almost identical wording in Matthew and Luke indicates that they both transposed the saying virtually verbatim from Q. However, during the course of the formation of Q, two modifications were made to the saying of Jesus to bring it into conformity with Christology: Jesus was made to refer to himself as "the Son of man," and a saying was added at the end: "Yet wisdom is justified by her deeds (Luke: children)." The appended saying interprets Jesus as the heavenly Wisdom who comes down to earth and calls to men in the market place but they do not heed (Proverbs 8), a quite natural interpretation, really, considering the metaphor which Jesus had used in his saying.

Having Jesus refer to himself as "the Son of man" is a bit more complicated. "The Son of man" is the title for a mythological figure in Jewish apocalyptic literature, a figure associated with the idea of a final judgment (Daniel 7; 4 Ezra 13; etc.). However, in this saying "Son of man" is used in a non-apocalyptic sense just as it is used in a proverb from Q: "Foxes have holes, and birds of the air have nests; but the Son of man has nowhere to lay his head" (Matt 8:20 = Luke 9:58). What the proverb and the similitude of the children in the market places have in common is the idea of *homelessness*, an idea associated with the figure of *Wisdom* in Proverbs, and it might be that the community (or communities) which produced Q used the

Son of man, a male figure, to take the place of Wisdom, who was always female. Whatever the explanation for its appearance here, though, it is obvious that the title belongs to early Christian efforts to explain theologically the meaning of Jesus, and that in the original saying Jesus referred simply to himself.

The saying is composed in three parts. It begins with a question: "To what shall I compare this generation?" Then comes the answer: "It is like children...." And then the application: "For John came...." Since the saying is based on a comparison between this generation and children sitting in the market places, we call it a similitude, and it is, in fact, the only similitude among the core material. The saying provides us with important historical information about John the Baptist and Jesus, and also with a unique insight into Jesus' understanding of how his generation viewed him and John the Baptist.

Group psychology

The similitude informs us that John the Baptist came neither eating nor drinking. In other words, he was an ascetic ("His food was locusts and wild honey" Matt 3:4). Jesus, on the other hand, although he had been baptized by John, did not observe the asceticism practised by John and by John's disciples (Mark 2:18 par.); indeed, public attention was attracted by Jesus' eating and drinking with his friends.

The expression "tax collectors and sinners" refers to all those whose occupations or ways of life would stigmatize them as non-conforming Jews, all those, in other words, with whom an observant Jew would not eat.

The history of religions shows that one of the distinguishing marks of the Jewish tradition from earliest biblical times down to the present has been its regulations surrounding the eating of food. In the Jewish tradition, one establishes one's identity according to the food one eats. This is not a matter of personal taste, but of group identification. The Jewish people have always constituted themselves as a group and have marked themselves out as different from others by their common eating customs. A "Jew" is, by definition, someone with whom other Jews share the same eating habits and with whom, therefore, they will have a meal.

The synoptic tradition has created the impression that Jesus gave offence to observant Jews because he ate and drank with "tax collectors and sinners" (Mark 2:15-17 par. and Luke 15:1-2). This impression has persisted down to the present day, and is an integral component in contemporary scholarly reconstructions of the mission of the historical Jesus. It is widely assumed that Jesus gave offence because he included in his "table fellowship" (the concept New Testament scholars use for Jesus' eating and drinking with friends) those with whom observant Jews would not eat.

However, the similitude itself states that both John the Baptist and Jesus were disparaged by their contemporaries. It is not the conceptual content of John's preaching or Jesus' language that gives offence, but ostensibly their eating practices. Even though John and Jesus were totally different from one another—one was an ascetic, one an eater and a drinker—both were denigrated. Quite *different* modes of behaviour evoke the *same* impulse to devaluate in sub-human terms: "John has a demon and Jesus is a glutton and a drunkard." Since totally different eating practices provoke the same response, it is obvious that more is at stake than disapproval of two men who no longer eat as conventional Jews (especially since there is no indication that John ate with tax collectors and sinners).

In the similitude, Jesus sees beneath their name-calling and describes the human dynamics of the situation. Jesus observes that the real reason for their hostility to John's asceticism and to his eating and drinking is not religious (in any sense of the term) but psychological, specifically the psychology of a group (to use the modern term). As the group sees it, John does not dance when it pipes and Jesus does not mourn when it wails. The group psychology which governs the reactions of Jesus' contemporaries is identical to that of a group of children playing games who resent those who refuse to submit to the rules that control the activities of the group. Those individuals who refuse to be tribalized are treated as defectors, viewed with suspicion and resentment, and branded as sub-human. Jesus' similitude, then, offers a lucid and penetrating description of the pathology of his contemporaries' socio-psychological condition.

The similitude illuminates the historical situation of Jesus and John the Baptist, but also, because it penetrates to the depths of the human dynamics in the situation, points beyond itself to a universally human experience. Those who establish their self-understanding by submitting to the canons that mark the identity of a group resent those persons who live out of a different mode of human existence. It is important to notice that Jesus and John are *not* like children who refuse to join in the games of their peers. Neither Jesus nor John rebels *against* Judaism. Each of them acts according to his own standards; neither of them pays any attention to the group. But their contemporaries *perceive* them as *defectors* from the group, since they categorize everyone as either a "member" of the group or as a "*non*-member"; even those whose being has nothing to do with the group's way of establishing its identity are defined with reference to the group.

The hostility and resentment of Jesus' contemporaries is still conscious and is directed at definite objects. Nevertheless, we can see here the obvious characteristics of the value delusion of *ressentiment* because the tribalized children *devaluate* both John the Baptist and Jesus, disparaging John as demon-possessed and Jesus as a glutton and a drunkard. Those who understand themselves in terms of group identity are governed by the impulse to denigrate those who act as free persons. The similitude shows that Jesus understood very clearly the instincts that control certain types. The traditional view that Jesus evoked opposition from his contemporaries because the friends he ate with were tax collectors and sinners (the early Christian picture) is not wrong, it is just superficial relative to Jesus' own perceptions.

From hatred to violence

A second saying of Jesus collected in Q supplements the similitude we have just examined, even though the picture we can derive from it is not so well focused:

> From the days of John the Baptist until now
> the kingdom of God has suffered violence,
> and men of violence take it by force (Matt 11:12;
> cf., Luke 16:16).

In Q, the saying had no context, and so Matthew and Luke have each placed the saying in a narrative context of their own. In this saying, Jesus also places John the Baptist on a plane equal to himself, this time in connection with "the kingdom of God." As we have already seen, this high evaluation of John the Baptist indicates that the saying is authentic and was not produced by the early Christians.

It is noteworthy that Jesus associates the language of "the kingdom of God" with the days of John the Baptist. Matthew reports that John preached "Repent, for the kingdom of [God] is at hand" (Matt 3:2; cf., Mark 1:14 which places this language in the mouth of Jesus: "The time is fulfilled, and the kingdom of God is at hand; repent"). Matthew is usually accused of Christianizing the preaching of John, but the evidence of Jesus' own saying strongly implies that John did use kingdom language.

John the Baptist was active in the wilderness of Judea, that is, in the Jordan Valley at the north end of the Dead Sea. He announced an impending judgment, exhorted his listeners to repent in preparation for that event, and baptized them as a sign that they had done so. If John did use the language of the kingdom, it was in connection with his preaching of God's impending judgment, when God would intervene in history to separate the righteous among his people from the wicked. In other words, John's understanding of the kingdom was squarely in line with the preaching of the prophets, as the sayings of John collected in Q make particularly clear (Matt 3:7-10 = Luke 3:7-9). John the Baptist, like the prophets, preached to the people of Israel and summoned them to repentance. But how does the language of the kingdom function for Jesus?

The saying has probably been modified somewhat in transmission, but we can see that it does *not* mention the kingdom in connection with an impending, transcendent judgment, nor with John the Baptist's characteristic themes of repentance and baptism. The appearance of the kingdom is spoken of in the *past*, as already occurring in the days of John the Baptist. The similitude we have just examined has shown that Jesus understood John and himself as persons who acted freely and so were hated by their contemporaries who submitted to control by the group.

This saying states that what John and Jesus represented elicited not only hostility but, from men of violence, it suffered violence. What both John the Baptist and Jesus represent, according to the saying, is the kingdom. But we have seen that it was not the content of John's preaching nor of Jesus' language that provided the occasion for their contemporaries' *ressentiment*. Rather, it was the very fact of their freedom that catalyzed hostility from the group.

In other words, Jesus does not use kingdom language here to refer to the whole range of ideas and associations evoked by John's preaching of an impending judgment, but to refer to John's mode of being as a free person. It is only in that sense that Jesus can speak of the kingdom's appearance as having already occurred, and as being active into Jesus' own time. Jesus, then, reinterprets the traditional symbol of the kingdom and now associates its power not with John's preaching but with the mode of being human that he shares with John (see further on this in Chapter Three).

It is not a very great distance from the hatred of those controlled by an impulse to denigrate and to disparage to an impulse to impose violence on the free person. The phenomenology of hate is brilliantly described by Jean-Paul Sartre in *Being and Nothingness*. As Sartre observes:

> Hate does not necessarily appear on the occasion of my being subjected to something evil. On the contrary, it can arise when one would theoretically expect gratitude—that is, on the occasion of a kindness. The occasion which arouses hate is simply an act by the Other which puts me in the state of *being subject to* his freedom. This act is in itself humiliating; it is humiliating as the concrete revelation of my objectness in the face of the Other's freedom. This revelation is immediately obscured, is buried in the past and becomes opaque. But it leaves in me the feeling that there is "something" to be destroyed if I am to free myself.[1]

Obviously, neither John the Baptist nor Jesus subjected their contemporaries to any evil. But their very freedom in contrast to their contemporaries' submission to tribalized control created a situation which their contemporaries found unendurable. John and Jesus' freedom by its very nature revealed that they lacked the freedom of persons, and in the face of it knew themselves to be objectified. In that sense, they thought of themselves as being subjected to Jesus and John, which left them with the feeling that there was something to be destroyed if they were to escape the subjection they felt in the face of freedom.

This saying, like the similitude on the children in the market places, refers to a specific historical situation but also, because of its

1. Jean-Paul Sartre, *Being and Nothingness: A Phenomenological Essay on Ontology*, translated and with an introduction by Hazel E. Barnes (New York: Washington Square Press, 1966), p. 533.

penetration into the human dynamics of that situation, points beyond itself to factors in human experience that are universally recognizable, to the way in which freedom elicits hatred and even violence.

Both the similitude and the saying of Jesus point to what has been traditionally called the problem of evil. What is the cause of the impulse to control, dominate, and even destroy? Is evil a super-terrestial force that enters human life from beyond, injecting itself into men, possessing them, and using them for its own destructive purposes? According to this view, evil is demonic, that is, a force which cannot be explained in human terms, but rather is construed as something trans-human, something for which human beings in the final analysis bear no responsibility. The saying and the simili-tude of Jesus take a different point of view. They characterize the impulse to control, dominate, and destroy as borne by specifically human agents—by a generation that is like resentful children, by men of violence. According to Jesus' own words, it is *human beings themselves* who are the agents of anti-human destructiveness. Evil has a human face, and the heart of darkness is not "out there" but is innate, as Kurtz discovered in Conrad's "Heart of Darkness." (When Francis Coppola used Conrad's "Heart of Darkness" as the basis for his film, "Apocalypse Now," he was making a somewhat different point, not that evil is innate in man, but that those who are protecting what they value, their wives and children, should be prepared to be agents of destruction).

CHAPTER THREE

The mythological and
the demonic

Jesus and the mythological

It would be interesting to know what brought Jesus from Galilee to the Jordan Valley where John the Baptist was active, why Jesus accepted baptism by John, and whether Jesus joined the baptist movement as a disciple of John for any time. Unfortunately, we could only speculate about these various matters, for our sources do not offer certain information. What *is* certain is that Jesus had a high regard for John the Baptist, for that is evident in Jesus' sayings.

John's baptism was a sign of repentance in anticipation of the imminent judgment of God which John was announcing. In other words, John's proclamation of an impending judgment was based on the assumption, shared with many of his contemporaries, that God would soon factually transform the world as it existed in order to begin it again. The cosmology that underlies these assumptions is of a three-storied universe with heaven above (the realm of God and his angels) and underworld below (variously named in our sources, but in any case the realm of Satan and demons). Such views were particularly common in Jewish circles from at least the time of the second century B.C. (see Daniel 7) well into the Christian period (see 4 Ezra = II Esdras 3—14 in the Apocrypha). Not confined to Jewish circles, these conceptions played a major role in the formation of early Christian thought. Paul, for example, draws on these ideas when he states that he expects to be alive when Jesus returns again:

> For this we declare to you by the word of the Lord, that we who are alive, who are left until the coming of the Lord, shall not precede those

who have fallen asleep. For the Lord himself will descend from heaven with a cry of command, with the archangel's call, and with the sound of the trumpet of God. And the dead in Christ will rise first; then we who are alive, who are left, shall be caught up together with them in the clouds to meet the Lord in the air; and so we shall always be with the Lord (1 Thessalonians 4:15-18).

Notice, incidentally, that Paul describes the picture as "a word of the Lord" which he delivers to the community, meaning a word of the risen Lord Jesus. Whether Paul himself received this word in prophecy or whether it is a word delivered through another early Christian prophet is impossible to know. But this word of the risen Lord Jesus concerning his second coming affords a particularly clear picture of the world-view of Paul and of other early Christians (Paul composed 1 Thessalonians in the early fifties).

Another example of a Christian prophet's receiving words from the risen Lord Jesus concerning "what must soon take place . . . . for the time is near" (Rev 1:1-3) is the Book of Revelation. The risen Lord Jesus appeared to the prophet John, who at that time was in Patmos, and dictated letters to seven early Christian communities concerning the impending transformation of the world (Revelation was written around the end of the first century).

In contemporary usage, "myth" means a fiction or something commonly held to be true but which is false. In the technical vocabulary of New Testament exegesis, however, the term "myth" is used in a very precise sense, borrowed from the discipline of history of religions. We use "mythological" to designate the type of language that utilizes symbols and pictures which presuppose a tripartite cosmology, without prejudice regarding the truth or falsity of the meaning of that language. If we designate the apostle Paul's or the prophet John's language as "mythological," we do not intend to prejudge the question as to whether by using that kind of language they were expressing something true (which is a separate issue from the obvious fact that they were mistaken regarding the factual palingenesis of the world). I will be using the term "mythological" in this restrictive sense, but the reader wishing to understand better how such language functioned in New Testament times could find no better guide than Amos Wilder's *Jesus' Parables and The War of Myths*.[1]

1. Amos Wilder, *Jesus' Parables and the War of Myths*, edited and with a preface by James Breech (Philadelphia: Fortress Press, 1982)

Mythological conceptions were not restricted to Jewish and Christian sources, but were widespread in Graeco-Roman antiquity, and they persist even now—the first Russian cosmonauts were reacting to this cosmology when they declared that they did not find God in outer space.

Kingdom of God as used in Jewish and Christian sources was mythological language in this technical sense. The New Testament scholar Norman Perrin recently formulated the present scholarly consensus about kingdom language in this way: "Kingdom of God is a symbol which evokes the myth of the activity of God as king on behalf of his people."[2] In the biblical tradition, mythological language was transmitted in the form of narratives recounting God's action in *history* (meaning the social and political spheres) on behalf of his *people* (meaning Israel). Such traditions go back to Israel's experience of being constituted as a people out of various slave groups who were delivered from Egyptian bondage by the God Yahweh. Thus, those Jewish and Christian prophetic preachers who proclaimed the imminence of the kingdom and of God's impending judgment drew from a tradition with a long pre-history, a tradition of pictures and conceptions intimately connected with a specific way of construing the world.

Surprisingly enough, it was only in the twentieth century that New Testament scholars began to recognize the full importance of this kind of language among those who produced the earliest Christian literature, and much of the discussion among interpreters of the New Testament in this century has centered on the question of the meaning and significance of mythological language in the New Testament, and with the question of how to translate this meaning into terms comprehensible to modern man.

During the course of this debate, the assumption has never been challenged that because Jesus employed the language of the kingdom, he also shared the mythological conceptions of his contemporaries. Part of the reason for the persistence of this assumption has been the corollary idea that Jesus "proclaimed" the kingdom, that is to say, that Jesus announced the imminence of God's breaking into history, and that he called his listeners to repentance to prepare for the event. But this is precisely the content of John the Baptist's preaching. Now of course it is possible, in theory, that

2. Norman Perrin, *Jesus and the Language of the Kingdom: Symbol and Metaphor in New Testament Interpretation* (Philadelphia: Fortress Press, 1976), p. 33.

Jesus did share the mythological conceptions of his contemporaries, and that he did preach a message virtually identical to that of John the Baptist and some of the early Christian missionaries. However, we cannot presuppose that this was the case. We must restrict our attention initially only to the core material, to see whether in these sayings Jesus appears as one who preaches the kingdom, announces an impending judgment, or calls for repentance.

We have already examined one of the core sayings in which Jesus uses kingdom language ("From the days of John the Baptist until now, the kingdom of God has suffered violence and men of violence take it by force"). In this saying, at least, none of the conceptions found in John the Baptist's message are evident. Jesus does not preach the kingdom, nor announce its coming as a future, transcendental event, but instead speaks of the kingdom as already active *since* the days of John the Baptist! This saying appears to take up the language of the kingdom in order to re-interpret its meaning and significance. Jesus associates the kingdom not with political or social events, not with conceptions of a transformation of the world, and not with imminent judgment, but rather with the individual, John the Baptist, and, implicitly, with the speaker himself, Jesus. The appearance of the kingdom is an event that provokes men of violence to wish to destroy John the Baptist and Jesus. If one *assumes* that John the Baptist's *preaching* of repentance evoked the desire to destroy him, then one will conclude that this saying asserts as much. But Jesus' similitude about children playing games shows quite clearly that, as Jesus understood the situation, it was not John's preaching or even his asceticism as such, but rather his mode of being as a free person, that his contemporaries found provocative, just as Jesus' mode of being as a free person elicited a similar hostility. If this analysis is correct, then we should conclude that this is the phenomenon to which Jesus' saying about men of violence refers. The corollary of this conclusion is a provisional hypothesis that Jesus re-interpreted the meaning of the kingdom in order to describe that power which generated the being of persons who acted in freedom from tribal controls—not only himself, but John the Baptist as well. But this hypothesis must be tested through an examination of the other core sayings which employ kingdom language.

Jesus and the symbol "kingdom of God"

An extremely important core saying in this connection is one preserved only by Luke:

> The kingdom of God is not coming
> with signs to be observed;
> nor will they say, "Lo, here it is!" or "There!"
> for behold, the kingdom of God is in the midst of you
> (Luke 17:20b-21).

Jesus states quite clearly that the kingdom of which he speaks is not a coming kingdom, a future kingdom, for it is already in the midst of his listeners. As soon as the kingdom is spoken of as a present reality, its character is changed. Obviously, the set of conceptions which associates the kingdom with a factual transformation or ending of the world is abrogated. Neither God, nor his Messiah, nor his angels, nor any other transcendental beings have intervened from a mythological heaven, for in that case Jesus' listeners would have seen them with their own eyes coming down through the clouds, as it were.

According to some expectations, various "signs" were expected to precede and to accompany the eschatological consummation. As Mark says, referring to such an event:

> But in those days, after that tribulation, the sun will be darkened, and the moon will not give its light, and the stars will be falling from heaven, and the powers in the heavens will be shaken. And then they will see the Son of man coming in clouds with great power and glory (Mark 13:24-26).

According to the angels in 4 Ezra, there will also be signs attending the event:

> ...the sun shall suddenly shine forth at night,
> and the moon during the day.
> Blood shall drip from wood,
> and the stone shall utter its voice;
> the peoples shall be troubled,
> and the stars shall fall   (II Esdras 5:4-5).

I could multiply examples of this sort, but these texts are sufficient to illustrate the kind of thing meant by "signs," and to show that they are quite visible.

Jesus explicitly repudiates the expectation that any prodigious signs accompany the appearance of the kingdom. At the least, this sets his conception of the kingdom apart from "apocalyptic" eschatology which, by definition, entailed speculation regarding such signs. There is no evidence that John's eschatology was of the apocalyptic variety; there is no reason to believe that John the Baptist speculated concerning apocalyptic signs. But John the Baptist did warn of the wrath to come which would involve a punishment by fire of the unrepentant (Matt 3:7-10 = Luke 3:7-9). In other words, John's preaching drew upon the conceptions and pictures of an eschatological tradition which was rooted in a mythological world-view. Therefore we must conclude that Jesus' saying not only distinguishes Jesus' understanding of the kingdom from apocalyptic expectation, but his saying also distinguishes his understanding of the kingdom from the kind of eschatological preaching represented by John the Baptist. In short, Jesus employs the language of the kingdom, but uses this language in a way that differs explicitly from the usage of his contemporaries, predecessors, and successors.

We have examined what the saying does say by way of distinguishing Jesus' understanding of the kingdom from apocalyptic expectation and from the preaching of eschatological prophecy. What about Jesus' silence? Jesus does *not* say that the kingdom will be evident in any political or social movements. Nor does he mention the kingdom in connection with traditional Jewish expectation that God would act in history on behalf of his *people*. In other words, Jesus does employ the language of the kingdom, which had rich associations among his listeners with conventional ways of understanding the history of the Hebrew people and of God's activity on behalf of them, but Jesus maintains a deafening silence with respect to these expectations.

The language and conceptions of eschatological prophecy (as with John the Baptist) are missing; the conceptions of apocalyptic are repudiated; and the expectations of the Jewish people are ignored. Instead, Jesus states that "the kingdom of God is in the midst of you." In other words, Jesus repudiates two ways of understanding the kingdom, is silent about a third, and instead he locates the kingdom in a quite unexpected quarter. What could he mean when he says "the kingdom of God is in the midst of you"?

The Greek which the R.S.V. translates "in your midst" can also be translated "within you," as the K.J.V. does. A decision between the two cannot be made philologically, since both translations are possible. If one translates "within you," however, the meaning is precisely that which Nietzsche analyzes under the rubric of the psychology of the redeemer as a retreat into the sweet blessedness of a purely inner world. It is remarkable that so much rests on a preposition! We cannot exclude "within you" simply because it would entail concluding that Jesus had the mentality of a retarded pubescent. On the other hand, in order to know which translation to adopt, we must consider the other kingdom sayings of Jesus, *none* of which points in the direction of an inner world as the location of the kingdom.

The kingdom sayings suggest that the kingdom is manifested in persons. So to say that "the kingdom of God is in your midst" is not to make the kingdom of God into a spatially restricted entity that is "between" human beings in the way that a chair is between two people standing on either side of it. The way in which Jesus uses kingdom language suggests that the kingdom manifests itself in and *among* persons, that it is a power in which human beings participate. Since Jesus associates the kingdom with John the Baptist, we cannot conclude that Jesus alone manifests the kingdom, as if "the kingdom of God is in your midst" meant "*I* am in your midst."

"In *your* midst" or "among *you*" points in the direction of the listeners' experience. The saying states, "Do not look to a future, eschatological kingdom that you would associate with conceptions of a tripartite universe whose heavenly entities will terminate the earthly realm as you know it; and do not think of the kingdom in apocalyptic terms, expecting prodigies to occur that will signal the dissolution of the present cosmic order; but what you think of as the kingdom of God is a phenomenon that is already among you and is, at least potentially, part of your present experience. Forget about your mythological conceptions for a moment, and just attend to what you might see and what you might hear."

It is possible that Jesus means that the kingdom of God is potentially part of his listeners' experience in the sense that *only* he and John the Baptist manifest the kingdom. It is true that they both manifest the kingdom of God, not in the sense that both "preached" the kingdom (for it was not on the level of ideas that they challenged their contemporaries) but in the sense that both manifested the power of the kingdom in their activity. Since the kingdom of

God reveals itself in the being of persons, that is, in and through more than one person, the kingdom of God is to be understood as a trans-personal power. That which establishes humans in the mode of being as free persons is a power in which human beings other than John the Baptist and Jesus can also participate. We can paraphrase Jesus' saying: "Your concept of the kingdom of God, whether it belongs to the future mythologically conceived in either eschatological or apocalyptic terms misses the reality of the kingdom, for the symbol really refers to a power that is a factor in human experience." In other words, Jesus *de-mythologized* the symbol kingdom of God!

Jesus and the demonic

The synoptic tradition tells us that there were exorcists among the early Christians, and that they interpreted their ability to cast out demons as deriving from Jesus (Mark 6:7 par.; Mark 3:13-15; 16:17). There were even itinerant Jewish exorcists who appeared in Ephesus and attempted to use the name of Jesus to cast out demons—unsuccessfully, according to Luke's account (Acts 19:11-17). Matthew finds it necessary to state that the ability to cast out demons in the name of Jesus was insufficient to guarantee entrance into the kingdom of heaven (Matt 7:21-23). The important point to note here is that exorcists were a common feature of the ancient world. There were pagan, Jewish (see also Matt 12:27—Luke 11:19), and Christian exorcists.

Several stories in the synoptic tradition describe Jesus as casting out demons: in the synagogue at Capernaum (Mark 1:21-28 par.); the Gerasene demoniac (Mark 5:1-20 par.); the epileptic boy (Mark 9:14-27 par.); the dumb demon (Matt 9:32-34). These stories function in order to give support to the early Christians' claims about Jesus—that he is the Holy One of God (Mark 1:24 par.) or the Son of the Most High God (Mark 5:7 par.). They are useful, therefore, as sources for reconstructing the earliest Christologies, but cannot serve as sources of information about the earthly Jesus.

That Jesus himself did cast out demons is confirmed by one of his own sayings preserved in Q:

> If it is by the finger of God that I cast out demons,
> then the kingdom of God has come upon you
> (Luke 11:20; cf., Matt 12:28).

According to popular belief, reflected in the stories told in the synoptic tradition about Jesus, various kinds of illness were thought to be caused by the invasion into human beings of forces hostile to physical and mental health. Thus, the Gerasene demoniac, according to the story, lived among the tombs, was always crying out, and bruising himself with stones. Not unnaturally, the story describes him as possessed by an unclean spirit (Mark 5:1-13 par.). A boy who fell to the ground, foamed at the mouth, gnashed his teeth, and became rigid is also described as being possessed by a spirit (Mark 9:14-27 par.). A man who is dumb is depicted as a demoniac (Matt 9:32-34). The close connection between illness and possession is also evident in Mark 1:32-34: "they brought to him all who were sick or possessed with demons .... and he healed many who were sick with various diseases, and cast out many demons."

How, then, did Jesus orient himself to popular belief? The circumspection of Jesus' saying is remarkable: "*If* it is by the finger of God that I cast out demons . . . ." By putting this acknowledgement of his healing power in the conditional, it is as if Jesus is saying: "According to popular understanding, it is by the power of God (= the finger of God) that I cast out what you would call 'demons.'" Jesus does *not* say: "Because I cast out demons by the power of God." Instead, he adopts the viewpoint of his listeners as a provisional way of construing the fact that there were those who felt mentally or physically restored by his power.

The experience of the demonic is a widespread one in human life, and was not restricted to the first century, nor to primitive cultures. It is the experience that some trans-human enormity has invaded human life from beyond, and has done so for destructive purposes.[3] Frequently the recognition of destructiveness in human experience is apprehended as being the cause of alien agencies; and in the ancient world such alien agencies were thought of as entities —"demons." In contemporary experience those alien forces that invade human life to destroy it are regarded with no less awesome a sense of fear and dread.

Contemporary films and novels are replete with images of creatures from outer space which enter earthly life and dispossess

---

3. For an analysis of the phenomenology of illness, and the experience of illness as "a living thing which has its form, its own duration, its habits," see Jean-Paul Sartre, *Being and Nothingness*, pp. 441-42.

humans, injecting themselves into human beings in order to carry out their dark purposes. Ours, too, is a time in which there is a widespread sense, reflected in contemporary art, film, and literature, that human life is surrounded by and vulnerable to super-terrestial agencies. One could multiply examples almost *ad infinitum*: science fiction ("Them," "The Thing," "War of the Worlds," "Close Encounters of the Third Kind"), the demonic ("The Exorcist," "Damien," "Omen"), and the catastrophe movies ("Jaws," "Earthquake"), etc. All of these films deal in various ways with the frailty of the human venture in the face of what are experienced as trans- and anti-human enormities.

In the contemporary world, it is particularly in connection with disease that conceptions associated with demonic possession are evident. The name for an alien force that invades human life for destructive purposes used to be "polio," now it is "cancer." In the face of the experience of the demonic, all the available medical and technological resources are marshalled in opposition, and those who are possessed, for example with cancer, as the literature on death and dying shows, are viewed in much the same way as popular superstition used to view those who were epileptic or dumb —as people controlled by an alien force and hence somehow not really human.

The experience of the demonic, in other words, does not necessarily entail the adoption of the language and conceptions of demonology, nor the actual belief in demons as factual entities. All the saying of Jesus tells us is that Jesus exercised power to free human beings from those forces which were *experienced* as having the character of the demonic. Jesus' own circumspection with respect to mythological thinking becomes particularly clear when one listens to Jesus' silence. He does *not* say: "If it is by the finger of God that I cast out demons, then I am the Son of God and you had best believe that I am." Nor does he say: "If it is by the finger of God that I cast out demons, then I am the Messiah, and you should repent for the judgment is coming and I am the judge." In other words, Jesus does *not* interpret the meaning of what was factually happening by appealing to the apocalyptic conceptions or messianic expectations of his listeners, nor does he, and this is crucial, make any claims for himself.

Given the tendency of the entire early Christian tradition which attributed a whole variety of Christological titles to Jesus, Jesus' own silence regarding his status is indeed earsplitting. Moreover, Jesus does not say: "If it is by the finger of God that I cast out demons, then this is a sign that a transcendent God is about to intervene in the social and political sphere on behalf of his people, Israel." Instead, Jesus once again re-interprets the symbol kingdom of God in terms of the human experience of particular individuals.

This saying states that one can discern the power of God, which people in their mythological thinking conceived of as an other-worldly reality, in the experience of those individuals who had been liberated from the demonic. In other words, the power which Jesus calls "God" is a power in human experience which opposes those forces that threaten to annihilate the bases of human life as human. This power is active in Jesus, and it can be communicated to others. It is called "God" because its character is to sustain individual life as human even where individuals are subjected to anti-human enormities. In that sense, the power of God is "creative" as opposed to "destructive."

The picture of Jesus' understanding of the kingdom of God (= God's power) which is emerging from his core sayings is a complex one, but one thing is clear: this power is repeatedly associated with the being of humans as free persons. Jesus associates it with his own and with John's activity, and observes that this power evokes contrary human impulses whose purpose is to control, dominate, and even destroy. We have used the traditional theological category "evil" to identify those anti-human impulses which have as their agents *human beings themselves*. On the other hand, those agencies which threaten to overwhelm human life and which are experienced as demonic (e.g., epilepsy, dumbness, insanity, and, in our day, cancer) are to be distinguished from the power of evil, which has a human face. The power of God is clearly effective in its opposition to anti- but non-human agencies. Whether or in what way Jesus considers the kingdom of God to be active in the face of the power of evil itself, however, is a question that must await our examination of Jesus' parable about the man going down the road who fell among robbers (Chapter Eleven).

CHAPTER FOUR

Receiving versus holding

Evil versus the demonic

Those who confuse evil with the demonic do not understand evil as a human phenomenon, as something for which human beings are responsible (in Dostoyevsky's *The Brothers Karamazov*, the Grand Inquisitor correctly predicts that modern man will say: "... There is no crime, and therefore no sin; there is only hunger. 'Feed men, and then ask of them virtue!'"[1]). In the contemporary world, the victim mentality has triumphed to such an extent that in virtually any dispute the side which succeeds in having itself understood as the victim is automatically considered to have the better position. To be a victim is to be in the *right* (supposedly from a *moral* point of view although the issue is not moral but one of propaganda, for the victim is exempted from virtue).

Those who confuse evil with the demonic frequently believe that evil can be avoided by returning to a pre-lapsarian state of innocence, before one was overtaken by this alien force for which one is not ultimately responsible. This view often looks nostalgically to childhood as a period of unqualified innocence and therefore as a model for human life remaining outside the demonic's sphere of control.

Matthew interpreted one of Jesus' sayings in this way, and his interpretation has dominated Christian thought ever since:

> Truly, I say to you, unless you turn and become like children, you will never enter the kingdom of heaven (Matt 18:3).

1. Dostoyevsky, *The Brothers Karamazov*, p. 262.

Writing about fifty years after the death of Jesus, Matthew has reworded Jesus' original saying in order to incorporate his view that in order to qualify for entrance into the kingdom of heaven (conceived of mythologically as a super-terrestial place), Christians must become like children, meaning that they must develop the humility consistent with obedience to and dependence on a heavenly Father. Indeed, all of Chapter 18 of Matthew's gospel delineates the appropriate attitudes of members of the Christian community if they are to gain entrance into heaven.

An inclusive awareness of children

The original wording of Jesus' saying is provided by Mark and by Luke:

> Truly, I say to you, whoever does not receive the kingdom of God like a child shall not enter it (Mark 10:15 = Luke 18:17).

No one who has carefully attended to Jesus' similitude on the children in the market places (Chapter Two) could possibly suppose that Jesus held a sentimental view of children. (I use the word sentimental here in the sense of an *exclusive* consciousness, that type which selects only certain aspects of experience to the exclusion of all others in order that it might retain *uncomplicated* feelings about the phenomenon. Even a totally cynical or purely intellectual view can be sentimental in this sense, whereas a very complex emotional understanding of a situation, on the other hand, can be an indication of an *inclusive* consciousness. The distinction is not between the mind and the heart but between the simplistic and the complex, between the exclusive and the inclusive.) No one who understands the psychological dynamics of children's games as acutely as Jesus does could be accused of holding a sentimental view of the innocence of children. Indeed, according to the saying, children exhibit the human impulse to control and to dominate in a more naked way than adults do.

In any case, Jesus speaks of *receiving* like a child, not of *becoming* like children. How, then, does a child receive? In the first place, a child does not receive something given by first organizing within itself any particular set of attitudes such as ready trust and instinctive obedience; the child receives what is offered. Receiving is not the same as taking, which implies grasping, capturing, seizing, or getting by conquest. Receiving implies accepting *freely* what is offered freely. Receiving precludes all calculation, all consideration of what is owing, all assessment of the situation in terms of sale and purchase, all consciousness of commerce, debt, right, obligation, or compensation. The child who receives has not yet developed the mental habit of measuring or calculating together with their psychological concomitants. In short, there is no sense of "justice" in the sense of measurement of equivalencies or of achieving equity. The child who receives has no consciousness of creditor or ower, no consciousness of indebtedness. In other words, the kingdom of God is not a commodity, not some *thing* the value of which can be calculated nor the reception of which entails commercial debt or obligation.

Jesus states that whoever does not receive the kingdom of God like a child shall not enter it. This is to make an observation of fact, not to set entrance requirements. Jesus does not exclude anyone from participation in the power of God; people exclude themselves when they choose contrary modes of being human. From the perspective of Jesus' sayings, there are various modes of being human, not all of them rooted in the kingdom of God.

The kingdom not only has the character of something which one receives, it also has the character of something into which one enters. This shows that the kingdom does not function in order to refer to a set of beliefs or concepts, but rather to a *dimension* of human experience. It is not a mythological place (heaven) for one does not "receive" heaven. The kingdom is a reality which Jesus speaks of in a variety of ways: it suffers violence, it comes upon individuals and frees them from trans- and anti-human forces, it is in the midst of persons, it is communicable, one receives it, and one can enter into it. Only a "power" can be spoken of in such a variety of ways, for power is polymorphous. It is a power which engenders specific modes of being human—those characterized by the freedom of persons. Since Jesus designates this power as "God," the implication is that it is ultimate. Those modes of being human grounded in the power of God are rooted in the real, as opposed to those modes of being human which are rooted in other, contrary, implicitly counterfeit, forces.

Holding on to what one does

Not every human being is fit for life in this mode. As Jesus says, in a core saying preserved only by Luke:

No one who puts his hand to the plow and looks back
is fit for the kingdom of God (Luke 9:62).

The plowman uses the plow to break open the soil. He who looks back while he plows tries to decide whether he is doing a good job by looking back on what he has done, so he does not pay attention to where he is headed. To use a modern analogy, he is like someone who drives his car while constantly looking in the rearview mirror. This kind of human being finds it difficult, or even impossible, to know the value of his present actions until he has judged their results. The value of no activity can be grasped in itself and for itself, but must be known through comparison, for judging by estimating results is a means of judging through comparison.

In other words, the man who puts his hand to the plow and looks back is someone who has to "hold on" to what he is doing in order to know its value. The image, then, is one of lack of confidence, an absence of a non-reflective awareness of the value of what he is doing. He lacks confidence in the activities of the self. The image of the man who puts his hand to the plow and *looks* back identifies a particular mode of being human from the perspective of its distinctive mode of *consciousness*, which is a *holding* mode. Jesus quite readily discriminates among various modes of being human and here he observes, with characteristic detachment, that the holding mode (that is to say, the comparing, calculating mode) is not fit for participation in that dimension of human reality nourished by the kingdom of God.

Treasure is treasure

It is probably Jesus' emphasis on "receiving" rather than "holding" that has caused many of the early Christians to conclude that those who had worldly riches were not fit for the kingdom. Luke has made this idea central to his view of Jesus, and so placed at the beginning of Jesus' public ministry a programmatic statement that Jesus came "to preach good news to the poor" (Luke 4:16-19), a New Testament passage that has proved to be extremely popular as a proof text for contemporary liberation theologians. The idea that

Jesus opposed the rich and sided with the poor was deeply embedded in the tradition from its earliest stages, and was connected with the Christian concept of reversal: "Many that are first will be last, and the last first" (Mark 10:31 par.; cf., Luke 18:19; and *passim*). This interpretation of Jesus' meaning was founded on the conception of the kingdom of God as heaven, and on a literal understanding of treasure as meaning material treasure; hence the long, and central, Christian tradition of developing world-negating attitudes.

Part of the reason for this development was the notion that religious treasure offers a better security than worldly treasure, a notion which is expressed, for example, in the advice given by an early Christian teacher which was collected in Q:

Do not lay up for yourselves treasures on earth,
where moth and rust consume and where thieves break in and steal,
but lay up for yourselves treasures in heaven,
whether neither moth nor rust consumes and where thieves do not break in and steal.
For where your treasure is, there will your heart be also
(Matt 6:19-21 = Luke 12:33-34).

This saying does not oppose the attitude of holding, but instead elevates it to a religious principle. Be acquisitive, it says, but strive to acquire those things which time does not erode.

That these New Testament passages have authorized within certain Christian circles the development of a repudiation of such positive values as beauty, health, freedom, independence, power (and one might add, the generosity of those who are rich enough to give), a repudiation infected by *ressentiment*, seems hardly to be denied. But quite apart from its role in feeding *ressentiment*, this tradition has failed to notice that it is not the possession nor lack of material goods that distinguishes those who live in the mode of holding from those who do not. This tradition fails to observe that different people can "hold on" to different things.

As Zooey says, in J.D. Salinger's novel, *Franny and Zooey*:

". . . as a matter of simple logic, there's no difference at all, that I can see, between the man who's greedy for material treasure—or even intellectual treasure—and the man who's greedy for spiritual treasure. As you say, treasure's treasure, God damn it, and it seems to me that ninety per cent of all the world-hating saints in history were just as acquisitive and unattractive, basically, as the rest of us are."[2]

2. Salinger, *Franny and Zooey*, pp. 147-48.

The core saying of Jesus which speaks to the matter of holding, acquisitiveness, and greed, is the following:

> It is easier for a camel to go through the eye of a needle than for a rich man to enter the kingdom of God (Mark 10:25 = Matt 19:24 = Luke 18:25).

The traditional interpretation of this saying presumes that the kingdom of God refers to a mythological place (heaven) and that the rich are prohibited entrance.

However, the saying speaks of the difficulty the rich man had in "entering" the kingdom of God, not of his being excluded. I do not think it is necessary to belabour the point that Jesus did not share his contemporaries' mythological conceptions about heaven. To paraphrase the saying: "It is easier for a camel to go through the eye of a needle than for a rich man to enter that dimension of human experience sustained by the power which generates the life of human beings as free persons." If the man who puts his hand to the plow and looks back serves as an image of those whose *consciousness* is characterized by holding on to their *activities*, then the rich man serves as an image of those whose orientation to *things* is characterized by holding.

Not everyone who is rich is a Scrooge, and not everyone who is poor is generous. Zooey's observation holds that ninety per cent of all the world-hating saints in history were basically acquisitive, as does Franny's observation that the acquisitive instinct is just as likely to be found among academics or the culturally sophisticated as it is among the wealthy. The point is that those who live out of the attitude of holding, of whatever kind, are not fit for, or cannot enter, that dimension of human experience characterized by receiving, any more than those who establish their identity through controlling and being controlled are fit for or can enter that same dimension marked by freedom.

Sartre's analysis of the phenomenology of hate is just as illuminating in this context as it was in the context of the interpretation of the meaning of violence. Sartre observes that the crux of the matter has to do with the way in which one responds to the free being of another, and the crisis becomes particularly acute when one is confronted with a freely enacted kindness. One can respond with love, or one can respond with hate, but one cannot remain neutral.

The kingdom of God is distinguished by free giving and free receiving. Those who live out of the attitude of holding find it extremely difficult, or even impossible, to accept presents. As we have seen, entering into the dimension sustained by the kingdom of God precludes any attitude of calculation, all consideration of compensation or commerce. To enter into that dimension is as hard for those intent on piling up treasure of whatever kind as it is for a camel to pass through the eye of a needle. This dimension is fraught with uncertainty, surprise, and risk. How many people are prepared to surrender the certainties of that to which they can hold on for the dubious advantages of living in the personal mode? The Christian tradition has circumvented this fundamental issue (and, incidentally, fed *ressentiment*) by promising a heavenly reward to all those who give away what they have. But Jesus himself does not trade in such ideas. His own sayings, instead, heighten the dilemma, if anything, because of their silence with respect to the human impulse for security.

All he can promise is that the mode of being human which is rooted in the kingdom of God is grounded in the real, that is oriented to the highest possibilities for the fulfillment of human existence. If this mode turns out in the particular circumstances of an individual's life to involve factual deprivation, judged from the point of view of mankind's basic desires not to be hungry, not to live in uncertainty, and not to be lonely, then it is not Jesus who tries to cushion his listeners from these consequences of living in the personal mode. From the Grand Inquisitor's point of view, this means that Jesus does not show a proper love for mankind, that he expects too much of man, and that his words are only for an elect— for the strong and powerful. On the other hand, perhaps holding out to man the possibility of greatness is also a form of love, strange thought it may seem to the humanitarian.

The two ways

There is one saying attributed to Jesus in the synoptic tradition that I would like to comment on in this connection:

The gate is wide and the way is easy, that leads to destruction,
and those who enter by it are many.
The gate is narrow and the way is hard, that leads to life,
and those who find it are few (Matt 7:13-14; cf., Luke 13:24).

Although this saying is not one of the core sayings, largely because the motif of the two ways was widely used in antiquity and is known from both pagan and Jewish sources, the thrust of this saying coheres with the meaning of Jesus' core sayings.

If Matthew had composed the saying, he would have spoken of entering the kingdom of heaven. Luke has characteristically reworded it in a moralizing sense and suggests that those who do not strive will be excluded: "Strive to enter by the narrow door; for many, I tell you, will seek to enter and will not be able" (Luke 13:24). The saying as transmitted by Matthew does not employ any mythological concepts such as heaven or hell, judgment or reward. It distinguishes simply between *life* and *destruction,* and both are spoken of matter of factly, with detachment.

The saying is a neutral observation by a keen observer of the human situation who notices that most people lead lives that issue in destruction. Only a few "find" (the gratuitousness implied in this verb is characteristic!) the way to life, a way that involves hardship —presumably, courage. The saying, if authentic, promises nothing to those who choose to enter the dimension sustained and nourished by the power of God other than *life.* There are no transcendental promises, no transcendental rewards or punishments. If authentic, it certainly is an eloquent expression of the observation that the fulfillment or destruction of human existence depends entirely on the mode of being human that one chooses. "Hell" then would be the destruction of human existence, and "heaven" would be life. There is nothing else.

CHAPTER FIVE

Jesus and his table companions

Prayer before eating and drinking

In the first of the core sayings which we examined, Jesus provided us with the information that he came eating and drinking. This refers to his drinking with friends who included, according to the similitude, people with whom observant Jews would not share a meal. Those who *held on* to their identity as members of the endogenous eating group were not "fit for" the risks and uncertainties of being in the receptive mode. They experienced themselves as objectified in the face of personal freedom, and hence gave in to the impulse to detract, trafficked in value delusion, and even became violent.

Is there any other saying of Jesus which might illuminate his practice of table fellowship, a practice which was central to his public activity? Yes, there is, and fortunately it has been preserved by Q and transmitted by both Matthew and Luke.

Luke 11:2-4

Father,
Hallowed be thy name.
Thy kingdom come.

Give us each day our daily bread;
And forgive us our sins
For we ourselves forgive everyone
who is indebted to us;
And put us not to the test.

Matthew 6:9-10

Our Father who art in heaven,
Hallowed be thy name.
Thy kingdom come,
Thy will be done,
On earth as it is in heaven.
Give us this day our daily bread,
And forgive us our debts,
As we also have forgiven our debtors;

And put us not to the test,
But deliver us from the evil one.

Synoptic comparison of Luke's version with that of Matthew makes it quite clear that Matthew transmits an expanded version of the prayer. "Who art in heaven" inserts the mythological conception of the Father as a transcendent being who resides in a superterrestial location. There, other transcendent beings (probably angels) are thought of as doing his will. Matthew shows a characteristic interest in the idea of doing the will of God, and this is evident in his expansion of the prayer, which also thereby imports into the prayer the conception of a tripartite universe. Luke preserves the original wording of the first three verses.

Since it is characteristic of Luke's editorializing to moralize sayings by giving them an iterative force, Matthew's "give us *this* day our daily bread" has a higher probability of being original. Both Luke and Matthew in the next two verses reflect the idea that what is forgiven is something for which people are indebted to one another. Luke's "sins" is likely due to secondary moralizing, if "sin" here means "transgression of a moral code." However, if "sin" is understood as "injury done to another," then the Greek words, which use the metaphor of debt and obligation, refer to "what we owe those whom we have injured." Obviously, the context of the prayer is not commerce, and no moral code or system of religious law is in view, but rather relationships between people. An approximate paraphrase of the sense of these verses is:

And forgive us what we owe those whom we have injured,
As we ourselves forgive what is owing from those who have injured us.

In other words, the ancient and universal principle of an eye for an eye and a tooth for a tooth is abrogated.

The R.S.V. translates the last petition as "lead us not into temptation," thus interpreting the petition morally, as a temptation to transgress ethical or religious prohibitions. However, the prayer deals with relationships between people, and so we should, in our translation, adhere more strictly to the Greek, which says "and put us not to the test." Matthew's gloss on the verse ("but deliver us from the evil one") shows that his tradition understood the petition to refer to a more fundamental conflict than temptation to transgress. Matthew's tradition, probably rightly, understood the petition as having to do with a potential encounter with evil. How evil might be encountered in the context of table fellowship, and how this encounter might be a test for those expressing their readiness to forgive injuries done to one another, remains still to be answered.

A close approximation of the prayer uttered by Jesus is:

Father,
Hallowed be thy name.
Thy kingdom come.
Give us this day our daily bread,
And forgive us what we owe those whom we have injured,
As we ourselves forgive what is owing from those who have injured us.
And put us not to the test.

Context and meaning of Jesus' prayer

The first principle of interpretation is to establish the context of a statement, for context always controls meaning. The saying was preserved without external narrative context in Q, and so Matthew and Luke have each placed the prayer in contexts which they have created. Matthew uses the prayer, along with numerous other previously detached sayings, in his composition of the Sermon on the Mount, and here sandwiches the prayer into a section dealing with instructions on religious practice—almsgiving, prayer, and fasting (Matt 6:1-18). Luke mentions that Jesus "was praying in a certain place," and then taught the disciples how to pray (Luke 11:1-4). The lack of specific context in Luke, and Matthew's use of the prayer in his Sermon on the Mount, show that each found the saying in Q unattached to any specific historical context. We are dependent on purely internal evidence for determining the historical context in which it was spoken and to which it refers. Fortunately, that is not difficult to determine.

The petition for bread shows that the saying belongs in the context of Jesus' table fellowship. This prayer was uttered by Jesus and his table companions on the occasions when they ate and drank together.

The prayer opens by addressing someone or something as "Father," blessing this name, and praying for the presence of his kingdom. The prayer addresses that power to which elsewhere Jesus refers as the kingdom of God, but here he addresses that power personally. Matthew's community understood the Father to be quite literally a person, a personal entity who inhabits a place above the earth (heaven). Whether or not Jesus himself shared this view of God as a mythological being is another matter. We have seen that Jesus speaks of the kingdom of God in a variety of ways which show clearly that he does *not* think of the kingdom of God in mythological terms, that he does not think of God as a heavenly being, but rather uses the symbol "kingdom of God" to refer to a power that is active in human experience. The important question is: why did Jesus address this power personally? We must leave that question in suspension until we have carefully considered other aspects of the prayer's meaning.

It is striking that Jesus teaches his table companions to pray for the coming of the kingdom of God when they are about to eat and drink together. Jesus' statement that the kingdom is not coming with signs to be observed, but is already in the midst of his hearers, shows that the prayer for the coming of the kingdom cannot be an expression of hope that a mythological kingdom will soon transform the earth. It is not a prayer for the "other" world to manifest itself in "this" world. Rather, it is an expression of hope that the power which sustains individuals as free persons will be active during table fellowship.

This is coupled with an expression of readiness on the part of those who gather to eat and drink together to transcend the imperatives of an eye for an eye and a tooth for a tooth—the *lex talionis*. In other words, the table companions express the hope that all present will have the strength communicated to them to overcome the human impulse to keep score of wrongs done to one another. In the context of the prayer, "forgiveness" does not mean the attitude that no longer discriminates among differing kinds of human behaviour, for example in the sense that Nietzsche speaks of when he describes the illusion-creating force of love that no longer notices any other because its impulse is to feel itself in union with everyone and everything. In this prayer, the otherness of other persons is acknowledged, and this is evident in the expressed consciousness that human beings *do* injure one another (the matter of "intentions" is left out entirely), and that consequently human beings do experience an impulse to keep score of wrongs.

Forgiveness in this prayer means a readiness to be strong enough to overcome the impulse for revenge. The existence of *conflict* among human beings is presupposed and accepted, and the remedy suggested is not the repression but the overcoming of impulses generated by such conflicts. The assumption is that it is "the kingdom of God" which can empower the table companions to forgive one another. In the midst of the quite natural conflicts and alienations which characterize human relationships, it is the power of the kingdom which, it is hoped, will provide them with the strength to overcome those impulses which would result in hatred.

Different people and groups eat for different reasons. For some, eating is solely for survival. For other groups, eating functions primarily as a means of perpetuating the endogenous (and endogamous!) group. Judging from Jesus' similitude on the children playing games, and from the wording of this prayer, it would appear that for Jesus eating and drinking was the occasion for fellowship among those against whom the tribalized children were prejudiced, and those whom they would segregate.

Fellowship is not the same as feeling oneself in union with everyone. Fellowship implies exchange among those who maintain their identities as separate persons. This observation leads us directly to the question with which we began our quest for the elusive reality of Jesus: can people be present with one another in their concrete particularity without having the situation degenerate into an occasion for the expression of evil impulses?

The wording of the prayer does not take the sanguine view that differences between people are only superficial, as if all would be well if each would only agree to overlook his difference from all others, so that all could experience mellow feelings of harmonious union with everyone else. For those oriented to social utility, one tries to produce a harmonious group usually by appealing to everyone's self-interest, particularly to everyone's narcissism: think of everyone not as an *other* but as your *self* so that your self-love can guide your behaviour and attitudes. The ethics of narcissism were utilized in both Hellenism and Judaism, in the form of the Golden Rule, and entered the synoptic tradition through Q (Matt 7:12 = Luke 6:31). That utilitarian narcissism is frequently held up as the epitome of Jesus' so-called "ethics" is most offensive.

The awareness of things ill-done and done to others' harm

Jesus' prayer acknowledges that when the table companions gather together for fellowship, negative human impulses may be evoked. So the table companions pray that their eating and drinking together will not be an occasion when they are put to the test, meaning that they pray that the power which sustains them in their being as free persons will enable those present at the meal to respond to the freedom of each *other* not with hatred (one possibility) but with a free and voluntary willingness to engage with the *freedom* of the *other*. This is what it means to "love" the "neighbour," an understanding of "love" to which this prayer gives expression, and to which Dostoyevsky devotes much of *The Brothers Karamazov*.

The capacity to engage voluntarily with the freedom of another is the exception, not the rule, in human experience. It is precisely when persons are present with one another in their freedom that the potency of destructive impulses is most powerful. At this level of inter-personal dynamics, intentions are irrelevant. As T.S. Eliot observes, reflecting on past relationships:

> ... the rending pain of re-enactment
> Of all that you have done, and been; the shame
> Of motives late revealed, and the awareness
> Of things ill done and done to others' harm
> Which once you took for exercise of virtue.[1]

It is precisely when people are oriented to one another in openness that they, if they are sensitive, experience the most acute awareness of how their most well-intended actions, those they take for exercise of virtue, are frequently either ill-done or done to the other's harm. The closer people are to one another, the more need there is for forgiveness.

From table fellowship to Eucharist

From its earliest stages, the Christian tradition struggled with the memory that it was one of Jesus' table companions who betrayed him into the hands of those who wished to destroy him, and with the memory that all of his table companions without exception abandoned him when he fell into the hands of his enemies. His friend, Peter, even denied that he had known Jesus. None of these pieces of information was invented by the earliest Christians. From the point of view of historical probability they enjoy the highest degree of certainty, because the kernels of these traditions are extremely embarrassing. In the successive stages of

1. T.S. Eliot, "Little Gidding," II, in *The Complete Poems and Plays*, p. 142.

the tradition, scholarly analysis can follow the tortured efforts of the Christian communities to come to grips with these memories. From the point of view of developing Christian theology, the greatest problem was the conflict between the Christological claims made about Jesus and these facts. How could one both make exalted Christological claims about Jesus and at the same time admit that he had been betrayed by a table companion, abandoned by the rest of them, and then denied by a friend?

The solution worked out in the pre-Markan tradition was to represent Jesus as predicting that all of these things would happen, and that they were necessary in the divine plan. Such a solution was apparently more or less satisfying to the early Christians, and remains so to many even today. But such a solution can be satisfying only for those who already hold certain beliefs about Jesus. For them, the narration of these events evokes a poignant response precisely because the narratives were composed out of a sense of dismay that the Son of God could have been so treated by those close to him. This solution does not touch the heart of the matter, because it represents a stage of development in Christian reflection that has already advanced beyond the point where Jesus' friends and table companions perceived the dimension of experience over which he presided, to which he introduced them, and into which he afforded them insight and understanding, as the dimension of the really real. In other words, this stage of reflection has already reached the conclusion that it was in table fellowship that the power which one can identify as "God" had entered human experience. They expressed this conclusion by attributing divine titles to Jesus. But all that is after the fact. At the point where Jesus was betrayed, abandoned, and denied, all of this was very much in question—so much in question that everyone close to him doubted, and acted upon their doubt, that the dimension of the personal was where the real was to be located.

Nevertheless, the fact that the canonical tradition took these occurrences seriously, attempting to understand them in terms of their own theological categories and perceptions, shows that the earliest Christians had at least grasped, however fragmentarily, where the issues lay. The point is not that God incarnate had been betrayed, abandoned, denied, and crucified, and later through his resurrection demonstrated his divinity. The point is that the earthly human being, Jesus of Nazareth, had invited his table companions to locate ultimate reality in the dimension of the personal, and that he himself lived out the consequences of having chosen this mode of being human while his table companions balked. The resurrection experiences are to be understood in this context, then, as the apprehension by, initially, Jesus' table companions that this mode of being human, though complicated and challenged by suffering and death, was by no means drained of its potency even by that person's death. Death cannot annihilate the reality revealed in Jesus' mode of being human. The early Christians expressed their apprehension of this, of course, in terms of ways of construing experience current at the time—for them, God had raised Jesus from the dead and they, as it were, experienced his continuing presence with them. Those who conceive of being human in terms of the mode of holding think of death as taking away what one has and of resurrection as giving it back. The resurrection experiences of the early Christians, however, are to be understood as their apprehension that the *receiving* mode was grounded in a reality whose potency could not be *taken* away. This is not to say that either Jesus or the early Christians held the Greek idea of immortality of the soul, for this idea infiltrated Christian doctrine much later, from around the second century onward. This idea does not fundamentally challenge the holding mode, but instead locates the reality of the individual in a supposed incorporeal essence which is immortal while only the body remains subject to time and death. Jesus' own sayings show that he construed human existence as a psycho-somatic totality. That is why suffering and death pose such crucial challenges to the viability of the personal mode; for those who have souls, like Socrates, suffering and death are not really issues at all, but merely, it is hoped, passage ways to a better existence.

We have so far found little evidence to support the view that the early Christians repeated Jesus' ideas and practice, that they thought in precisely the same way that he did. Whatever continuity there might have been between Jesus and the early Christians, it was not a continuity of a superficial kind. They appropriated what they believed Jesus to be saying in terms of their own religious categories and in terms of concepts borrowed from the various religious cultures in which the Christian movement spread. And they expressed the significance they saw in Jesus in terms of these same categories, all of which are rooted totally in the culture of the first century. Their continuity with Jesus was not one of language and ideas but of attempting to live in that dimension of human experience which Jesus had revealed to them. They felt that Jesus had put them into contact with ultimate reality, and so they expressed Jesus' significance by attributing divine titles and attributes to him. That is not surprising. After all, they had to understand him as best they could, considering that they felt he had truly disclosed the highest possibilities for human existence. One of the primary ways in which they attempted to continue living in the dimension which Jesus had revealed was through the early Christian practice of engaging in communal meals, enacted in memory of Jesus' table fellowship. This is where the continuity between Jesus and early Christianity is to be found. However, this is not the place to attempt to adumbrate a theological analysis of the early Christian movement and its continuities and discontinuities with Jesus. Our present concern is to try to comprehend better the dynamics of table fellowship as understood by Jesus himself.

Eating with the actual other

We have seen that Jesus' prayer acknowledges the conflict inherent in efforts to engage openly with the freedom of others. We can turn to modern literature for some assistance in thinking through the problems involved with table fellowship. We have already seen that in *The Brothers Karamazov* Ivan believes this kind of voluntary engagement with the actual other ("love of neighbour") to be virtually impossible. A similar opinion is expressed by another character in the novel, Mme. Hohlakov, when she is speaking to the monk Zossima. She professes to be in agony about her faith because she's afraid that death will be the end. She claims to have considered leaving all that she has and serving humanity, but realizes that if her charitable services were not met with gratitude she could hardly persevere:

> "... if anything could dissipate my love to humanity, it would be ingratitude. In short, I am a hired servant, I expect my payment at once—that is, praise, and the repayment of love with love. Otherwise I am incapable of loving any one."[2]

2. Dostoyevsky, *The Brothers Karamazov*, p. 56.

She believes that there should be some reward for love beyond the activity itself. Zossima informs her that this is exactly the same sort of thing a doctor had told him a long time ago:

> "I love humanity . . . but I wonder at myself. The more I love humanity in general, the less I love man in particular. In my dreams . . . I have often come to making enthusiastic schemes for the service of humanity, and perhaps I might actually have faced crucifixion if it had been suddenly necessary; and yet I am incapable of living in the same room with any one for two days together, as I know by experience. As soon as any one is near me, his personality disturbs my self-complacency and restricts my freedom. In twenty-four hours I begin to hate the best of men: one because he's too long over his dinner; another because he has a cold and keeps on blowing his nose. I become hostile to people the moment they come close to me. But it has always happened that the more I detest men individually the more ardent becomes my love for humanity."[3]

The crisis of open engagement occurs most acutely when people sit down to eat and drink together. It is then that forgiveness is most required. Table fellowship is not a business luncheon nor a romantic dinner, where those involved expect to get something from one another. When people eat and drink together and they have nothing to gain from one another, it all too easily happens that they disturb each other's self-complacency and restrict each other's freedom.

In Flaubert's novel, *Madame Bovary*, Emma becomes increasingly irritated by her husband, Charles:

> She was increasingly annoyed with him in general. As he grew older his manners became cruder than ever: he whittled the corks of empty wine bottles at the end of the meal, he ran his tongue over his teeth after eating, he made a gulping sound each time he swallowed a spoonful of soup; and as he became fatter his eyes, already small, seemed to be pushed up toward his temples by the puffiness of his cheeks.[4]

Simply by describing the specific details which Emma notices, and which her consciousness selects, Flaubert conveys the way this other human being beside her provokes a feeling of irritation. Indeed, the entire novel explores the contradiction between

---

3. Dostoyevsky, *The Brothers Karamazov*, p. 56.

4. Gustave Flaubert, *Madame Bovary*, translated by Lowell Blair, edited and with an introduction by Leo Bersani (New York: Bantam Books, 1972), p. 53.

Emma's desires for romantic transport and her distaste for people who are nearby. She experiences romantic feelings most intensely when thinking of people or places that are far away. All that is actual in her experience shatters her romantic longings. Even the presence of her various lovers interferes with the voluptuous pleasures of her reveries. In fact, the entire novel can be read as an exploration of man's offence at the actual, an offence which Emma experiences most acutely when eating with Charles:

> But it was especially at mealtimes that she felt she could bear her life no longer, in that little room on the ground floor with its smoking stove, squeaking door, sweating walls and damp stone floor. All the bitterness of life seemed to be served up to her on her plate, and as the steam rose from the boiled meat, waves of nausea rose from the depths of her soul. Charles was a slow eater; she would nibble a few hazelnuts, or lean on her elbow and idly make lines in the oilcloth with her knife.[5]

Many people would be willing to sacrifice their lives, if necessary, out of "love" for another. But such acts of immediate heroism which occur as it were on a stage with everyone watching, and which terminate the ordeal of living in the presence of the concrete other, are not to be confused with love of neighbour, which means hard work and tenacity, and which involves learning to affirm the actual other who sits across from one at the table, whether his or her table manners are graceful or ungraceful, his or her conversation engaging or boring, his or her habits mannerly or ill-mannered. The prayer that Jesus taught his table companions to say before sitting down to eat and drink together shows that Jesus understood the fundamental dynamics of such occasions, that it was during that time, as perhaps at no other, that they were most in need of that power which would sustain them in their readiness to be present in fellowship.

We are now in a position to understand why Jesus did address the power usually referred to as "God" or "kingdom of God" as a person, even though he did not think of God as a mythological entity residing in heaven. This particular power communicates to human beings the possibility of living in that mode which involves the free and voluntary engagement of persons with one another. To be a person is not a mode that one lives alone. The isolated individual is not a person, but an atom whose contacts with others

5. Flaubert, *Madame Bovary*, p. 56.

are purely external. The personal mode entails that each find his own proper reality, for only then can there be free giving and free receiving with others who have also achieved their own proper realities. These are the marks of personal life, and according to Jesus' sayings this mode of being human is a possibility only for those whose being is rooted in that power which engenders this mode, the power which Jesus therefore addresses as "Father." It is the father who engenders, whereas the mother nurtures. Since this power generates or *engenders personal* life, it too has the *characteristics of the personal*. It is not, for example, an impersonal force which has its being in itself, is utterly self-enclosed, and only acts *on* others, externally. An impersonal force never communicates its own being but only imposes itself on other things, other human beings, and other persons. From Jesus' perspective, such a force would not be "God."

Jesus came eating and drinking

The preceding analysis of Jesus' core sayings, as my colleagues will recognize, owes a great deal to previous scholarship on the historical Jesus, and yet the approach has been different. I have employed the historical-critical version of Ockham's razor, and have utilized as few historical hypotheses as possible in order to reconstruct a picture of Jesus in history by using only the evidence that the sayings themselves provide. The resulting picture is, in its most important features, consonant with the prevailing consensus regarding the historical Jesus, but with crucial differences in emphasis and interpretation.

The most distinctive feature of Jesus' activity was his eating and drinking with friends, a practice that differed completely from John's asceticism. It was not the content of their differing languages, nor even the differing forms of their public behaviour, that provoked their contemporaries. Rather, it was their existence as free persons that provided the occasion for the venting of impulses rooted in *ressentiment*, leading even to violence.

Jesus expressly rejected the mythological thinking of apocalypticists, and did not continue John's eschatological prophesying, but instead reinterpreted the traditional symbol "kingdom of God." Although Jesus did not share the mythological conceptions of first-century people, he did not attempt to correct their defective concepts. Instead, he directed their attention to specific phenomena as the locus for the revelation of the power he called "God." He implied that it was evident in his own and in John's mode of being as free persons, and asserted that it had come upon those individuals who had been liberated from possession by anti-personal enormities. It is not a force which imposes *on* human beings, but a power which one receives, opening up a dimension of existence into which one enters. Those who exist in the mode of holding are not fit for, or find it virtually impossible to enter into, the dimension characterized by receptivity, and even those who do enter discover that it offers no more and no less than life. Far from shielding them from the shocks and surprises of earthly human life, this mode of being exposes persons in the most acute way to human evil, not only to external evil, in the form of violence perpetrated against those who are free, but also to internal evil, in the form of negative energies in themselves and others, even in those oriented to the risks and ambiguities of life in the personal mode.

Jesus taught his table companions to be open to receive that power which engenders the being of free persons in the hope that it would enable them to overcome their own negative impulses and to be energetically active in the face of seemingly overwhelming deprivations or fulfillments. To exist actively in this mode, with one's being continually nourished by the superabundant power which can be called "God" is, according to Jesus, the way to life. Nothing else is promised in his core sayings. There is no evidence of the mythology of transcendental reward or punishment to compensate for the *apparent* deficiencies of life in the personal mode. In these sayings, Jesus does not promise a heaven which might make up for the meagreness which people might have tasted in their experience of the world, nor does he instruct people *how* to find life.

That the early Christians translated the meaning of Jesus' sayings and actions into the religious concepts and practices with which they construed their world is not surprising considering the reality which his *words* revealed to them, nor is it surprising that they borrowed various messianic and divine titles from contemporary usage in order to highlight the significance which they saw in him. (A personal favourite of mine in this connection is an early Christian dialogue in the Gospel of John: "Jesus said to the twelve, 'Do you wish to go away?' Simon Peter answered him, 'Lord, to whom shall we go? You have the *words* of eternal *life,* and we have believed, and have come to know, that you are the Holy One of God'" (John 6:67-69).)

There are, to be sure, ethical, religious, social, and political implications to the understanding of reality expressed in Jesus' sayings. However, it is my opinion that we must admit that Jesus himself refrained from working out these implications and therefore refrained from setting men's minds at ease by instructing then *how* to live. Could he have done otherwise? For was not Dostoyevsky essentially correct when he supposed that in answer to such questions Jesus, to remain faithful to his perceptions, chose to remain silent? Where human existence in its highest possibilities is envisioned as free being, the articulation of ethics becomes extremely complicated. All ethical systems, whether liberal or laissez-faire or whatever, entail compulsion of some kind, as parents and educators know full well. How could Jesus "compel" people to be free? He could not, of course, but what he could do is to compose and narrate parables that might provide the opportunity for others to share in the consciousness of a free being. And so we now turn to the analysis and interpretation of Jesus' core parables.

PART TWO

When Jesus smiled

CHAPTER SIX

Jesus' photodramatic parables

Jesus' parables and the kingdom

Having analyzed and interpreted Jesus' core sayings, we now turn to a consideration of the core parables. These twelve parables can be divided into two groups, which I am going to call the *photo*dramatic and the *phono*dramatic parables. Both groups describe what human beings *do*; hence, their dramatic character (from the etymology of the Greek word for "drama," which means "to do"). One group limits itself to the external description of what men and women do, and so I call them photodramatic because they report *visible* actions. The other group describes what people *do* and what they *say*, and so I call them phonodramatic because they report *visible* actions and *audible* words.

The photodramatic parables are those traditionally entitled "The Sower," "The Mustard Seed," "The Leaven," "The Hidden Treasure," "The Pearl," "The Lost Sheep," and "The Lost Coin." The phonodramatic parables have been known traditionally as "The Unjust Steward," "The Great Supper," "The Labourers in the Vineyard," "The Prodigal Son," and "The Good Samaritan."

A number of these parables are introduced in the synoptic tradition with words to this effect. "The kingdom of God (Matthew: heaven) is like . . . ." We must ask at the outset whether Jesus did originally introduce his parables in this way. This question has a direct bearing on the interpretation of Jesus' core parables, and to answer it we must first critically examine the sources.

Matthew introduces his version of "The Great Supper" as follows:

> The kingdom of heaven may be compared to a king who gave a marriage feast for his son... (Matt 22:1-14).

In addition, Matthew introduces two other parables with almost exactly the same words:

> Then the kingdom of heaven shall be compared to ten maidens... (Matt 25:1-13);
> Therefore the kingdom of heaven may be compared to a king who wished to settle accounts with his servants... (Matt 18:23-35).

Each one of these three parables, as Matthew narrates them, deals with the characteristically Matthean notion that the Church is a mixed body of good and bad who will be judged on the eschatological judgment day when Jesus as the Son of man comes to separate the sheep from the goats (Matt 25:31-46). In short, the introductions to these three parables are totally Matthean in terms of language and ideas, and can offer us no information about the way in which Jesus might have introduced his parables.

There is a fourth Matthean parable with the same introduction, "The Parable of the Weeds" (Matt 13:24-30), which has come to Matthew either from Q, in which case Luke has omitted it, or from Matthew's special source. We can conclude that Matthew found this parable in a source, and did not himself compose it, because there is another version extant in the so-called "Gospel of Thomas." The Gospel of Thomas, so named from its subscription, was discovered at Nag Hammadi in upper Egypt in 1945-46 along the thirteen Coptic codices containing fourty-four separate works which all, apparently, belonged to the collection of a monastic library.[1] The Gospel of Thomas, written in Sahidic Coptic around A.D. 400, is a translation from a Greek original, of which several fragments survive and which can be dated to about A.D. 200.

This so-called "gospel" is not really in the gospel form at all, that is, in the form of our synoptic gospels and the Gospel of John. The inscription reads: "These are the secret sayings which the living

---

1. James M. Robinson, ed., *The Nag Hammadi Library in English* (Leiden: E.J. Brill, 1977), pp. 1-25. All references to the Gospel of Thomas are from this edition, introduced by Helmut Koester, p. 117, and translated by Thomas O. Lambdin, pp. 118-30.

Jesus spoke and which Didymos Judas Thomas wrote down."
("Didymos" means "the twin," and he was thought in Syrian tradition to be Jesus' twin brother.) The text proceeds to list one
hundred and fourteen sayings attributed to Jesus. They occur one
after the other with no narrative context and few connectives,
except that occasionally a disciple, or the disciples as a group, asks
Jesus a question which he then answers with a saying. The question and answer form was widespread in antiquity as a form for
transmitting the sayings of sages, and there are numerous examples in the synoptic tradition. For the most part, however, the text
simply reiterates: "Jesus said . . . . Jesus said . . . . And He said . . .," etc.

Before the discovery of this collection of sayings attributed to
Jesus, the existence of a written sayings-source (Q) utilized by both
Matthew and Luke remained without analogy. If only Matthew
and Luke, but not Mark, for example, survived, we could still use
source-criticism to show that they must have both utilized a written gospel as a source. Fortunately the gospel of Mark *has* survived,
and so we can compare this source empirically with Matthew and
Luke in order to determine how each one has used his source. But
no copy of Q has survived and, until the discovery of Thomas,
there was no empirical evidence that the early Christians created
collections of "the sayings of Jesus." The discovery of Thomas has
thus provided important corroboration for the view that both
Matthew and Luke did utilize a sayings-source in addition to utiliz-
ing Mark as a source when they composed their own gospels.
Essentially, both Matthew and Luke are revised, expanded editions
of Mark.

Thomas is also important in another way. There are many
points of contact between this collection of Jesus' sayings and the
sayings collected in Q, connections which suggest that Thomas'
tradition has had contact with the Q tradition. "The Parable of the
Weeds" affords a good example of this kind of contact between Q
traditions and the Thomas tradition. Matthew and Thomas introduce the parable in the same way:

> The kingdom of heaven may be compared to a man who sowed good
> seed in his field . . . . (Matt 13:24);
> The kingdom of the Father is like a man who had [good] seed.
> (Thomas 57).

Both Matthew's parable and Thomas' parable compare the kingdom to a situation in which the wheat or grain and the weeds are
allowed to grow together until the time when the weeds will be
68

burned. In both parables, the bad seed is sown by the man's enemy, that is, the devil. Both parables reflect the situation of the early Christian community which thought of itself as being composed of both good and bad who would be separated on the judgment day. The Thomas parallel shows that this idea was already present in Matthew's source; he has developed it and made it a central theme in his gospel. However, since the parable, together with its introduction, contains the idea of the kingdom as the Church, and mirrors the situation of the early Christians, it can be used for reconstructing the history of early Christian ideas, but tells us nothing about how Jesus thought of the kingdom nor whether he thought of his parables in connection with the kingdom.

Before the development of techniques of analysis which permit scholars to identify the motivations, theological and otherwise, that early Christian authors had when using their sources (we call these techniques "redaction criticism"), scholars were accustomed to employing the criterion of multiple attestation to establish the authenticity of Jesus material. The criterion of multiple attestation says that if material is attested in several different sources and traditions, then that material can be considered authentic. Using the criterion of multiple attestation, one could argue that since both Matthew and Thomas compare the kingdom with "The Parable of the Weeds," the material must be very old, and some would even say that it goes back to Jesus. But we have already noted that Matthew did not write until fifty years after the death of Jesus. It was during that period that collections of sayings were made, collections that issued in both Q and the Thomas tradition. Using both Matthew and Thomas, then, can take us back to that formative period of the tradition, sometime between A.D. 32 and A.D. 80. But once we have gone back that far, we still have further work to do. We must still ask ourselves, what situation does the saying or parable reflect? Does the parable serve the interests and needs of the early Christian community? If so, then we cannot assume that the parable was composed by the historical Jesus, and "The Parable of the Weeds" offers a good example of how parables composed by early Christian teachers in order to illustrate their understanding of their own situation have come to be attributed to Jesus as the sayings tradition developed.

There are seven other parables in the synoptic tradition which have been given similar introductions to the Matthean parables just examined.

(1)

	With what	What
The kingdom of heaven is like a grain of mustard seed.... (Matt 13:31)	can we compare the kingdom of God, or what parable shall we use for it? It is like a grain of mustard seed.... (Mark 4:30-32)	is the kingdom of God like? And to what shall I compare it? It is like a grain of mustard seed.... (Luke 13:18-19)

"The disciples said to Jesus, 'Tell us what *the Kingdom of Heaven is like.*' He said to them, *'It is like* a mustard seed...."* (Thomas 20)

(2) *The kingdom of heaven is like* leaven.... (Matt 13:33)	(Unknown to Mark)	*To what shall I compare the kingdom of God? It is like* leaven.... (Luke 13:20-21)

"*The Kingdom of the Father is like* a certain woman." (Thomas 96)

(3) *The kingdom of heaven is like* treasure hidden in a field... (Matt 13:44)		(Unknown to Mark and unknown to, or not used by, Luke)

"*The Kingdom is like* a man who had a [hidden] treasure in his field...." (Thomas 109)

(4) *The kingdom of heaven is like* a merchant.... (Matt 13:45)		(Unknown to Mark and unknown to, or not used by, Luke)

"*The Kingdom of the [Father] is like* a merchant...." (Thomas 76)

(5) Again, *the kingdom of heaven is like* a net.... (Matt 13:47)		(A Matthean composition and so unknown to either Mark or Luke)

(6) (Unknown to, or not used by, Matthew)	The kingdom of God is as if a man should scatter seed.... (Mark 4:26)	(Unknown to, or not used by, Luke)

(7) For *the kingdom of heaven is like* a householder.... (Matt 20:1)	(Unknown to Mark)	(Unknown to or not used by, Luke)

An examination of the parallel version of these introductions shows that Matthew characteristically introduces his parables with the phrase "The kingdom of heaven is like...," an introduction which is also characteristic of Thomas (Thomas also uses this introduction for parables in Thomas 97 and Thomas 98, which are not in the synoptic tradition). This evidence shows that at least as early as the period when the sayings collections were being formed, parables were introduced as illustrations of the kingdom. Matthew has changed the introductions to the "Parable of the Mustard Seed" and the "Parable of the Leaven" to make them conform with his favorite wording.

Looking at Luke's introductions to the "Parable of the Mustard Seed" (1) and the "Parable of the Leaven" (2), we can see that Luke has a question in both cases: "To what shall I compare the kingdom of God?" This shows that in Q the parables were introduced with a question. Matthew's versions tell us nothing about Q, since Matthew has used his own form of introduction. Luke's versions of these two parables show that the Q community understood both the mustard seed and the leaven as illustrations of the way the community grew and spread in the ancient world. The Q versions of these parables, then, together with their introductions, give evidence of early Christian thinking, but do not provide evidence of how Jesus might have connected the kingdom and his parables.

The "Parable of the Net" (5) is an early Christian, perhaps Matthean, composition illustrating Matthew's favourite idea of the Church as a mixed body of good and evil who will be separated on the judgment day. The "Parable of the Labourers in the Vineyard" (7) is also used by Matthew to provide an illustration of the judgment day, when "the last will be first, and the first last" (Matt 20:16 = 19:30). The use of kingdom language in connection with ideas about the Church and the last judgment is extremely valuable for understanding the development of early Christian thought.

Thomas' version of the "Parable of the Merchant" is more developed than Matthew's: "The Kingdom of the Father is like a merchant who had a consignment of merchandise and who discovered a pearl. That merchant was shrewd. He sold the merchandise and bought the pearl alone for himself. You, too, seek his unfailing and enduring treasure where no moth comes near to devour and no worm destroys" (Thomas 76). Here we see the situation of the Christian teacher who is exhorting his listener to give up all that he has, to follow the example of the shrewd merchant and get for himself treasure that time will not erode. According to Thomas, contrary to his own introduction, the kingdom is *like a pearl* (*not* a merchant) which "no moth comes near to devour and no worm destroys." In other words, the kingdom is understood in Gnostic terms, and neither the parable nor its introduction takes us back further than the period of early Christian teaching.

Matthew's versions of the "Parable of the Treasure" and the "Parable of the Pearl" also take us back to the situation of early Christian teaching about the kingdom. For him, as for Thomas, though in different ways, the kingdom is a supernatural treasure for which the listener should be prepared to give up everything. By introducing these parables with the comparison, "The kingdom of heaven is like...," the early Christian teacher makes the parable into an example story, an example of how the listener should act. That is to say, the listener should act as the man does who finds a treasure, or as the merchant does who finds a pearl, for the treasure and the pearl are thought of allegorically as illustrations of the kingdom.

The fact that these are secondary additions to the stories can be seen quite clearly by noticing that Thomas' "Parable of the Treasure" is not about the treasure at all, as Thomas thinks, but about the man. Similarly, although both Matthew and Thomas think of the "Parable of the Pearl" as being about the pearl, that is that the pearl illustrates what the kingdom is, their wording shows that the story was originally about the merchant, not about the pearl! The incongruity between the subject matter of these stories and the uses to which they were put by early Christian teachers who wanted to employ them as example stories to illustrate to their listeners how they should act, is important evidence showing that the introductions are secondary, Christian additions.

This leaves us with three parabolic introductions to examine: (1), (2), and (6). In the Markan version of "The Parable of the Mustard Seed" and in the Markan "Parable of the Seed Growing Secretly," the kingdom is understood as the Church which had small beginnings but which quickly grew and spread. In the first example, the kingdom of God (= the Christian community) is compared with a mustard seed ("the smallest of all the seeds on earth" (Mark 4:31), which nevertheless grows up "and becomes the greatest of all shrubs, and puts forth large branches, so that the birds of the air can make nests in its shade" (Mark 4:32). The meaning is that the Christian community, although it had small beginnings, will become as great as the cedars of Lebanon envisioned by the prophet Ezechiel (17:23; 31:6) into whose branches the "birds of the air," (Ezechiel 31:6), namely Christian converts, will make their homes. In other words, the parable has been reworded and interpreted in the light of the early Christian community's understanding of its missionary past. Therefore the parable, as it now stands, with its identification of the kingdom of God and the Church, cannot tell us how Jesus understood the kingdom.

The Markan "Parable of the Seed Growing Secretly" (Mark 4:26-29), our sixth example, reflects the same understanding, namely that the kingdom of God is the Church which grows in a mysterious fashion until the harvest, that is, the judgment. Thus, our examination of these examples, (1) and (6), has shown that, in the Christian traditions used by Mark, these stories were used by early Christian teachers and preachers in order to illustrate their understanding of the spread of their movement, and so we cannot conclude from these examples how Jesus might have related the kingdom to his stories.

It should not surprise us that separate groups of early Christians should have utilized these stories in similar ways, nor that they should have found remarkable the spread of their movement. Nevertheless, the fact remains that the connection between the kingdom of God, understood as the Church, and these stories was made by the earliest Christian teachers and missionaries, and that they therefore cannot be used as evidence to reconstruct the connection that Jesus might have made between the kingdom of God as he understood it and the stories which he composed and narrated. Indeed, the introductions to every single one of the eleven parables as they have been preserved and transmitted in the synoptic tradition are evidently products of the early Christian communities. In each case, the kingdom is compared either to some item in the parable which grows (a mustard seed), or spreads (the leaven), just as the Church grew and spread. Or, in the case of the Matthean and Thomas versions, the kingdom of heaven (for Matthew, the Church; for Thomas, the Gnostic Kingdom of the Father) is compared with an item in the parable (the treasure or the pearl). Many people did join the early Christian communities during the fifty-year period in which these traditions were formulated. However, not everyone lived up to the standards set by their teachers. In their view, the communities contained both bad and good, righteous and evil. Matthew has made this idea central to his gospel, and has used six parables to warn his listeners that on the judgment day the Son of man will separate those who are worthy from those who are unworthy of his heavenly reward.

Source criticism can take us back to the formative stage of the

Christian tradition, to the stage when early Christian teachers used stories composed by Jesus in order to illustrate their own ideas and experiences. Since the interpretative framework accompanying all of the so-called "kingdom parables" is clearly the product of early Christian teachers, we cannot use them as evidence in our effort to discover how the earthly Jesus himself might have made connections between his understanding of the kingdom, as expressed in the seven kingdoms sayings examined in Part One, and the subject matter that he disclosed through his parables, which we will examine in Parts Two and Three. Obviously, Jesus did not think of the kingdom as the Church, nor as heaven, nor as the judgment day. All of these concepts were developed in the early Christian communities. All we have, then, are the kingdom sayings on the one hand, and the parables on the other. Whatever relationships there might be between them will have to be discovered solely through internal analysis of the parables themselves. As in dealing with the core sayings of Jesus, our approach dictates that we employ as few hypotheses as possible when we listen to Jesus' parables, that we attempt to suspend our preconceptions regarding their meaning, and that, instead, we attend carefully to precisely what Jesus says and does not say as he narrates these stories.

Reconstructing Jesus' seven photodramatic parables

We now turn to the seven core parables which describe what men and women do—the photodramatic parables. We have already seen that source-criticism and redaction-criticism show that the traditional introductions to some of these parables ("The kingdom of God is like . . .," etc.) were secondarily added, probably almost as soon as the parables were used in Christian teaching. Now we must reconstruct, as closely as possible, the more or less original introductions to these parables and we must also attempt to restore their original wording in so far as our methods will allow.

*　　　*　　　*

The most important clue for recovering the original introductions to these parables is provided through a source-critical and redaction-critical analysis of two parables recorded by Matthew from his special source:

The kingdom of heaven is like treasure hidden in a field . . .
(Matt 13:44);

Again, the kingdom of heaven is like a merchant in search of fine pearls, who... (Matt 13:45-46).

Matthew wants to say that the kingdom of heaven is like a treasure and that the kingdom of heaven is also like a pearl. But in the second instance, his editorial work has not been thorough, and we can discern behind his version the original wording: "There was a merchant in search of fine pearls who...."

That the parables were originally worded in this way is confirmed by comparison with Thomas' versions:

The Kingdom is like a man who has a [hidden] treasure in his field... (Thomas 109);
The Kingdom of the Father is like a merchant... (Thomas 76).

Not only is Thomas' pearl parable *about a merchant,* but his treasure parable is *about the man* who, as Thomas has edited it, "had a treasure." Source criticism, then, confirms our redaction-critical conclusions: originally these parables were *about specific men,* not about what they found, which is, in the view of the early Christian teacher, the kingdom. Even though Thomas' versions exhibit complete re-writing of the original stories, they still retain signs of their original subject matter, namely the man who found treasure and the merchant who was in search of fine pearls. In comparison with Thomas, Matthew's versions are patently more original.

The only obvious alteration Matthew has made to the parable of the man who found treasure hidden in a field is to insert the phrase "in his joy." This phrase is secondary according to both stylistic and redaction-critical criteria. The phrase can be explained as Matthew's addition in order to make explicit his idea that the treasure found is "the kingdom of heaven." Stylistically, the phrase is extraneous to the wording, and can be removed without affecting the meaning of the story. Moreover, comparison with the other core parables of Jesus shows that he only describes what is externally observable (actions) or what is audible (words). The only emotion ascribed to his characters is anger, and anger is something one can observe. To observe that someone is angry is not to switch into the voice of an omniscient narrator, nor is it to make a judgment, but only to call attention to an observable phenomenon.

Matthew's insertion of "in search of fine pearls" is also an explanatory phrase. The phrase breaks the narrative sequence by anticipating what happens in the story, and also lends point to the merchant's behaviour by making it appear that his purpose was to find "fine pearls." Elsewhere in the core parables, Jesus never describes the motivations of his characters; he only describes what they do or what they say. By removing this insertion, we recover a perfectly well-narrated story.

With a high degree of certainty, then, we can recover the original wording of these two stories:

> There was a man who found treasure hidden in a field, which he covered up; then he went and sold all that he had and bought that field.

> There was a merchant who, on finding one pearl of great value, went and sold all that he had and bought it.

*   *   *

"The Parable of the Mustard Seed" was also originally a story about a man, the man who took a mustard seed and planted it, not about the seed (= the kingdom), which is how the early Christians teachers told the story. We have three sources for this story: Mark, Q, and Thomas. Matthew has, as he usually does, combined both Mark and Q, while Luke has characteristically shown a preference for the Q version.

Matt 13:31-32	Mark 4:30-32	Luke 13:18-19
[The kingdom of heaven is like]	[With what can we compare the kingdom of God, or what parable shall we use for it?	[What is the kingdom of God like? And to what shall I compare it?
a grain of mustard seed which *a man* took and *sowed in his field;* [it is the smallest of all seeds,	It is like] *a grain of mustard seed,* [which, when sown upon the ground, is the smallest of all the seeds on earth;	It is like] *a grain of mustard seed* which *a man took* and *sowed in his garden;*
but when it has grown it is the greatest of all] *shrubs* [and becomes a tree,	yet when it is sown it grows up and becomes the greatest of all] *shrubs,* [and puts forth large	*and it* [grew]
so that] *the birds* [of the air come and] *make nests in its* branches.	branches, so that the] *birds* [of the air can]*make nests in its shade.*	and *became a* [tree,] *and the birds* [of the air] *made nests in its* branches.

Thomas (20):
It [the Kingdom of Heaven] is like a mustard seed, the smallest of all seeds. But when it falls on tilled soil, it produces a great *plant* and becomes a shelter for the birds of the sky.

Thomas' version shows that at a very early stage the Christians used this story to illustrate the contrast between the small beginnings of the Christian movement and its later growth. (This is not to say that Thomas himself understands the Kingdom as the Church, but only that his source did.)

Mark's version is more thoroughly reworded than Q's; in his effort to have the story tell about the small Christian community which eventually became the greatest of all, the man (preserved in Q), who sowed the mustard seed, has disappeared. Judging from Luke's version, Q had already altered the mustard plant, which is a seasonal shrub, into a tree, so that the picture would conform with Ezechiel's vision of the ingathering of the nations to Israel. The early Christians applied this vision to their own experience, because they felt that they had "grown" to be like a cedar of Lebanon, which "towered high above all the trees of the forest; its boughs grew large and its branches long, from abundant water in its shoots. All the birds of the air made their nests in its boughs" (Ezek 31:3-6; cf., 17:22-24). Both Mark and Thomas retain the correct, and original, information that the mustard seed grows into a shrub or plant, and is not a tree at all. The mustard is an annual plant, which can grow to a size of about ten feet, but its branches are not suitable for nesting. The birds in question nest on the ground, as do lapwings, partridges, and grouse, all of which were found in Palestine in biblical times, and still are.

Like the other parables we have examined, this one was originally about a man:

There was a man who took a grain of mustard seed and sowed it in his garden. It became a shrub, and the birds made nests in its shade.

*　　　*　　　*

There are two sources for the "Parable of the Leaven", Thomas and Q.

Matt 13:33	Luke 13:20-21	Thomas 96
	[To what shall I compare	
[The kingdom of heaven	the kingdom of God? It is	[The Kingdom of the
is like] *leaven* [which] *a*	like] *leaven* [which] *a*	Father is like a certain]
woman took and hid in three	*woman took and hid in three*	*woman.* She *took* [a little]
measures of meal, till it was all	*measures of meal, till it was all*	*leaven,* [concealed] *it is some*
leavened	*leavened*	*dough,* [and made it into large loaves.]

In this case, Thomas provides the source-critical evidence for our growing suspicion that Jesus told his stories about particular persons. Thomas has rationalized the woman's activity by representing her as making loaves out of the leavened dough. The original story as Jesus told it was probably as follows:

There was a woman who took leaven, and hid it in three measures of meal, till it was all leavened.

*   *   *

There are two sources for the parable of "The Lost Sheep," Q and Thomas.

Matt 18:12-14	Luke 15:4-6	Thomas 107
What do you think? If *a man has a hundred sheep, and one of them* has gone *astray, does he not leave the ninety-nine on the hills and go in search of the one that went astray? And if he finds it,* truly, I say to you, he rejoices over it more than over the ninety-nine that never went astray.	What *man* of you, having *a hundred sheep,* if he has lost one of them, does he not *leave the ninety-nine* in the wilderness, and go after the one which is lost, until he finds it? And when he has found it, he lays it on his shoulders, rejoicing. And when he comes home, he calls together his neighbours, saying to them, 'Rejoice with me, for I have found my sheep which was lost.'	The Kingdom is like a *shepherd who had a hundred sheep. One of them,* the largest, *went astray. He left the ninety-nine and looked for that one* until he found it. When he had gone to such trouble, he said to the sheep, 'I care for you more than the ninety-nine.'

As in the case of the story of "The Woman Who Took Leaven," Thomas preserves the original subject matter of this parable, namely the shepherd who had a hundred sheep. Matthew and Luke have both used Q as their source for this story, which was already changed into question form in that version. Matthew and Luke have used the story in different ways. Matthew uses it in the context of Jesus' discourse on the rules governing behaviour within the Christian community (Matt 18), and uses the sheep who went astray as an example of the deviant Christian, whom the community, according to Matthew, should seek out and return to fellowship.

Luke has used this story in a section of his gospel which he has constructed in order to illustrate his view that Jesus' practice of eating with "tax collectors and sinners" (Luke 15:1) is defensible because they were in fact "repentant" sinners. They were formerly "lost" in sin but have now been "found" since they have repented, and that is why Jesus grants them entrance to his table; repentance of a sinner, in Luke's view, is an occasion for rejoicing. Luke has completely recast the parable in order to conform with this teaching. There remains some incongruity, however, in the situation where the sinner is allegorized as a lost sheep, because the logic of Luke's redaction would appear to necessitate that the man invite his sheep to have dinner with him at the end, when he has found his sheep. Luke gets around this by having the man invite his friends and neighbours to the celebration. Luke 15:4f-6 is identical in wording to Luke 15:8e-9, which is further evidence that Luke has himself provided the context for interpreting the sheep who was "lost" but then "found" as a sinner who repented. Indeed, the idea that Jesus came to call sinners *to repentance* is characteristic of Luke (see Luke 5:32 in comparison with his source, Mark 2:17c = Matt 9:13b).

Thomas has also interpreted the story allegorically, and views the sheep who went astray as the true Gnostic who got lost in the world but whom the redeemer, Jesus, sought for and found, and whom he preferred anyway to all the other merely human beings who have become caught in the world (Thomas' picture of Jesus talking to the sheep is more logical, if more amusing, than Luke's). In any case, Thomas' allegory demands that the shepherd in fact find his sheep, as does Luke's. They both, therefore, have redactional motives for giving a happy ending to the story. Matthew's version, on the other hand, reflects the possibility that the shepherd did not find what he was looking for, and one cannot explain why Matthew would have *inserted* this element of uncertainty into the story if he found it told with a happy ending in Q. This means, then, that source-critical and redaction-critical criteria point to the conclusion that Q did not report that the man found his sheep.

Source-critical, redaction-critical, and stylistic evidence thus lead us to conclude that the original wording of the story was approximately as follows:

There was a shepherd who had a hundred sheep, and one of them went astray. He left the ninety-nine on the hills and looked for that one.

*   *   *

There is only one source for the parable of "The Lost Coin," Luke:

> Or what woman, having ten silver coins, if she loses one coin, does not light a lamp and sweep diligently until she finds it? [And when she has found it, she calls together her friends and neighbours, saying 'Rejoice with me, for I have found the coin which I have lost.'] (Just so, I tell you, there is joy before the angels of God over one sinner who repents) (Luke 15:8-10).

If the Thomas tradition was familiar with this story, it has left it out because of Thomas' aversion to tradesmen and merchants, and presumably to anyone who handles money. Our efforts to reconstruct the wording of this parable must depend on analogy, particularly with the analogy of the way Luke has handled the story of "The Shepherd Who Had a Hundred Sheep."

We have seen that Q had already transformed that story into a question, so it is very likely that the story of "The Lost Coin" had also already been changed into a question in Q. Matthew, then, would have left it out altogether for reasons we cannot discern. The words in brackets are identical to Luke 15:5-9, and Luke has inserted them so that the story will illustrate his idea (stated explicitly at the end) that since the angels of God rejoice over the "finding" of the sinner who was "lost," Jesus' allowing ostensible sinners to eat with him is defensible; after all, Jesus, says Luke, only ate with tax collectors and non-observant Jews *who had repented* of their sins.

Luke, apparently, does not realize just how profoundly Jesus' eating and drinking with non-observers of religious codes did call into question the fundamental world-attitudes of Jesus' contemporaries, as we have seen in our examination of Jesus' similitude about the children playing games. Moreover, by answering the objections of Jews in his own time who oriticized the reported practice of Jesus, Luke implicitly affirmed their own religious presuppositions.

With so little source-critical evidence to go on, one can only guess as to the original wording of the parable. Proceeding on the analogy of the others we have recovered with much firmer evidence, we can propose the following, very hypothetical, reconstruction:

> There was a woman who had ten silver coins, and she lost one. She lit a lamp and swept diligently looking for that one.

*   *   *

We have seen that the early Christians changed the wording of what we may now call "The Man Who Took a Grain of Mustard Seed" so that their versions would tell about the fate of the seed itself, that is, the kingdom. As early Christian teachers re-told the story, they re-worded it so that it would better reflect the point that they wished to make about the spread of Christianity. The same thing happened to what Matthew calls "The Parable of the Sower" (Matt 13:18), because it seemed to serve well as an illustration of their missionary experience.

There are two extant sources for the story, Mark and Thomas. It seems not to have been in Q because in spite of its appearance in Thomas neither Matthew nor Luke reflects any knowledge of a source other than Mark.

Each has altered Mark's version in a characteristic way. Luke has abbreviated Mark's version, smoothed out its language, and altered its emphasis, in order to make explicit his view that the seed is the word of God (Luke 8:11) preached by the Christian missionaries, and that the word of God is inevitably fruitful regardless of apparent obstacles. Matthew has also smoothed out Mark's language, but has not abbreviated so radically as Luke. Instead, Matthew has changed Mark's "seed" to the plural, "seeds," because he thinks of "the word of the kingdom" (Matt 13:19) as multiform, including not only the preached gospel but also, especially, early Christian ethical teaching. Matthew has in mind here his view of the Christian community as a mixed group of both bad and good, and so has altered the ending of the parable to show that "the word of the kingdom" has mixed results—some Christians represent a hundred-fold product of the word of the kingdom, some sixty, and some only thirty.

Since, then, the versions of both Matthew and Luke have been produced by modifying their Markan source, we have only Mark and Thomas as sources on which to base our efforts to reconstruct a hypothetically more original story.

Mark 4:3-8	Thomas 9
A sower *went out to sow.* *And as he sowed,* some seed *fell along the path,* and the birds came and devoured it. *Other seed fell on rocky ground,* where it had not much soil, and immediately it sprang up, since it has no depth of soil; and when the sun rose it was scorched, and since it had no root it withered away. *Other seed fell among thorns* and the thorns grew up and choked it, and it yielded no grain. And other *seeds fell into good soil,* and brought forth grain, growing up and increasing and yielding thirty-fold and sixtyfold and a hundredfold.	Now the *sower went out, took a handful* (*of seeds*), *and scattered them.* Some *fell on the road;* the birds came and gathered them up. *Others fell on rock,* did not take root in the soil, and did not produce ears. *And others fell on thorns;* they choked the seeds and worms ate them. *And others fell on good soil* and produced good fruit: it bore sixty per measure and a hundred and twenty per measure.

Thomas' version is the more original, for Mark's awkward wording in verses 5-6 ("where it had not much soil...it was scorched") indicates that he has inserted these phrases, particularly since he resumes the sequence of Thomas ("and since it had no root it withered away"). Mark was writing out of a concern for what was happening among the Christian communities which were being persecuted, and in his interpretation of this story (Mark 4:13-20) he tells us that those seeds which fell on rocky ground were shallow Christians who fall away in times of persecution (Mark 4:16-17). This is an excellent example of the way redaction criticism and source criticism complement one another.

The earliest version which we can reconstruct using source criticism was very close to Thomas' version, for once Mark's redaction has been removed, Mark and Thomas are very similar to one another. This means that Mark must have known a version of the parable very much like the one known in Thomas' tradition. But was this the original wording of the parable?

What is the parable about? (1) It is about the sower. (2) It is about the seed. (3) It is about the different types of ground on which the seed falls. (4) It is about the different things that prevent the seed from bearing fruit. And (5) it is about the wonderful yield of the seed when it falls on good ground. The story is about any one or all of these themes.

The earliest Christian teachers found this parable to be very useful for illustrating (1) their missionary experience; (2) their comparison of the seed with their message (sometimes the message was accepted, sometimes not); (3) their comparison of the different kinds of ground with the different kinds of listeners (sometimes they were receptive, sometimes not); (4) their comparison of the different things that prevented the seed from reaching fruition with the different things that prevented converts from being good Christians. They thought of Satan as being like birds which devour, or gather up, the seeds, because "Satan immediately comes and takes away the word which is sown in them" (Mark 4:15). They thought of some Christians as being shallow, and as falling away when there is the least trouble (Mark 4:16-17; Mark himself has added the scorching sun in Mark 4:6 and the mention of persecution in Mark 4:17). They thought of the cares of the world and the desire for material things (Mark 4:19) as being like thorns that choke the fledgling Christians or worms that eat away at them (so Thomas).

Nevertheless, these Christian teachers wished to assure their listeners that there were good Christians, ones who not only received the word but (5) were fruitful in spite of everything; in those Christians, the message was fruitful "thirtyfold and sixtyfold and a hundredfold" (Mark 4:8, 20; cf. Thomas: "it bore sixty per measure and a hundred and twenty per measure"). As soon as one begins using the story to illustrate the missionary experience of the community, it is difficult to stop allegorizing, because all of these different aspects of the experience are felt to be so important. Even at the earliest stage which we can recover source-critically, the story has at least five different foci—a lot of themes for a little story to carry!

Although we have not analyzed, yet, the other six, briefer parables reconstructed above, one can see that those stories display a characteristic economy in their narrative style. This means that there are also strong reasons, using stylistic criteria, for viewing all explanatory phrases in the parable as secondary efforts to clarify its meaning as the early Christians understood it.

Using stylistic criteria, we can tentatively conclude that the birds are secondary, because their introduction shifts the focus of the story to the question of the fate of the seed (viz., the word), and to the factors that might have prevented those who heard it from reaching fruition as Christians. Reporting that the seed did not take root when it fell on the rock is also an explanation, in the interest of answering questions about the different types of people who heard the Christian message. Thorns do not "choke" the *seeds*, but the *fledgling Christians* who are produced by the spreading of the word. When the Christian teacher tells that the thorns "choked" them, again there is a blurring of focus, and a deflection of interest to the inter-related questions of the fate of the message, the differing types of persons who receive the message, and the various worldly temptations that cause them to waver in their faith. The statement that the seed which fell on good soil produced a bountiful yield again deflects attention to the fate of the seed; moreover, the statement functions in order to reassure those who listened to the story that the word would, in the end, be truly fruitful.

But is there a story which could be reconstructed without all these additions which would make sense and, more importantly, conform in terms of the criteria of form, content, style, and function with the other core photodramatic parables of Jesus? The only way to answer that crucial question is to list the core parables whose original we have been attempting to recover, in descending order according to the weight of source- and redaction-critical evidence supporting our reconstruction. The next step is to analyze all of them as a group, to see whether they do display similar characteristics.

We can be most certain about the wording of these four stories:

(1) There was a man who found treasure hidden in a field, which he covered up; then he went and sold all that he had and bought that field.

(2) There was a merchant who, on finding one pearl of great value, went and sold all that he had and bought it.

(3) There was a man who took a grain of mustard seed and sowed it in his garden, and it became a shrub, and the birds made nests in its shade.

(4) There was a shepherd who had a hundred sheep, and one of them went astray. He left the ninety-nine on the hills and looked for that one.

The evidence is less firm for the wording of this story:

(5) There was a woman who took leaven, and hid it in three measures of meal, till it was all leavened.

Reconstruction of these two stories proceeds with a considerable admixture of uncertainty:

(6) There was a man who went out to sow, and as he sowed,

some seed fell on the road, other seed fell on rocky ground, other seed fell on thorns, and other seed fell on good soil.

(7) There was a woman who had ten silver coins, and she lost one. She lit a lamp and swept diligently looking for that one.

It must be remembered that when we note the varying degrees of certainty which attend our reconstruction of these stories, we have to do with degrees of probability within a definite range. These reconstructions are neither purely speculative and fanciful, nor are they purely and absolutely certain. They fall within a middle range of probability, from the relatively less certain to the relatively more certain. This means, then, that interpretation will not be able to proceed by making much of this or that word in any of the stories, but rather will have to content itself with observing the general narrative characteristics of each—plot patterns, style, methods of characterization, choice of subject matter, and the way the stories function.

CHAPTER SEVEN

What I do is me

What I do is me

Each of Jesus' photodramatic parables is about some person —a man, a merchant, a man, a shepherd, a woman, a man, and a woman, respectively—and not, as the traditional titles suggest, about some thing (the treasure, the pearl, the mustard seed, the sheep, the leaven, the seed, or the coin). We should re-title them as follows: "The Man Who Found Treasure," "The Merchant Who Found a Pearl," "The Man Who Took a Grain of Mustard Seed," "The Shepherd Who Had a Hundred Sheep," "The Woman Who Took Leaven," "The Woman Who Had Ten Silver Coins," and "The Man Who Went Out to Sow."

Each story consists in a description of how the person acted in connection with some things. The descriptions are purely external, and only that which can be observed is narrated. The storyteller does not assume the role of an omniscient narrator who knows the feelings or intentions of any of these characters, but knows them only through *what they do*. Jesus does not even use adjectives to describe them (such as "wise," "foolish," "vain," "humble," or the like). In other words, there are no value judgments of any kind, only detached descriptions of behaviour. The storyteller, furthermore, makes no reference or allusion of any kind to any system of valuation by which we might judge the behaviour of these characters. There is absolutely no reference to the Law, to any moral system, nor even to an ideal of man against which to judge their actions. Tha narrative style of these stories has the effect of concentrating attention, of creating an extremely sharp focus on what these people do, and it contains an implicit assumption regarding human activities, an assumption expressed very well in the octet of one of Gerard Manley Hopkins' sonnets:

> As kingfishers catch fire, dragonflies draw flame;
> As tumbled over rim in roundy wells
> Stones ring; like each tucked string tells, each hung bell's
> Bow swung finds tongue to fling out broad its name;
> Each mortal thing does one thing and the same:
> Deals out that being indoors each one dwells;
> Selves—goes itself; *myself* it speaks and spells;
> Crying *What I do is me: for that I came.*[1]

What, then, does each one of Jesus' characters do?

The man who found a treasure hidden in a field covered it up, obviously so that neither the owner of the field nor anyone else would find it while he went to raise the cash to buy the field. The man went and sold all that he had so that he would have enough money to buy the field and so gain possession of the treasure, and bought it from the owner, obviously without telling the owner that there was a treasure in the field. The storyteller gives absolutely no indication as to whether he thinks the man's actions were justified or unjustified, moral or immoral, the kind of thing one ought to do or not do. Jesus simply describes *what* the man *did.*

There was a merchant, someone whose occupation was buying and selling goods, who found a pearl of great value. What did he do? He, too, went and sold all that he had in order to raise the cash to buy the pearl he valued. His action means something completely different, however, than the action of the man who found treasure hidden in a field. That man stood to gain quite a bit by acquiring the field together with its treasure from the owner of the field. He paid for a field, but got a treasure, and thus enriched himself. The merchant, on the other hand, had to turn all that he owned into cash in order to acquire the pearl that he valued. All of his assets are tied up in the ownership of one pearl. Different listeners will evaluate his action in different ways. The storyteller, however, does not himself say whether this was a prudent or a foolish act, the act of a man enraptured by beauty or the act of a man obsessed

1. *Poems of Gerard Manley Hopkins*, the first edition with preface and notes by Robert Bridges, enlarged and edited with notes and a biographical introduction by W.H. Gardner (London: Oxford University Press, 1956), p. 95.

(magnificently or otherwise). Jesus simply describes *what* the man *did*.

The mustard is a common annual plant; it grows rapidly and is to be found everywhere in Palestine. Ordinarily, it is thought of not as something desirable but as a weed, something like a dandelion. Dandelion leaves are valued by some people as salad greens, and the mustard does produce a spice for food. But why did the man take a grain of mustard seed and plant it in his garden? The question arises naturally from the action which Jesus describes, but he does not tell us what motivated the man to do this. The time for planting in that part of the world is the fall, during the rainy season. By springtime, when the birds were nesting, the mustard plant would have been large enough to provide shade for them. But Jesus does not say that the man planted the mustard seed in his garden in order to provide shade for birds that nest on the ground; he only tells us that this is what in fact happened. Although the man's behaviour is puzzling, the picture of birds nesting on the ground in its shade is entirely realistic and the product of precise observation.

There was a shepherd who had a hundred sheep, a medium-sized flock. He is neither poor nor wealthy. One of his sheep went astray. He left the ninety-nine on the hills and looked for that one. Thomas tries to rationalize his behaviour by indicating that the sheep which went astray was the largest one, which he cared for more than the ninety-nine. Another way of rationalizing his behaviour is to assume that he must have left the ninety-nine in the care of another shepherd; but Jesus does not say that. He only tells us what the man did when one of his hundred sheep went astray, namely that he left the ninety-nine on the hills and went to look for that one. Jesus does not even say that the man found the sheep for which he was looking. The story as told evokes inevitably the question as to why the shepherd left the ninety-nine and went looking for the one that went astray, but the question is not answered, nor should the listener provide an answer, unless he wants to write his own story. Jesus' story tells us only *what* the man *did*.

There was a woman who took leaven and hid it in three measures of meal, which is over sixty pounds of flour;[2] a lot of flour!

2. The Greek "saton," Hebrew "seah," is about a peck and a half. Three measures would be 4½ pecks, or slightly over a bushel. A bushel of wheat weighs about sixty pounds.

Again, the narrative evokes the question: Why? Why would a woman "hide" leaven in over sixty pounds of flour? Thomas, again, attempts to rationalize her action by saying that she made the leavened flour into large loaves, which would be enough bread to feed over a hundred people. But, again, Jesus does not tell us "why" the woman "hid" the leaven in so much flour. Jesus tells us only *what* she *did*, and the telling prompts our questioning which, however, receives no answer.

The man who went out to sow let some seed fall on the road, other seed fell on rocky ground, other seed fell on thorns, and some did fall on good soil. He went out with a purpose, and his purpose was to sow. Does the description indicate that the man was absent-minded, just plain careless, or are we to assume that he was following the standard practices of his day? Even granting that the standard practice is to plough after sowing, half of the seed, according to the description, fell in places where it would be difficult to plough! One cannot plough the road, or the rocky ground. Even ploughing the ground where there were thorns would have mixed results, because the seed fell on the thorns. There is something strange about the way the man sows, and the fact that people feel a need to explain what he has done only underscores the fact that the narrative evokes questions about his activity. But the storyteller does not himself provide any answers; he only tells *what* the man *did*.

There was a woman who had ten silver coins, and she lost one. Where did she lose it? The storyteller does not say; he only says that she lost it. Was she careless or absent-minded? We don't know. She lit a lamp and swept diligently looking for that one. To say that she swept "diligently" is not to judge, but to report what can be observed, that her work was careful and steady. Why did she light a lamp? Was it nighttime? Or was her house dark? How did she know that she had lost the coin in her house, in any case? Why did she "sweep" when she was looking for her lost coin? Was she a peasant woman who lived in a hut with a dirt floor? Or was she someone who had a wooden or tiled floor in her house, but whose house was so dirty that she would not have been able to see the coin unless she swept away the dust? All of these questions are evoked by the simple narrative, but none of them is answered. Jesus, once again, only tells us *what* she *did*. He does not even mention why she was so careful and steady in her search for the coin. We don't know whether she prized that coin especially, or whether she feared what others (her husband or family, if she had any) might say, or whether she lived alone and could not afford to lose a single coin.

All things counter, original, spare, strange

T.S. Eliot makes the following observation regarding the way experience governs perception:

> There is, it seems to us,
> At best, only a limited value
> In the knowledge derived from experience.
> The knowledge imposes a pattern, and falsifies,
> For the pattern is new in every moment
> And every moment is a new and shocking
> Valuation of all we have been....
> The only wisdom we can hope to acquire
> Is the wisdom of humility: humility is endless.[3]

There are those who believe that pure consciousness of "reality" can be achieved by short-circuiting the operations of the mind. This belief was especially popular in the sixties. It fails to recognize that all consciousness imposes a pattern, that consciousness is always intentional rather than merely passive, and that there is, therefore, no such thing as neutral awareness. All that a person ever has been determines to some extent the nature and quality of the way he construes his experience, and this happens quite unconsciously. The knowledge we derive from experience imposes a pattern that falsifies.

There is, for example, a character in Margaret Atwood's novel, *Surfacing*, who is making a movie which he calls "Random Samples." He believes that if he knew in advance what to film, he would close his mind. "What you need is flow."[4] He believes that by suspending thought he is achieving pure consciousness of what is real. Among all the things and persons that this man, David, meets, he selects six images for his film: the lunatic, the grotesque, the disgusting, the violated, the dead, and the humiliated. Although he believes that his samples are random, in fact he has unconsciously selected images that correlate with the pre-conscious mood by which he

3. T.S. Eliot, "East Coker," II, *The Complete Poems and Plays*, p. 125.

4. Margaret Atwood, *Surfacing* (Toronto: McClelland and Stewart Limited, 1972), p. 10.

apprehends the world—*ressentiment*. Without realizing it, he has a "knowledge" of the world which imposes a pattern, a pattern that selects only those aspects of experience which are meagre, detestable, or revolting.

Differing patterns of feeling predispose people to construe their experience in different ways. The images which David's consciousness selects are of the terminal, the cut-off, and the mutilated. In J.D. Salinger's novel, *Franny and Zooey,* by contrast, Zooey, while standing at the window of his parents' Manhattan apartment, lets his attention be drawn to quite a different kind of scene —that of a child hiding behind a schoolyard maple tree until her young dachshund picks up her scent and they are joyfully reunited. The scene is "nice," Zooey says. Why is it nice—because of its content, which some might find sentimental? No, it's nice because the schoolgirl and her dachshund play out a *story* of separation and reunion, a story which has a meaning and coherence of its own. They play out this little story regardless of the approval or disapproval of those who presume to dictate what is or is not valid—specifically, New York writers, producers, and directors. They represent all those who take the ego to be the final arbiter of what is real. For Zooey, the case is different:

> "God damn it...there are nice things in the world—and I mean *nice* things. We're all such morons to get so sidetracked. Always, always, always referring every goddam thing that happens right back to our lousy little egos."[5]

Which experiences reveal reality, David's or Zooey's, the grotesque or the "nice," the truncated or the storied? And which experiences should be determinative for *our* understanding of what is real? That depends almost entirely on the fundamental, consciousness-informing attitude of the person in question.

Gerard Manley Hopkins, for example, selects the following subject matter for his sonnet, "Pied Beauty":

> Glory be to God for dappled things—
>   For skies of couple-colour as a brinded cow;
>   For rose-moles all in stipple upon trout that swim;
> Fresh-firecoal chestnut-falls; finches' wings;
>   Landscape plotted and pieced—fold, fallow, and plough;
>   And all trades, their gear and tackle and trim.

5. Salinger, *Franny and Zooey*, p. 151.

All things counter, original, spare, strange;
　　Whatever is fickle, freckled (who knows how?)
　　With swift, slow; sweet, sour; adazzle, dim;
He fathers-forth whose beauty is past change:
　　　　Praise him.[6]

If Gerard Manley Hopkins had gone into the backwoods of Quebec with the narrator of *Surfacing*, we can be sure that he would have had quite different "Random Samples" than David did—rose-moles all in stipple upon trout that swim rather than the innards of dead fish. Hopkins selects from the totality of his experience those things that are counter, original, spare, strange, and concludes that *these* items reveal what really is; for him, the power that fathers-forth beauty is "God" and elicits his praise. David, on the other hand, does not have to make his theology explicit because it is implicit in the sum total of his random samples. For him, the ultimate realities are destructive and anti-human. For him, death is ultimate and functions as "God."

Now it is one thing to be captivated by the couple-colour of skies, or by fresh-firecoal chestnut falls, or finches' wings, but what about man and man's activities in the world? Zooey lets his attention be drawn to a scene acted out between the little girl and her pet dog, and calls it sublime, because it is a scene filled with "joy" and "ecstasy." But what about adults? It is one thing for Hopkins to praise the pied beauty of nature, or for Salinger to have Zooey affirm that the reunion of the girl and her dachshund is a nice thing, but is it possible to observe the varied activities, pursuits, and concerns of grown men and women in their "newness" without imposing on them patterns of feeling created by the knowledge we have gained from our own experience?

Of all the things and people that Jesus happened to come across, to what scenes did he let his attention be drawn? What did his sensibility select, and what images are correlative of his implicit understanding of what is real?

The pattern is new in every moment

Each one of Jesus' photodramatic parables describes a particular, interesting person and what he or she did. We cannot say

---

6. *Poems of Gerard Manley Hopkins*, p. 74.

that any of the characters is typical, that any of them behaves the way everyone would behave in that situation. The man who found treasure hidden in a field, covered it up, and sold all that he had to raise the money to buy that field, does not exhibit typical behaviour. The merchant is not typical either; who could say that he would sell all he owned to buy a single pearl? Would every shepherd who had one sheep that went astray leave all the others on the hills while he went to look for that one? How many people would plant a mustard in their garden? How many women would think that sixty pounds of meal was a good place to hide leaven? It's not the case that every man who goes out to sow lets some fall on the road, some on rocky ground, and other on thorns. Nor would every woman who lost one of her silver coins light a lamp and sweep carefully and steadily until she found it. The listener to these photodramatic narratives can neither say, "Yes, that person is typical," nor can the listener identify with any one of these characters, saying, "That's just what I would do in that situation!" Each of these characters remains outside standard categories, and each one remains strange to the listener, thus retaining his or her individuality which is irreducible to general categories and precludes the listener's impulse to find himself in the picture.

We can't say, either, that any one of these characters provides a model of ideal behaviour, or acts in a way that represents the way one should or ought to act in a similar situation, for each situation is particular, and each character behaves in a particular way that transcends the apparent givens of the situation. There is nothing idealized about the actions of any one of them.

The man who found a treasure hidden in a field and the merchant who found a pearl of great value appear to be oriented, in their responses to those very different situations, to their own fulfillment, but each situation and each response differs completely from the other. It is one thing to sell all that one has in order to enrich oneself, another to sell all that one has in order to acquire some one, highly-valued thing. The shepherd whose sheep went astray left in search of that one, and the woman who lost one of her ten silver coins and searched diligently for it, are each looking for something each has lost. But the meaning of each one's activity differs completely from the other. It is one thing to leave ninety-nine sheep on the hills, and quite another to light a lamp and sweep diligently in one's house.

The man who went out to sow has a purpose, but with reference to that purpose his actions appear distracted. The listener is not quite sure what to think. But the most opaque activities are those of the man who took a mustard seed and planted it in his garden, and of the woman who took leaven and hid it in sixty pounds of meal. Why in the world did they do that? To be sure, the birds came and nested in the shade of the mustard plant when it grew in the spring, and the meal was all leavened, but the very incongruity of those results and the initial actions of each character provoke puzzlement. Did the man intend to provide shade for the birds, and was the woman intending to bake bread for over a hundred people? We don't know. Jesus' characters do not act as if they were just "anybodys" who fit themselves into the world given as an instrumental complex. On the contrary, in their incongruity, they emerge as free persons who do not just use things for the purposes which appear to be indicated by the situation.

The distinctiveness of Jesus' attitude as a storyteller towards his characters can be seen more clearly by comparing it with the Epicurean attitude toward human beings. Epicurus founded a philosophy, a system of thought and a mode of behaviour, that flourished from the late fourth century B.C. through the time of Jesus and well into the fourth or fifth century A.D., when it quietly vanished. There were no changes in Epicurus' philosophical system during this period; the adherents of his school transmitted his teachings faithfully for this entire period of almost seven hundred years. Epicurus' philosophy was designed to produce "happiness" (Greek "hedone," which is the root of our word "hedonism"), and this was to be achieved both by adherence to Epicurus' doctrines and to his ethics. His doctrines told people what to think and his ethics told people how to behave in order to achieve happiness. The company of like-minded people was held to be one of life's greatest pleasures, and friendship was therefore the basis and goal of the Epicurean community. Is there any similarity between Epicurean friendship and the fellowship which Jesus enjoyed when he ate and drank with his friends? A considerable body of Epicurean writings has survived, but neither Epicurus nor any of his followers produced *any stories at all* about *particular people* which are in any way comparable with the photodramatic parables of Jesus![7]

7. Since 1978, I have directed a research project, funded by the Social Sciences and Humanities Research Council of Canada, which has read all the extant literature

Where happiness is the goal of one's activity and thought, and where the company of others is sought for the pleasure it affords, then there can be no question of an interest in the concrete particularities of persons, of all that renders them *other* than oneself. In order to derive pleasure from the company of others, one must eat only with people who think and act like oneself; otherwise, as both Ivan and the doctor in *The Brothers Karamazov* observe, their otherness would threaten to disturb one's self-complacency and restrict one's sense of freedom. That Jesus composed such photodramatic parables, is entirely consonant with his eating and drinking in fellowship with friends, each of whom had his or her own reality and who, therefore, had to be prepared to engage freely with the freedom of each other.

How do Jesus' parables reveal the reality of the other? There is today a widespread popular assumption that the reality of others is given to us through their bodies, and it would be difficult to find an example in contemporary literature which does not begin with a bodily description of what people look like. Is it not remarkable that not one of the core parables of Jesus provides a bodily description? Jesus' parables represent the reality of people not in terms of their bodies, but in terms of their *activities* in *relationship* with things. In other words, the parables suggest that the reality of others is given in terms of a situation in which the other is active. It is not the body of another which manifests his reality to me, but rather his *freedom* in relationship to things, and the way Jesus describes these activities communicates the sense that the reality of persons *transcends* the facticity of things which they manipulate.

This perception of the freedom of others stands in marked contrast with the assumption that we know people through their bodies, for to know others through their bodies is to know them through a purely external relation as belonging to the instrumental complex of things-to-be-used. The corollary of this way of knowing others is that my own reality is primarily to be a body, that is, as something-to-be-used. For the body is that which is factually *given* (birth, race, class, nationality, physiological structure, character,

---

from the Hellenistic and Graeco-Roman periods with the purpose of collecting all stories from antiquity into a *Sourcebook on Parabolic Narrative*. This *Sourcebook* will facilitate the comparative analysis of genres of narrative discourse employed in late Western antiquity, and will be published within the next few years.

past, etc.).[8] Jesus' parables, on the other hand, function in order to disclose others not in terms of an instrumental complex of given things, but rather in terms of their possibilities in contrast to the givenness of things. It is in this sense that the parables function in order to disclose the proper reality of others and, in so doing, they function in order to restore the listener to his or her own proper reality.

The photodramatic parables describe individuals who act, each one, in a completely idiosyncratic way, yet not eccentrically in the sense of being foolish or queer. We call someone an eccentric if he wears overshoes in the heat of summer or if she sits in the upstairs bedroom of an enormous house dressed in her bridal gown. The eccentric provokes laughter.

Laughter is profoundly human

Baudelaire, in his essay "On the Essence of Laughter and, in General, on the Comic in the Plastic Arts,"[9] observes that "Laughter comes from the idea of one's own superiority. A Satanic idea, if ever there was one!"[10] Baulelaire notes that laughter is most often prompted by the sight of someone else's misfortune, almost always at the sight of someone else's mental failing, although sometimes the sight of someone else's physical misfortune also makes us laugh, as, for example, when someone slips and falls.

Baudelaire notices that laughter arises from the tension between a sense of being superior to the conditions which govern the lives of ordinary human beings and a sense of being inferior to the ideal:

> Laughter is Satanic: it is thus profoundly human. It is the consequence in man of the idea of his own superiority. And since laughter is essentially human, it is, in fact, essentially contradictory; that is to say that it is at once a token of an infinite grandeur and an infinite misery —the latter in relation to the absolute Being of whom man has an inkling, the former in relation to the beasts. It is from the perpetual collision of these two infinites that laughter is struck. The comic and

8. For a phenomenological analysis of how we know the Other, see Jean-Paul Sartre, *Being and Nothingness*, pp. 301-470.

9. In Charles Baudelaire, *The Painter of Modern Life and Other Essays*, translated and edited by Jonathan Mayne (London: Phaidon Press, 1964), pp. 147-65.

10. Baudelaire, "On the Essence of Laughter," *The Painter of Modern Life*, p. 152.

the capacity for laughter are situated in the laugher and by no means in the object of his mirth.[11]

Laughter is the expression, simultaneously, of a feeling of superiority to others and of inferiority to the absolute, and so is the symptom of man's misery. According to Baudelaire, Jesus never laughed because he was the Word Incarnate.[12] But perhaps the reason he was apprehended as the Word Incarnate is that he never laughed. In other words, the answer is *not* that Jesus was divine, but that he *was* a different type of human being, a type that neither felt superior to others nor inferior to an absolute.

The idiosyncratic actions of the seven characters in Jesus' photo-dramatic parables do not appeal to a feeling of superiority in the listener. Laughter is symptomatic of man's misery, as illustrated by Georges Rouault's marvellous etching of the clown, "Qui ne se grime pas?" The opposite of laughter is ecstasy. "*Ecstasy* only *smiles* — despair laughs...."[13] There is absolutely no room for the feeling of superiority towards the characters whom Jesus creates, and so the listener does not experience the profoundly human—and Satanic —feelings which elicit laughter.

Ecstasy does not refer to feelings, any more than despair does. Feelings are relatively superficial, as Nietzsche and Scheler have observed. It is what underlies feelings and intentions that determines one's mode of being. Despair refers to a fundamental orientation toward existence, and is based on the feeling that death is the ultimate reality, and so there is no point in striving for any higher human possibilities: "Eat, drink, and be merry, for tomorrow we die." That is the voice of despair.

Ecstasy refers to a mode of being, and etymologically is the same word as existence. Literally translated, both mean "to stand out," that is, to stand out of oneself. To exist is more than to persist or to subsist. To exist, to be ecstatic, is not to be locked in on one's self. The depressed are locked in on themselves, and so they content themselves with playing irrelevant games. But to exist means to go out of oneself, to be vital. The fundamental mood of this mode of existence is joy which, like despair, is a preconscious apprehension of all of one's experience—an apprehension of the superabundance of the actual.

11. Baudelaire, "On the Essence of Laughter," *The Painter of Modern Life*, pp. 153-54.

12. Baudelaire, "On the Essence of Laughter," *The Painter of Modern Life*, p. 149.

13. Baudelaire, "On the Essence of Laughter," *The Painter of Modern Life*, p. 153, n. 2.

Each of Jesus' photodramatic parables describes the activities of various people and the kinds of being that they deal out in their actions. It has been customary among some New Testament scholars either to assert that these characters behave in perfectly normal ways, or to claim that their surprising behaviour points to some meaning beyond the world of the everyday. In other words, scholars have frequently brought to their interpretation of these stories the assumption that the everyday is itself "predictable," that is to say "meagre." But the everyday appears predictable only to the consciousness that imposes a particular pattern of feeling on its experience.

Jesus' photodramatic parables force the listener to focus *on* the phenomena of human actions, and not to look beyond them nor to impose categories on them. These stories look directly *at* human beings in their activities, not *through* them. Each character emerges in his or her own sensible idiosyncrasy. Each is interesting, thus challenging the self-complacency of those who are indifferent or insensible to what men and women do, and the parables challenge those who regularize the everyday by imposing their normalizing patterns of feeling on their experience. The stories achieve this without in any way appealing to the sense that the listener might have of being superior to others, of feeling that "for me the conditions of being human do not obtain." In other words, these stories function by restoring the reality of particular individuals, in order to restore the listener to his or her own reality—his or her non-Satanic reality—and thus they function to restore persons to a consciousness of the superabundant reality which engenders personal life.

They accomplish what is extraordinarily difficult to do in narrative. In his sonnet, "Pied Beauty," Hopkins selects samples only of that which is beautiful—dappled things, skies of couple-colour, rose-moles all in stipple upon trout that swim, fresh-firecoal chestnut-falls, finches' wings, landscape plotted and pieced, and the gear, tackle, and trim of the trades. In his sonnet, "Kingfishers Catch Fire," Hopkins selects only the inanimate—stones that ring when tumbled over the ring of round wells, the sound of tucked strings, the tongue of each hung bell—and the natural—the kingfisher and the dragonfly. All of these stimulate his praise of God. When Salinger describes the scene to which Zooey allows his attention to be drawn, it is a scene acted out "sublimely" on a side of the street which is "fortunate," the girl's tam "was very nearly the same shade of red as the blanket on the bed in van Gogh's room at Arles," and their reunion was filled with "joy" for both, with the dachshund "shimmying with ecstasy." Both Hopkins and Salinger have a strong aesthetic sense. In contrast, the photodramatic parables do not depend on aesthetics for their effect. Without appealing to either the profoundly human and Satanic, and without appealing to the aesthetic, they nevertheless succeed in representing the reality of particular human beings in their actuality.

In common usage, "ecstasy" often refers to an extremely pleasurable experience, and in this sense it means enjoying the pleasure produced by certain kinds of experience. In other words, it means enjoying one's own feelings, a form of self-centred hedonism. This is abundantly clear in the case of Mme. Bovary, who finds the actual other an impediment to her romantic transports.

But if ecstasy is understood as going out of oneself in conscious enjoyment of *the other*, then even ambiguous feelings may be included in the ecstatic mode. Jesus' photodramatic parables draw attention outward to the fact that "each mortal thing does one thing and the same"—"selves"—and the parables do this in a way that makes irrelevant the feelings of the observer; in fact, the listener's ego is transcended, producing an attitude akin to selflessness.

These parables reflect a world-attitude that has an extreme capacity for delighting in all mortal things who "deal out that being indoors each one dwells," who playfully express the vitality of personal being. They are interesting in themselves, quite apart from reference to anyone's ego. Their very being attracts the storyteller's attention and engages his interest. He enjoys them; and that is why, when listening to these stories, we can say that, when he told them, Jesus smiled.

PART THREE

The teller of stories

Jesus' sayings and his photodramatic parables have provided us with preliminary access to his sense of the actual and to his sense of where the reality of human being is to be located. If these eight sayings and seven parables alone had survived, we would consider ourselves fortunate in having received material which, after more than nineteen centuries, still carries the power to disclose these dimensions of existence. And yet there is more material to be considered—the five phonodramatic parables. It is these parables which, above all, communicate Jesus' own particular vision into the complex and enigmatic depths of human reality, and which afford us the opportunity to understand more completely what it means to live in the personal mode—namely, to live in story.

CHAPTER EIGHT

The rich man who had
a steward

The original story

We have only one source for the parable known tradition-ally as "The Unjust Steward" (Luke 16:1-8a). The earliest Christians had a great deal of difficulty fitting this story into their systems of thought, and a whole series of attempts to interpret it has been attached to the end (Luke 16:8b-15). Since none of these attempted explanations reflect characteristically Lukan ideas, it is safe to assume that Luke found the parable, together with these glosses, in either Q or in his special source. The wording of the parable has been preserved perfectly intact, except that the ending was damaged in transmission.

The rich man who had a steward

(1) There was a rich man who had a steward,

(2) and charges were brought to him that this man was squander-ing his goods. And he called him and said to him, "What is this that I hear about you? Turn in the account of your stewardship, for you are no longer able to be steward."

(3) And the steward said to himself, "What shall I do, since my master is taking the stewardship away from me? I am not strong enough to dig, and I am ashamed to beg. I have decided what to do, so that people may receive me into their houses when I am put out of the stewardship."

(4) So, summoning his master's debtors one by one, he said to the first, "How much do you owe my master?" He said, "A hundred measures of oil." And he said to him, "Take your bill, and sit down quickly and write fifty." Then he said to another, "And how much do you owe?" He said, "A hundred measures of wheat." He said to him, "Take your bill, and write eighty."

(5) (The master commended the steward for his shrewdness.)

The introduction to the story has not been altered by the early Christian teachers, probably because its subject matter was not at all amenable to being used as an illustration of their favourite themes, the growth of the Church and the need to be prepared for the final judgment. The fact that this parable is so ill-suited to early Christian teaching or doctrine is, indeed, one of the strongest and clearest signs that the parable was composed by the historical Jesus.

All of the sayings in verses 8b-15 were added by early Christian teachers. There remains an indication in verse 8a (5) that the rich man was originally speaking to his steward at the end, but his words have been lost. Whoever truncated the parable has understood the rich man's speech to be a commendation of the steward, whom the abbreviator thinks of as "dishonest." It is a very superficial reading of the story to see the steward as merely dishonest. In any case, we cannot accept the abbreviator's interpretation of the rich man's words with any confidence, and we must for the time being remain agnostic rather than attempt to restore this unfortunate omission from the story. Nevertheless, we can be grateful that the tradition has preserved this indication that the rich man *was* speaking at the end of his story. This shows that the story displays the same formal structure as the other four core phonodramatic parables of Jesus: each story is about a man who is speaking at the end.

Listening to the story

As we turn to the story, we will rely only on what Jesus has himself said. In listening to any story, it is quite a natural impulse to fill in the lacuna left with information drawn from our own doctrinal systems (as in the case of the earliest Christians), or from our knowledge of history (as in the case of scholarly interpretation), or, more importantly, from our own presuppositions about how

stories are told or how people behave ("it must have been that . . .").
As we shall see, Jesus' stories function in order to create certain
narrative expectations, some of which are realized and some of
which are not. In many cases, the listener's narrative expectations
are not met nor are his questions answered. In other words, these
stories function as narratives in order to create internal silence, and
it is the silence of Jesus as storyteller that provides the most
important context for understanding the meaning of the story.

This story begins, as all oral narratives do, by telling what the
story is about—it is *about* the rich man, it is *his* story. Recognizing
just what the subject matter of the story is provides an important
clue to its meaning. As in the other core phonodramatic parables,
the rich man is introduced as having a relationship with another
human being—he had a steward.

The narrative immediately raises a number of questions. How
rich is he? What of his other relationships—wife, family, friends?
Some of these questions will be answered, others will not. The
story's beginning opens up a practically infinite set of narrative
possibilities regarding the relationship between the rich man and
the steward, but those possibilities are narrowed to a single set in
the next sentence, "and charges were brought to him that this man
was squandering his goods." The verb translated as "squandering"
etymologically means "scattering," as in the "scattering" of seeds or
the "scattering" of sheep; it is the same verb used to describe what
the younger son did in the story of "The Man Who Had Two Sons,"
when he "squandered his property in loose living."

Since his responsibility was to manage the rich man's business,
the charge means that the steward was not an efficient manager. It
could be that his inefficiency was due to extravagance, or it could be
due simply to incompetence. In any case, the rich man has not
himself scrutinized the steward's activities, nor has he himself
audited the steward's accounts. *Others* have brought charges to him
that the steward was squandering his goods. This indicates two
things: that the steward's activities attracted the attention of
others, and that the rich man himself was, for whatever reasons,
not himself making sure that the steward handled his affairs
efficiently.

At this point in the narrative, there are several future possibilities: the rich man could have a hearing to determine whether or not
there was any basis for the charges; the rich man could begin legal

action against his steward; or the rich man could simply dismiss the steward. The rich man called his steward and said to him, "What is this that I hear about you? Turn in the account of your stewardship, for you are no longer able to be steward." The storyteller selects the third possibility. Had he selected either of the first two narrative possibilities, then the issue would have been whether or not there was sufficient evidence to dismiss the steward, and the narrative would have cast the listener in the role of judge. But the issue is not whether or not the rich man has sufficient grounds for dismissing the steward, or whether or not the steward is guilty as charged.

The rich man "calls" his steward, that is, he summons him, because he is in charge. He then asks, "What is this I *hear* about you?" Jesus underscores the fact that the rich man has not himself looked into his steward's activities, that he has only heard what the steward has been doing. Does this motif suggest that the rich man is indifferent to his own business affairs or that he is too busy to be bothered?

He has heard what the steward has been doing—or not doing!—and this tells the rich man something *about the steward*: "What is this I hear *about you*?" He has heard that the steward has been squandering his goods. The rich man concludes from this that the steward is no longer capable of fulfilling his responsibilities, and can no longer be trusted to manage his affairs efficiently and responsibly. In other words, the narrative focuses on the issue of *trust*: the rich man is not primarily concerned about his possessions, but about the steward whom he has entrusted to be responsible for them.

The rich man says simply, "You are no longer able to be steward." From his point of view, it does not matter whether or not the charges are justified, and the storyteller prevents the question of the steward's culpability from arising. The charges that have been brought to him that the steward has been squandering his goods makes trusting his competence and responsibility as a steward no longer possible. This is the dynamic of any relationship based on trust; any time that outsiders question the behaviour of one of the parties in the relationship, the other one can no longer trust in the same way. In a different kind of relationship, for example a marriage, one would likely want to go on trusting the other whose behaviour has been called into question. But nevertheless, even if innocence is established, the terms of the relationship have been forever changed. Trust would become trust in the context of tolerance, no longer unquestioning.

In a business relationship such as this, there are two aspects to trust. The rich man trusts his steward to be competent, and he trusts his steward to be honest. Charges have been brought to the rich man that the steward is irresponsible in the management of his goods, and so one half of his basis for trusting his steward has been destroyed. So the rich man tells the steward that he is no longer able to be steward. Acting decisively in this new situation, he dismisses his steward. This decisiveness of the rich man in the context contrasts with his previous relative indifference to the management of his affairs. He did not concern himself with the details of the management of his affairs, but trusted his steward to handle them for him. Now that the rich man can no longer trust his steward, he decisively tells him that he is no longer able to be steward.

The rich man says, "Turn in the account of your stewardship," not: "I am seizing your accounts and will audit them myself." This shows that the rich man still trusts the steward to be *honest,* and that the steward's honesty has not been challenged nor called into question. He is dismissing the steward because he is, in one respect, unreliable; he does not want such a person as his steward. But he still trusts that the steward will turn in a true account of his stewardship. Jesus develops the narrative in such a way that it focuses on the issue of trust between the rich man and his steward; in other words, on the inter-personal basis of their relationship.

"And the steward said to himself." In two of his core phono-dramatic parables Jesus relates to us the secret thoughts of a character. Here, and also in the story of "The Man Who Had Two Sons," where he relates the thoughts of the younger son (Luke 15:18-19). What will the steward say to himself? Will he express sorrow for having betrayed the trust of his employer? No, he says, "What shall I do?" Does this mean "what shall I do while I am preparing the accounts?" or "what shall I do afterwards?" or does it mean "what shall I do to regain my employer's trust?" Will he acknowledge his responsibility for the erosion of trust? No, he exhibits no awareness whatsoever that he has any responsibility for the destruction of his employer's trust. Instead, he deflects responsibility onto the rich man: "since my master is taking the stewardship away from me." He understands himself as passive, and does not think of himself as having done anything to cause his master to dismiss him. He talks like a victim.

So far, what do we know about this steward from his actions and his words? We know that he is: (1) incompetent as a steward, that he has squandered his master's goods; (2) selfish, that he is concerned about himself (What am I to do?); and (3) irresponsible, that he has no awareness whatsoever of contributing to the situation in which he now finds himself.

We learn, too, how the steward understands himself: as weak and proud. "I am not strong enough to dig, and I am ashamed to beg." He feels that he is not physically strong enough to support himself by manual labour, and he feels that he is too ashamed to ask others to give him money. He considers two extremes, working to support himself, and begging, and rejects both possibilities because of his self-understanding. He does not consider any other possibilities, which tells a lot about his character.

"I have decided what to do." In this crisis, he is decisive. Having considered and rejected the extreme possibilities, having only concern for his own welfare, and having no awareness of any responsibility for having broken the trust of his master, the steward has decided what he will do . . . "so that people may receive me into their houses when I am put out of the stewardship." His decisiveness is guided by his concern to look out for his own best interests. He is guided by no loyalty to any person, but only by the determination to make the situation work for himself. He has judged that the situation offers him an opportunity to turn matters to his own advantage. He will somehow make people feel indebted to him, so that they will receive him into their houses when he is put out of the stewardship for squandering his master's goods.

He is reckoning on having some time to turn the situation to his own advantage because he has not yet turned in his account. "When he will be put out of the stewardship" still lies in the future; his master still trusts him to be honest, and has asked for an account of his stewardship. There is still time to exploit the master's trust in him that he is honest, because he is still steward. He does not envisage himself being hired as a steward by other people because he speaks of "people receiving him into their houses," rather than of someone hiring him as his steward. In other words, he envisages himself existing as a sponger. He won't work, but people will house and feed him because he will have made them indebted to him in some still unspecified way.

"So, summoning *his master's* debtors one by one . . ." Jesus reminds us of the master, the rich man who has trusted the steward to turn in an account of his stewardship. Jesus keeps the issue of the personal relationship in the forefront of the narrative. The master has debtors who are either tenants who deliver a portion of their yield as rent, or wholesale merchants who have received goods on credit. In either case, the master's relationship with his debtors is also a business relationship based on trust. The fact that the steward has explicitly stated that what he is about to do will serve his purpose of ingratiating himself with his master's debtors makes irrelevant the whole scholarly discussion of whether or not the steward had received the goods on consignment from his master and had the authority to dispose of the goods at a price he himself has set. The fact is that he is looking out for number one. Whether he is a survivor who is dishonest or a survivor who is honest does not change the fact the he is a *survivor*. However, the weight of probability lies far on the side of his being dishonest, for the storyteller describes the debtors as *"his master's"* debtors, not the steward's. Moreover, the fact that the steward tells the first debtor to change his bill "quickly" suggests, at the least, that something unsavoury is going on. The steward summons his master's debtors "one by one," meaning that the story gives us only two examples of what might well be a whole series of debtors.

"He said to the first, 'How much do you owe my master?'" Why does the steward have to ask what the first debtor owes? Is this an example of his incompetence as steward, that he does not have records of the debts owing his master? It is difficult to imagine that his man, whose whole natural inclination is to look out for his own best interests, would not know what was owing if he himself was the beneficiary of the transaction. This is further evidence that the rationalization which wants to see the steward as simply reducing debts owed to himself is utterly fanciful. The question is, "How much do you owe *my master*?" It is *to the rich man* that these business-men are indebted, and Jesus once again reminds us that the rich man is the steward's *master,* someone who trusts his steward to be *honest.*

"He said, 'A hundred measures of oil.'" We now learn approximately how rich the master is. One hundred measures of oil is between eight and nine hundred gallons of oil, the yield of about one hundred and fifty olive trees, worth about three years' wages for the average worker in that time! (To give some rough idea, using a modern equivalent: olive oil today sells for about twelve dollars a gallon, so nine hundred gallons would retail for almost $11,000. On the other hand, if we think in terms of an average year's wage for workers, that would, today, be about $15,000, and the oil in question would be worth the equivalent of about $45,000.) However one tries to imagine the size of the debt, it is clear that the debt is a large one, and that the rich man is indeed wealthy.

"And he said to him, 'Take your bill, and sit down quickly and write fifty.'" The steward tells the debtor to alter his bill so that it will appear that he owes the rich man half of what he actually owes.

"Then he said to another, 'And how much do you owe?' He said, 'A hundred measures of wheat.' He said to him, 'Take your bill, and write eighty.'" One hundred measures of wheat is about eleven hundred bushels, the produce of about one hundred acres, worth the equivalent of a wage earner's income for seven and a half years—well over $100,000 in today's terms! The steward tells this debtor to alter his bill so that it will appear that he owes the rich man four-fifths of what he actually owes. In both cases, he has reduced the bill by exactly the same amount, the equivalent of one and a half year's earnings. The total reductions amount to the equivalent of three years' wages—approximately $45,000 today.

The debtors go along with the steward. They, too, act in their own self-interest, but at the steward's instigation. His attitudes and activities corrupt his master's debtors, or at least permit already corrupted people to make real their corruption. The steward interferes in the master's relationship with his debtors—whatever it was. He had given them goods on credit, or was expecting to receive a portion of their yield; in other words, he had a business relationship with them, also based on trust. He counted on them to pay what they owed for what they had received from him. The steward interferes destructively in this relationship.

The steward gains a double advantage for himself. He not only makes people indebted to him by encouraging them to defraud his master, but he also ensures that his accounts will now look better. Whatever he had squandered will be at least partially covered up. We remember that he still must turn in an account of his stewardship.

Even if it were the case that the steward is merely reducing the amount of profit which he stood to make on these transactions, the fact remains that his actions show him to be the kind of person who in a crisis thinks only of ways to use people to his own advantage. He is incompetent (he squanders his master's goods), concerned only about his own interests (What am I to do?), irresponsible (my master is taking the stewardship away from me), weak (I am too weak to dig), proud (I am ashamed to beg), a sponger (. . . . so that people will receive me into their houses . . .), a conniving opportunist with no sense of responsibility to others (he takes advantage of his master's trust), a survivor, and someone who corrupts others. To assert that he was dishonest is to call attention to his *least* unattractive quality.

For two thousand years the dominant Christian and scholarly interpretation of this parable has been that its point lies in the example of the steward's decisiveness; he is seen as an example of how the Christian should behave when confronted by "the preaching of the kingdom," in other words, the Christian should act in his own best interests, since the kingdom is thought of as a better security than worldly goods. It is no wonder that Nietzsche bridled at this attitude. In this view, the religious person is just as acquisitive and unattractive, basically, as anyone concerned with piling up treasure. The only difference is that moths don't eat and rust does not destroy what he wants. But the same personality configuration is evident in the steward and in this type of Christian.

It is truly regrettable that the rich man's words to his steward when he turned in his account have been lost in transmission. Judging from the words of the man who had two sons to his elder son, judging from the words of the householder who went out early in the morning to one of the labourers he had hired to work in ·the vineyard, and judging from the words to his servant of the man who once gave a dinner, it is safe to say that the ending would have held some surprises.

The traditional interpretation, evident in Luke 16:8a and repeated even to the most recent scholarly analyses, has been that the rich man knew that his steward was a survivor, and that he commended his steward for acting decisively to secure his own advantage in the situation. I have already commented on how unacceptable this interpretation is, and would add that it does not develop out of the whole narrative situation, which has made the rich man's trust in his steward the central issue.

The story says that when the rich man lost his trust in the steward's competence, he dismissed him, but still trusted him enough to turn in an account of his stewardship; the issue initially was not the steward's honesty. We then see the steward exploiting his master's trust in order to turn the situation to his own advantage. It is extremely important to keep in mind that the rich man has not been primarily concerned about his goods *per se*, but rather with his relationship to the steward whom he trusted to manage his affairs competently. If he had been primarily concerned about finances, he would have himself noticed that the steward had been squandering his goods, and he would have decided to audit the steward's accounts immediately. But he did not. He told the steward that because *he was the kind of person* about whom charges had been brought that he was squandering his goods, he could no longer have him as his steward.

A second possibility, then, is that in his final words the rich man indicated to the steward that he knew the steward was "shrewd," that is to say, dishonest, and that his commendation was in fact a caustic sign of disapproval. Although what we know of the rich man suggests that he would *not* approve of the steward's looking-out-for-himself behaviour, there is no analogy in the other core phonodramatic parables for this kind of sarcasm, nor would what we know of the rich man lead us to expect that he would express his thoughts in a veiled way with intent to hurt or ridicule. Sarcasm is the tone of the person who feels superior but does not want to be forthright about it. In the opening scene, the rich man *was* forthright and decisive, taking responsibility for the conclusions he had drawn from what he had heard about the steward.

A third possibility is that the rich man did not know that his steward had defrauded him of the equivalent of more than three years' wages, but that he commended the steward for his prudence in turning in the account as demanded. In this case, the picture would be of a trusting man who is hoodwinked by his clever employee, and the listener would be in what Baudelaire calls the Satanic position of feeling superior to the mental deficiency of the rich man. Such an ending would run counter to everything we have so far discovered about the way Jesus' language functions.

The fact is, we do not know what the rich man said to his steward at the end of the story; we only know, from the indication in Luke 16:8a, that he did say something, something that was crucial to the dimensions of inter-personal life that Jesus was uncovering in his story. We will have a better understanding of how Jesus does this when we examine the remaining phonodramatic parables. In the case of this parable, we must content ourselves with the truncated version which has been transmitted to us by the early Christians.

Story versus picaresque

The parable treats the steward as an individual, not as a type or as an example to be avoided, and yet his mode of being human is familiar to us. In *Franny and Zooey*, Lane Coutell writes an essay on Flaubert that tore him down in order to gratify Lane's conceit. And, when Franny was recovering after fainting in a restaurant, Lane was thinking only how he might turn the situation to his own advantage by sneaking up to Franny's room where she would be recuperating. One could multiply examples of this sort. In *The Brothers Karamazov*, Rakitin tries to ingratiate himself into a rich widow's affections so that he can use her money to buy his own newspaper, uses Dmitry's trial as an opportunity to launch his literary career, and even goes so far as to use Alyosha, who was very attached to him. After Zossima's death, Alyosha was so grieved that he felt all his ideals were in question, and Rakitin saw in his grief two ways of furthering his interests:

> He was a practical person and never undertook anything without a prospect of gain for himself. His object in this case was twofold, first a revengeful desire to see "the downfall of the righteous," and Alyosha's fall "from the saints to the sinners," over which he was already gloating in his imagination, and in the second place he had in view a certain material gain for himself. . . . [1]

One of the best known opportunists in English literature is Edmund in *King Lear*. Like Rakitin, he has enough detachment from others to see how their characters might offer him a chance to secure some gain for himself:

> A credulous father, and a brother noble,
> Whose nature is so far from doing harms
> That he suspects none; on whose foolish honesty
> My practices ride easy. (I, ii, 172-75)[2]

1. Dostoyevsky, *The Brothers Karamazov*, p. 359.
2. William Shakespeare, *King Lear*, edited by Alfred Harbage (New York: Penguin Books, 1970).

This sort of person sees everything in terms of its utility value, sees people and things only in terms of their usefulness to him. He thus reduces the entire world to the level of dead matter. His is a mechanistic universe, an instrumental complex with a clever intellect at the center, manipulating and using, taking but never receiving, for receiving implies a human bond.

This mode of being human is a vitally deficient one. As Scheler points out, " ... all specific 'egoism,' the concern for oneself and one's interest, and even the instinct of 'self-preservation' are signs of a blocked and weakened life."[3] The steward is an egoist in this sense, that his instinct is for self-preservation and for his own interests. To him, the rich man is someone to use, and so are his master's debtors. He is guided only by his wits, and uses his cleverness to turn the situation to his own advantage. He trusts no one but himself.

Why is this story *not* about the unjust steward? Because the egoist, the survivor, the opportunist, does not live in story. He is just a rolling stone, a man perpetually on the road. He has one adventure or experience after another, and there is no unifying principle except his own survival. Such a mode of being human is episodic and sequential, with each day linked to each other day only by one following after another. Things happen to him in linear fashion. From the point of view of genre, the only kind of narrative to be told about such a human being is the picaresque (the best contemporary example of which is probably Fellini's film, "The Satyricon").

To live in story, one must live out of a commitment to someone or something beyond one's self, and this is possible, perhaps paradoxically, only for those who are not anxious about self-preservation, those who are conscious of the fullness of being. What the rich man says and does suggests that he is such a person, someone with autonomous roots, and so capable of paying attention to other values than merely self-preservation. Like Edgar in *King Lear*, "whose nature is so far from doing harms that he suspects none", the rich man does not suspect his steward. Initially, charges were brought to him by others that the steward had been wasting his goods, yet even after hearing this information he still trusts the steward to be honest in submitting his account! People with this

3. Scheler, *Ressentiment*, p. 89.

nature appear somehow vulnerable, even foolish, to those who are habituated to distrusting others and to selecting always that which permits them to detest others. (One thinks of Prince Charles, who appears in this light to the eyes of cynical journalists and commentators).

What concerns the rich man is not his money, but his relationship with the steward. He asks, "What is this I hear *about you*?" He dismisses the steward because he can no longer *trust* him, and that is quite different than dispensing with someone because he is no longer useful. In other words, this man's concern is with the human relationship; *that* is what is important to him. And because he lives in the mode of the personal, Jesus tells the story about him, suggesting therefore that to be a person is to live in story.

This parable demonstrates that Jesus harboured no covert *ressentiment* against the higher positive values, and should always be taken together with Jesus' saying about the camel going through the eye of a needle:

It is easier for a camel to go through the eye of a needle
than for a rich man to enter the kingdom of God.

The interpretation of the saying must proceed from an awareness of precisely how Jesus told his story about a rich man, for the parable shows that Jesus could not have been speaking about wealth as such in his saying. This rich man, at least, did live in story, and was oriented to the dimension of the personal. Indeed, it is not he but the steward and his creditors who live out of the attitude of holding, which prevents them from living in story.

CHAPTER NINE

The man who once gave a dinner and invited guests

Reconstructing the wording of Jesus' story

Jesus' story about a man who once gave a dinner and invited guests has been preserved in three different versions, Matthew 22:1-14, Luke 14:16-24, and Thomas 64. Thomas' version, if analyzed with the appropriate source-critical and redaction-critical methods, can be quite helpful in the attempt to reconstruct the story composed by Jesus.

It has been rightly pointed out that we cannot proceed on the assumption that there was a single, definitive, wording of any of Jesus' sayings or parables. The probability is that he uttered these stories on different occasions and that the precise wording varied from time to time. And, indeed, we can only approximate the "original" wording of the story of the man who once gave a dinner and invited guests. But, as we shall see when examining Jesus' four other phonodramatic parables, the degree to which each word and phrase in these stories has been carefully selected is striking; how difficult it is to change a single word without altering the meaning of the story! In other words, I believe that our examination of these stories will show that we can develop fairly reliable criteria for determining with a very high degree of probability the original words of the stories narrated by Jesus.

In order to facilitate our analysis, I have printed the English translation of the three extant versions in parallelism with one another. Italics indicate the original words, and brackets surround secondary additions to the story.

Matthew 22:1-14	Luke 14:16-24	Thomas 64

1. [The kingdom of heaven may be compared to a king who gave a marriage feast for his son,]

A man once gave a [great] banquet, *and invited* [many];

A man had received visitors.

2. and *sent his servant*[s] to call *those who were invited to the* [marriage] feast;

and at the time for the banquet *he sent his servant* to say to those who had been invited, 'Come, for all is now ready.'

And when he had prepared *the dinner, he sent his servant to* invite *the guests.*

3. [but they would not come.]

[But they all alike began to make excuses.]

4. [Again he sent other servants, saying, 'Tell those who are invited, "Behold, I have made ready *my dinner,* my oxen and my fat calves are killed, and everything is ready; come to the marriage feast."'' But they made light of it, and went off,]

5.

[He went to the first one and said to him, 'My master invites you.' He said, 'I have claims against some merchants. They are coming to me this evening. I must go and give them my orders. I ask to be excused from the dinner.'

6. [one to his *farm,*]

The first said to him, 'I have bought a field, *and I must go out and see it; I pray you, have me excused.'*

[He went to another and said to him, 'My master invites you.' He said to him, 'I *have* just *bought* a house and I am required for the day. I shall not have any spare time.']

7. [another to his business,]

And another said, 'I have bought five yoke of oxen, and I go to examine them; I pray you, have me excused.'

8. [while the rest seized his servants, treated them shamefully, and killed them. The king] *was angry,* [and he sent his troops and destroyed those murderers and burned their city.]

9. (The motif of the marriage feast has become the basis for Matthew's revision, and so has dropped out here)

And another said, 'I have married a wife

and therefore I cannot come.'

[He went to another and said to him, 'My master invites you.' He said to him, 'My friend is going to get married, and I am to prepare the banquet.] I shall not be able to come. [I ask to be excused from *the dinner.'*]

10.

(Compare Luke's first refusal)

[He went to another and said to him, 'My master invites you.' He said to him, 'I *have* just *bought a farm,* and I am on my way to collect the rent. I shall not be able to come. I ask to be excused.']

11.

So the servant came and reported this to his master.

The servant returned [and said] *to his master,* ['Those whom you invited to the dinner have asked to be excused.']

12. *Then he said to his servant*[s], ['The wedding is ready, but those invited were not worthy.]

Then the householder *in anger said to his servant,* ['Go out quickly to the streets and lanes of the city, and bring in the poor and maimed and blind and lame.']

The master *said to his servant,*

13.

[And the servant said, 'Sir, what you command-ed has been done, and still there is room.' And the master said to the servant,]

Go [therefore] *to the* thoroughfares, and invite [to the mar-riage feast] *as many as you find.'* [And those servants went out into the streets and gathered all whom they found, both bad and good; so the wedding hall was fil-led with guests.]

'*Go out to* the highways [and hedges], and compel people to come in, [that my house may be filled. For I tell you, none of those men who were in-vited shall taste my banquet.']

'*Go outside to the streets and bring back those whom you happen to meet,* [so that they may dine.' Businessmen and mer-chants will not enter the Places of My Father.]

14. [But when the king came in to look at the guests, he saw there a man who had no wedding gar-ment; and he said to him, 'Friend, how did you get in here with-out a wedding gar-ment?' And he was speechless. Then the king said to his at-tendants, 'Bind him hand and foot, and cast him into the outerdarkness;there men will weep and gnash their teeth.' For many are called, but few are chosen.]

One notices immediately that Matthew has added an additional scene to his version of the story (14) which tells how the king found a man at the marriage feast who did not have a wedding garment, and so had him cast into the outer darkness: "'there men will weep and gnash their teeth.' For many are called, but few are chosen." The idea reflected in this scene as well as its language are totally Matthean, and correspond with his view that both good and bad enter the Church (many are called) but on the day of judgment the unrighteous will be separated out, and will be cast into outer darkness (this theme recurs frequently in Matthew, and we have already had occasion to note it in his "Parable of the Net" (Matt 13:47-50), as well as in his handling of several other parables).

In comparison with both the Gospels of Thomas and Luke, Matthew has changed the banquet or dinner into a "marriage feast" given by a "king" (rather than by a man or a householder) for his "son" (1). Matthew has, then, reworded the story in order to make it serve as an illustration for his idea that Jesus was the Son of God, and that his ministry was, in effect, an invitation to the future, other-worldly, messianic banquet. In Matthew's version alone, the king's servants are treated shamefully and killed (8). Again, this reflects Matthew's idea that God's messengers were put to death by the Jewish leaders (see especially in the Matthean "woe to the scribes and Pharisees," (Matt 23:29-36) which accuses them of having murdered the prophets (23:31) and of killing and crucifying Christian missionaries (23:34).

Matthew then says that because of this, "the king was angry, and he sent his troops and destroyed those murderers and burned their city" (8). In other words, Matthew, writing around A.D. 80, asserts that the destruction of Jerusalem in A.D. 70 was God's punishment of Israel for rejecting, and even murdering, God's messengers. According to Matthew, because Israel rejected God's messengers (from the prophets through Jesus and the early Christian missionaries), God had his servants (subsequent Christian missionaries), invite as many as they found, meaning non-Jews, and they gathered in "both bad and good" into the Church (13), but few of these will be "chosen" on the judgment day (14).

Matthew has altered the details of the story in order to change it into an illustration of his view that Jesus is the Son of God (the king) and in order to illustrate his understanding of the meaning of the destruction of Jerusalem and, indeed, of the history of the Christian mission up to his own time. And, in fact, Matthew's handling of this story is one of the most important internal pieces of evidence for dating the composition of his gospel to approximately A.D. 80, that is, about half a century after the death of Jesus, rather as if Jesus had died in the early 1930's and Matthew were writing his gospel this year.

Luke has also revised the story in some of its details in order to illustrate the spread of Christianity, but his transformation of the story is not as thorough as Matthew's. Luke has changed the "dinner" into a "great banquet," thereby emphasizing that he is talking about a supernatural event (1).

Luke has inserted an additional sending of the servant (12) to bring in the poor, the maimed, the blind and the lame. From the point of view of source-criticism this is secondary, because neither Matthew nor Thomas has a parallel. From the point of view of redaction-criticism, we can explain why Luke would have added this first mission of the servant. In the context of Luke's gospel immediately preceding this parable, Luke's Jesus offers the following advice: "When you give a dinner or a banquet, do not invite your friends or your brothers or your kinsmen or rich neighbours, lest they also invite you in return, and you be repaid. But when you give a feast, *invite the poor, the maimed, the lame, the blind,* and you will be blessed, because they cannot repay you. You will be repaid at the resurrection of the just" (Luke 14:12-14). This is a piece of instruction from an early Christian teacher, possibly from Luke's own community, but certainly one who flourished sometime during the approximately sixty years that passed between the death of Jesus and the writing of Luke's gospel. The instruction reflects early Christian ideas about how to secure for oneself a heavenly reward, and also reflects Luke's special interest in the physically and materially impoverished (see, for example, the programmatic passage in Luke 4:16-19, a pure Lukan composition). Luke has inserted the invitation to the poor, the maimed, the blind, and the lame into the parable in order to illustrate his understanding that the Christian mission did reach out to these groups. The phrase is source-critically and redaction-critically secondary. It is also a secondary insertion from a stylistic point of view. Once this second invitation is removed, there is a smooth transition in Luke: "Then the householder in anger said to his servant ... 'Go out to the highways and hedges and compel people to come in.'"

The man's anger (8, 12) is original for both source-critical and redaction-critical reasons. Its appearance in both Matthew and Luke shows that in the Q version the man was angry. Matthew has clearly interpreted the anger as divine wrath, but his householder is nonetheless allegorized as a divine figure. Since these explanations were added by Matthew and Luke, we can assume that Q did not explain the man's anger. And that means, in turn, that Q had no reason for having added this motif. We can conclude, therefore, that the man's anger is original.

The case is different with the idea that the host wanted to exclude those who had refused to come (13). Luke rationalizes that the host sent his servant to compel people to come in "that my house may be filled. For I tell you, none of those men who were invited shall taste my banquet." Luke wants to turn things around, so that the invited guests who refused instead are excluded by the host. Thomas has a similar idea. His Jesus says "Businessmen and merchants will not enter the Places of My Father," as if they had been excluded when in fact the story says that they refused to come. Not only do these phrases of exclusion reflect Christian ideas and terminology, not only are they secondary from a source-critical point of view, but they also conflict with the wording of the story. These incongruities are good signs of secondary expansion and interpretation, and are to be understood as efforts to explain the man's otherwise puzzling command to his servant to bring back those he happens to meet (13).

Thomas' version of this command has more claim to originality than either Matthew's or Luke's. Luke's "compel" is a stronger version of "bring back," and reflects his idea that the servant's mission illustrates the Christian mission. Matthew's "invite" is also a variation of Thomas'"bring back," again in the terminology of the Christian mission. Similarly, Luke's "highways and hedges" and Matthew's "thoroughfares," reflect their view that this mission of the servant illustrates the Christian mission to the Gentiles, to those outside Israel. Thomas' "Go outside to the streets" is, in comparison, a neutral command, and so we can regard it as closer to the original wording of the story.

So far, source-critical and redaction-critical analysis of the three versions of this story have shown that there was a considerable degree of revision made to the second part of the story, principally by Matthew and Luke in order to illustrate the progress of the Christian mission after its failure among the Jews. When we turn to the first half, we see that Luke's version is very close to the original, since both Matthew's and Thomas' versions can be explained as redactions of his wording.

All three versions show that the story was about the man (Matthew: king) who once gave a dinner. In the middle of his version, Luke calls him "a householder" (12), and it must be considered a possibility that the story was originally about "a householder who once gave a dinner." Jesus tells another story about a householder, the one who went out early in the morning to hire labourers for his vineyard (Matt 20:1-15). However, since Luke thinks of the host as executing judgment on his invited visitors (13), and since elsewhere Luke represents Jesus as a householder who shuts the door, at the judgment day, on those who are not worthy to receive his heavenly reward (Luke 13:22-30), the weight of probability is on the side of a "man" rather than a "householder."

Who did the man invite to his dinner—Luke's "many" or Thomas' "visitors" (1)? Our choice must be based on purely redaction-critical criteria. In this case we can see that Luke has a reason for changing "visitors" to "many," because he uses the parable to illustrate his idea that Jesus made an invitation to all to follow him, "but they all alike began to make excuses." Thomas, on the other hand, has no redactorial motive for changing "many" to "visitors" so we can regard his "visitors" as closer to the original wording.

All three versions retain the information that the man sent his servant to call his guests when the dinner was ready (2). Matthew has the servant say: "Behold, I have made ready my dinner . . . everything is ready; come to the marriage feast." That Matthew's version is the result of secondary expansion is evident from the repetitiousness of the servant's message. Luke's version says: "at the time for the (dinner) he sent his servant to say to those who had been invited, 'Come; for all is now ready'" (Luke 14:17). Matthew and Luke both reflect the original picture that the guests had been invited, and that when the dinner was ready, the man sent his servant to call his guests. Thomas, who seems unaware of the Palestinian custom of sending a servant to call the invited guests at the time for the dinner, says: "and when he had prepared the dinner, he sent his servant *to invite* the guests." There are no particular source-critical nor redaction-critical reasons for preferring either Thomas' "And when he had prepared the dinner," or Luke's "and at the time for the (dinner)"; the meaning of both is the same. However, on stylistic grounds, Luke's wording is preferable. We have to decide between Thomas' and Luke's invitation. Since Luke's version reflects the language of the Christian mission, we can conclude that Thomas' version of the servant's summons is closer to the original, which simply stated that the servant went to (call) the invited guests.

In Luke's version, before his three refusals, the text says, "But they all alike began to make excuses" (3). It will be recalled that Luke has changed an invitation from "visitors" to "many," and that he does this in order to make the story illustrate Luke's view of why the Jews refused to follow Jesus. His picture is of a *"great* banquet" to which *many* people are invited. The original story, however, dealt only with a dinner which a man intended to give for his guests, that is three guests, because there were only three refusals in the original (and in Luke's version for that matter, too). This means that Luke has added the phrase "But they all alike began to make excuses" in order to give the impression that the three refusals are only examples of the kind of thing the "many" said to excuse themselves. And, moreover, the third refusal did not involve a prayer to be excused, as we have seen, but rather a statement from the man to the effect that "he could not" come.

That Luke's generalizing summary in anticipation of the three refusals is a secondary expansion of the story can be corroborated by comparing the Thomas version which lacks a statement to this effect, but instead reports the exchange between the servant and the invited guests immediately after the man has sent his servant to summon them to dinner. Matthew, on the other hand, has expanded the series of refusals so that first the servants call those who were invited to the marriage feast, but they would not come (Matt 22:3). Again he sent other servants, who were treated shamefully and killed. And finally he sent a third group of servants out into the streets to gather in both the bad and good. Matthew, then, has altered the whole picture to coincide with his belief in the successive stages of Christian missionary activity.

We can more easily reconstruct the content and order of the three guests' refusals if we compare the three versions:

Matthew	Luke	Thomas
(1) farm	(1) field	(1) merchant
(2) business	(2) oxen	(2) house
(3) [the marriage motif has been used as the basis for the parable]	(3) wife	(3) marriage
		(4) farm

Apparently, Luke retains the original order and content of the refusals, because both Matthew's and Thomas' versions can be explained as variations from the order retained in Luke. The first guest had bought a farm or field. Thomas has moved this into fourth place to make room for the merchant, in line with his aversion to those involved in business. In all three versions, the second refusal has to do with a business transaction. Since both Matthew and Thomas have made other alterations, Luke's wording here is preferable. The marriage motif is evident in the third place of all versions.

What did the servant say when he returned to his master? Thomas' version that the servant said "Those whom you invited to the dinner have asked to be excused" (11) cannot be original, since in fact not all the invited guests did excuse themselves. Luke's statement that "the servant came and reported this to his master" seems preferable, because this implies that he repeated the guests' refusals to his master. This is an important feature of the narrative structure, because it provides the catalyst for the man's anger.

We can now see what results our source-critical and redaction-critical analysis has produced. The original version is most nearly preserved by Luke.[1]

The man who gave a dinner and invited guests

(1) There was a man who once gave a dinner, and invited guests.

(2) And at the time for the dinner, he sent his servant to call those who had been invited.

(3) The first said to him, 'I have bought a farm, and I must go out to see it; I pray you, have me excused.'
And the second said, 'I have bought five yoke of oxen, and I go to examine them; I pray you, have me excused.'
And the third said, 'I have married a wife, and therefore I cannot come.'

(4) So the servant came and reported this to his master.

(5) Then the man in anger said to his servant, 'Go outside to the streets and bring back those whom you happen to meet.'

1. All the words for the reconstructed story have been taken from the extant versions, with the exception of the enumeration for the "second" and "third" invited guests. Luke and Thomas speak of "another," Luke because he wishes the series to represent "many" who "all alike began to make excuses," and Thomas because he has expanded the refusals to four. On the basis of Luke's statement that "The *first* said to him," I have restored what I take to be the original enumeration. This does not change the meaning, but does make the story easier to follow.

Comparing the versions with the original

When examining the wording of "The Man Who Once Gave a Dinner," one is struck by its economy of language. In comparison with this reconstructed wording, which hypothetically is very close to the pre-Q version used by both Q and Thomas, Thomas' version is noticeably expanded. We have already observed that Thomas has recast the story in order to illustrate the idea that businessmen and merchants will not enter the Places of the Gnostic Jesus' Father. (Thomas reflects an advanced stage in the early Christian loss of 'world.') In order to accomplish this, Thomas has replaced the first refusal with an excuse by a man who has business with merchants. This has caused a displacement of the refusal by the man who bought a farm (Luke: field) from the first into the fourth position. These alterations, motivated by specific Gnostic ideas, are easy to identify. But the difference in style between Thomas and the pre-Q, more original version, is also noteworthy. Thomas has both standardized the excuses and has expanded them, in a very specific way; the invited guests now offer reasons for their excuses:

(5) "They are coming to me this evening. I must go and give them my orders."

(6) "...and am required for the day. I shall not have any spare time."

(9) "My friend is going to get married, and I am to prepare the banquet."

(10) "I am on my way to collect the rent."

All of the reasons offered show the invited guests as being involved in business, a motif which is characteristic of Thomas' tendency. The fact that these expanded explanations are made on the basis of the more simple refusals evident in Luke confirms our source-critical reconstruction of the content and order of the refusals. That is, clearly Thomas has produced a *version* of the more original text, which does not offer such explanations. Instead, each guest simply says what he is going to do that evening instead of attending the dinner; no explicit reason or explanation is offered.

The man's anger is not explained in the original version, nor his reason for instructing the servant to bring back those whom he happens to meet on the street. Luke adds a reason for this: the man in anger wishes to fill his house *so that* the invited guests cannot attend his banquet. Thomas has Jesus explain that the man's actions show that businessmen and merchants will not enter the Places of Jesus' Father. (Matthew does reflect the idea of the house being full, but does not connect this with the exclusion of the previously invited guests.) In short, the various attempts by the different editors to explain the man's behaviour show that in the original his behaviour was left unexplained.

In all three early Christian versions, the invited guests who refuse to come to the dinner are interpreted negatively within the revised story. Luke is the most reticent in this respect; nevertheless his redaction, particularly in the context which he has provided for the story (Luke 14:7-14), reflecting the stages of the Christian mission, interprets the refusals as analogous to the rejection of the gospel of the earliest Christian missionaries (or, more probably, as the rejection of Jesus by, however anachronistically, the Pharisees). Thomas equates those who refuse with businessmen and tradesmen, who will not enter the Places of Jesus' Father. Matthew has the harshest judgment on the invited guests, a judgment which we have already examined in some detail.

In the original story, however, there are no criteria provided internally for making a judgment on the invited guests' refusal to come to the dinner. The narrator does not describe them adjectivally as "good" or "bad," nor does he include in the story any moral, religious, or legal system which could guide the listener's evaluation of what has transpired. The listener must judge for himself by attending only to what has been said and what has been done. The narrative style of the original is sober and detached.

The original story deals only with a man who once invited guests to a dinner and sent his servant to call them. There is no attempt to allegorize the characters in order to make them function as surrogates for any set of transcendental or mythological figures or concepts. The situation is rooted totally in the world of everyday experience. The characters in the story are all particular human beings, and with an astonishing economy of language the narrator makes each character come alive in his particularity.

The formal structure of Jesus' phonodramatic parables

All of Jesus' five core phonodramatic parables begin in the same way, either with "There was a man who . . ." or "A man . . . ."

125

The meaning is the same, and I have chosen the alternative "There was ... who ..." because of the analogy between it and Matthew's introduction to his version of "The Labourers in the Vineyard": "The kingdom of heaven is like a householder who ...." We have already examined the way in which Matthew characteristically introduces parables, by using them as illustrations for his views regarding the kingdom of heaven. This suggests that the original beginning of this story was: "There was a householder who ...," and so offers support for that particular form of introduction. There are two stories which do open in this way:

"There was a rich man who had a steward..." (Luke 16:1-8a);

"There was a man who had two sons..." (Luke 15:11-32).

Source-criticism and redaction-criticism, then, together with form-criticism all point us to the conclusion that the other stories also opened in the same way:

"There was a man who once gave a dinner..." (Luke 14:16-24 and parallels);

"There was a householder who went out early in the morning to hire labourers for his vineyard..." (Matt 20:1-15); and

"There was a man going down from Jerusalem to Jericho, who fell among robbers..." (Luke 10:30-35).

This brings us to a crucial form-critical observation which, as in the case of the preceding observation regarding the opening of Jesus' stories, has not previously been noticed. Every one of these narratives ends with someone speaking. The story of the man who had two sons ends with the father speaking to his elder son (Luke 15:31-32a). The story of the man who once gave a dinner ends with him speaking to his servant (the ending as reconstructed above). The story of the householder who went out early in the morning ends with the householder speaking to one of the labourers whom he had hired early in the morning (Matt 20:13-15). The ending to the story of the rich man who had a steward has been damaged in transmission, but even the damaged ending indicates that what has been lost is a speech by the rich man to his steward (Luke 16:8a). In short, all four of these stories end with the man about whom the story is told speaking in direct discourse. In the fifth story, the one about the man going down the road, the ending has the Samaritan speaking to the innkeeper (Luke 10:35). The man who was going down the road was beaten and left half dead by the robbers, and he does not, within the story, resume an active

126

role. The Samaritan, as it were, speaks in his stead, a form-critical variation on the standard pattern the significance of which we shall examine in Chapter Eleven.

These observations indicate that in each of these five parables there was a formal correlation between the beginning and the ending of the story. In each of them, with the significant exception of the story about the man going down the road, Jesus tells a story about a man and the story ends with that same man speaking. This observation gives us an important criterion for identifying narrative parables composed by the historical Jesus. Not only are the five narrative parables which we will examine recognized by a consensus of scholars as authentic, but this recognition, which has been based on a variety of historical-critical criteria, can now be reinforced by our form-critical observations. None of the example stories, illustrative stories, or allegories attributed to Jesus display these same formal characteristics, which means that any scholar wishing to expand the concentric circles of authenticity outward to include other materials must reckon with these five core phonodramatic parables as the norm against which all other parables must be judged.

One further observation, from source-criticism. Before the development of fairly sophisticated redaction-critical methods in the fifties and sixties, scholars were accustomed to employing the criterion of multiple attestation to establish the authenticity of the Jesus material. We have seen in our examination of the so-called kingdom parables that source-criticism can take us back to the formative stage of Christianity when the sayings were being collected and used in Christian teaching and preaching. The source of Mark, the source Q, and Thomas' source all give evidence of that formative period, and we can say, therefore, that the evidence has multiple attestation. However, multiple attestation cannot take us back behind the period between the death of Jesus and the first extant gospels. Having reconstructed how the sayings were used in that period, we have discovered that in every single case the kingdom was interpreted in terms of early Christian ideas—about the spread of the Christian mission, and about the judgment which the early Christians anticipated in the future.

However, the case is different with the form-criticism of Jesus' parables. We have seen that five of them are composed in the same form: each story is about a man who is speaking at the end of the story (this is why we have termed them *phonodramatic* parables). This formal characteristic of Jesus' parables has the strongest possible source-critical support: the story of the householder who went out early in the morning comes from Matthew's special source; the stories of the man who had two sons, of the rich man who had a steward, and of the man going down from Jerusalem to Jericho all come from Luke's special source; and the story of the man who once gave a dinner comes from the Q source and is also attested to by Thomas. In other words, the criterion of multiple attestation functions supremely well in support of our conclusion regarding the original form of Jesus' parables: that he composed stories about particular men who were speaking at the end of their stories.

The story of the man who once gave a dinner and invited visitors is formally structured so that the ending correlates with the beginning. But even the internal components of this story are symmetrically arranged. In the centre stand the three refusals of the invited visitors. To either side of this center stand the man's sending of his servant to summon his invited visitors, and the servant's report to his master concerning their replies.

Fortunately, this is the only one of Jesus' core phonodramatic parables whose original wording must be reconstructed from the extant versions. The wording of the other four has been preserved almost intact. If this reconstructed story turns out to be identical in terms of style, content, and form with the other four whose wording has been preserved virtually intact, then we will have important corroborative evidence to guide our analysis of these parables.

Listening to the story

"There was a man who once gave a dinner, and invited guests." The story is about a man, a particular man, identified only as a man who once gave a dinner. We know nothing else about him: whether he is old or young, rich or poor, married or unmarried, religious or non-religious, Jewish or non-Jewish. He is defined only in terms of a relationship with his invited guests. This opening corresponds stylistically with that of "The Householder Who Went Out Early in the Morning to Hire Labourers for his Vineyard," a story which begins by saying that the story will be about the householder and the labourers whom he will hire. Also comparable are the story of "The Man Who Had Two Sons" and the story of "The Rich Man Who Had a Steward." Four out of five stories begin with a particular man, and the story concerns his relationship with other particular people. The first line of the story indicates its subject matter, and shows that the traditional title ("The Great Supper" or "The Marriage Feast") misrepresents the subject of the story.

The storyteller does not explain why the man decided to give this dinner. Other storytellers might wish to explain that the dinner is given because the man's son will be married (Matthew), or say that the dinner is "a great banquet" (Luke), thus implying that the dinner is to be viewed allegorically. Jesus remains silent about the man's reasons for giving the dinner. Hypothetically, the man could have been repaying past social obligations, or he could have been a social climber, or he could have been spontaneously generous and sociable, or even lonely and needing company. There are numerous other possibilities, but none of them is mentioned by Jesus. If we knew why the man was giving the dinner, the whole meaning of the story would be deflected toward a single interpretation. Jesus' technique of narration opens up possibilities for understanding rather than closing them down.

Jesus does tell us that the man invited "guests," meaning that he was not giving a dinner for his family. By planning a dinner and inviting guests the definite possibility emerges that those invited will not come at the time for the dinner, a possibility built into the situation of issuing an invitation. One can always be rebuffed; people can always refuse to come, can always say "no."

"And at the time for the dinner, he sent his servant to call those who had been invited." We now learn that the man is not poor, but is sufficiently well off to enjoy the services of at least one servant. As was the custom, the man sends his servant round to call the guests who had been previously invited.

The storyteller devotes an entire verse to the moment when eveything hangs in the balance. The guests had been invited, dinner time has arrived, and now he has sent his servant to bring his guests to the dinner. This sentence evokes that particular uncertainty attending a space of time which is fraught with possibilities, both positive and negative, a period of time which has its own particular kind of lack and absence, waiting to be filled by the guests as expected and hoped. There is no reason whatsoever to fear that the guests will not come when called, of course; but the very situation which Jesus describes nevertheless holds out that possibility as an undercurrent to the certainty that the guests will arrive as planned.

Had the storyteller told us "why" the man was giving this dinner, we might have already been anticipating various specific possibilities. For example, if he were a social climber, we might have speculated that some, at least, of the guests might rebuff the man. Or, for example, if this were a wedding feast, there might be last-minute cancellations, as we all know from experience. In short, if we knew something about this man or about his reasons for giving the party we might already be anticipating various possible responses, including various reasons why people might want to, or have to, cancel at the last minute.

Anyone who has given a dinner has known the experience of the last hour before the guests' expected arrival. It is not unusual for a host to attempt to control the situation, to think up some pretext for calling one or more of the invited guests: "Would you mind bringing me . . . ?" or "I know that so and so will be driving and could offer you a ride," and so forth. In short, Jesus' narrative evokes the situation of this man in his hopefulness and his vulnerability, in his openness to the possibility that his expectations and plans will be met as well as his openness to the possibility that his expectations and plans will *not* be fulfilled.

Naturally, the listener assumes that the guests will arrive and that the story will have to do with what happened during the dinner, since that is the specific set of narrative expectations which the storyteller has created. There is absolutely no hint that those invited might not come back with the servant.

"The first said to him . . ." We expect quite naturally for him to say something like: "Thank you, I have been looking forward to this dinner, and I am on my way."

"I have bought a farm." Fair enough. Perhaps he will say: "And I'm anxious to discuss my purchase with your master this evening."

"I must go out to see it; I pray you, have me excused." The first guest simply says that he feels he "must go and see" the farm he has bought. Jesus does not explain why the man feels he "must" go to see the farm. Hasn't the deal been closed yet? Or is he fearful that he has been sold a piece of land that is not what he thought it was?

130

In Jesus' story, he gives no reasons. Thomas, on the other hand, fills this gap by reporting that the man who had just bought a farm was on his way to collect the rent (#10 above). That, at least, is a logical explanation, one the reader can accept as at least understandable, though still rude.

When someone says "I must do something," we aren't inclined to challenge the person, although we might wonder why he feels the compulsion of necessity. Someone who says "I must" and who does not give reasons either *cannot* give a reason (he says "I must" to disguise the fact that he wants to decline the invitation because of sheer caprice, impulse, or for his own private reasons, but does not want to admit as much) or he *does not want* to disclose the nature of his obligation (for example: "I have bought a farm and I must go and see it because I am dying and I want to ensure that my dependents receive a good property;" or "I feel that I must go because I am concerned that I have been deceived or defrauded, and I will not be able to enjoy the dinner until my mind is at rest;" or "I have bought a farm and it's a deal that will make me a rich man—it's a deal on which my whole future depends"). The necessity which the first guest feels could be personal, moral, or financial; but Jesus does not confirm any of these possibilities. We do not understand why he cannot come later, after he has seen the farm (after all, how much could he "see" of a farm in the dark?). In short, we do not really know why he asks to be excused.

So the narrative leaves us wondering about all of these unanswered questions when the servant goes to call the second guest who had been invited. The optimism of waiting for the guests to arrive and for the account of their evening with the man has vanished, and now all the indications are ominous. Things are not developing as they should.

"And the second said ...." Again, the second guest could, hypothetically, say almost anything in response to the servant's summons. However, because the first guest has responded negatively, the actual possibilities are in total disarray, and uncertainty dominates the narrative. Nevertheless, it could be that the first guest was an exception.

"I have bought five yoke of oxen ...." We learn that the man who once gave a dinner moves in affluent circles. His first invited guest has just bought a farm, and his second guest has just bought five yoke of oxen. Since the average farmer owned one yoke of oxen, which was sufficient to plow a single field, the second guest has bought enough oxen for five times the average! His having made this purchase, however, does not determine whether or not he will come to the dinner when called.

"And I go to examine them." In comparison with the first guest's excuse, this one comes as a relief. The second guest does not appeal to some vague sense of felt necessity. He is decisive ("I go"), and takes full responsibility for his actions. Now we are dealing with a man of substance who does not attempt to deflect responsibility for his actions onto some vaguely felt sense of duty.

"I pray you, have me excused." But that's just what the first guest said. The first guest seemed to have reasons which he could not or did not wish to state, but the second guest offers neither excuse nor reason for his refusal to come. Are we to conclude that seeing the oxen prevents him from coming? But that's impossible; he cannot very well examine the oxen he has bought after nightfall, any more than the first guest can "see" his farm in the dark, during the time of the dinner.

The second guest does not even allude to vague reasons for refusing to come. He just says in effect: "I have other plans for the evening (which are more important than coming to your master's dinner)." The second guest offers no reasons, logical or otherwise, but simply says, "I pray you, have me excused."

The whole situation has become very unsettled. The dinner is now ready. The man who planned the dinner is waiting for his servant to bring home his guests, but the first two guests have each asked to be excused—one for vaguely suggested obligations and the other because he has decided to do something else instead. What is going on?

Fortunately, the law of threefold repetition is at work here. According to the canons of popular storytelling, we can confidently expect that the third man will be different from the first two, and that he will come when called, as expected. Relief is in sight; and on behalf of the man who planned the dinner and invited guests, we anticipate a change in fortune.

"And the third said, 'I have married a wife....'" Perhaps the third man will ask whether he can bring his new bride to dinner.

"....and therefore...'" The third guest, unlike the first and second guests, is a logical man. He recognizes premises and knows how to draw conclusions from those premises. Good, we are finally listening to someone who is rational and who holds himself to the standards of reason.

"'I cannot come.'" He *"can* not" come!? What does he mean, he *cannot* come? That's ridiculous. That *is* ridiculous. The first and second guests did not explain themselves fully, but at least the first guest knows what he feels he must do—he's his own man in that sense—and the second guest knows what he wants to do and has chosen to do—he's decisive. But this third guest is a snivelling fellow. What does he mean, he has a wife, and THEREFORE— therefore he cannot come—what's logical about that? Does he really think that his conclusion follows from his premise? The third guest is totally exasperating, because he disguises his weakness with fabricated logic.

"So the servant came and reported this to his master." The servant came and repeated the refusals of the invited guests to his master, who has been waiting for the servant to bring his invited guests for the dinner. How will the man respond to this news?

"Then the man in anger said to his servant . . . ." Jesus' deft use of the triadic form makes the man's angry explosion come inevitably. Optimistic anticipation of the dinner to come has been swept away by a succession of totally unforeseen refusals by the invited guests —one irresponsible, one decisive in his refusal, one weak. In the vulnerability of one's concrete entanglements with other human beings, this is how one's best-laid plans are shattered. It is perhaps difficult today to imagine the man's situation without uncon- sciously thinking either that there must be something wrong with him or with his guests. But the story does not say so.

The story raises the question as to how the man will express his anger. Will he retaliate, go and burn down the first guest's farm, kill the second guest's oxen, and injure the third guest's wife? Will he seek revenge? (Matthew's king is not vengeful, for he acts to punish murderers, as Matthew states. This act is not retaliation, but the enactment of a specific kind of justice.) Or will the man, like Luke's and Thomas' host, fill the house with anyone he finds from the streets and lanes, highways, and hedges, convincing himself that he can somehow *exclude* those who were invited, even though they refused to come? In other words, will he affirm A in order to deny B? Is the host a man of *ressentiment*?

A lot depends on how he construes the refusal of his invited guests. If he takes their refusal as a personal injury, he might, if he were impotent, respond as Luke's and Thomas' hosts did. Both Luke and Thomas have unwittingly turned the story into the fable of the fox and the sour grapes! On the other hand, if the host were an angry man, with a bad temper, these refusals would trigger an irruption of his ugliness. In that case, one might expect him to react destructively, by beating someone up, for example, or throwing the dinner into the garbage.

The incongruities of this story are so intense, the directions in which the drama is pulling are so varied, that the whole account is threatening to dissolve into nonsense. It all seems so crazy: a man giving a dinner and all of his invited guests refusing to come for reasons that we don't understand, aren't stated, or that we find ridiculous. At every single stage of the story, Jesus has raised a certain set of narrative expectations and then frustrated them with a completely unexpected turn of events. There is no anticipating what the man might now say to his servant.

"Go outside to the streets and bring back those whom you happen to meet." Why does the man choose this alternative? Puzzling over what the man has ordered his servant to do will perhaps help us to understand the narrative better.

How the story means

Neither this parable nor the preceding one can be reduced to an ideational content. Each functions strictly as narrative and never simply as, for example, illustration for ideas that could be stated in other terms. The question "*What* does it mean?" usually presupposes an answer that is reductionist. The question "*How* does it function?" expects an answer that ignores meaning. Jesus' parables, however, posit a meaning in the way that they function, and so we must ask: "How does the story mean?"

The subject matter of the story selected by Jesus is itself significant. He has chosen to tell a story *about* a specific man who never becomes an example or a type, nor do the invited guests, for that matter. Each of them is also characterized with complete particularity. The whole situation, then, develops as one representing an individual man in his actual entanglements with other individual men.

Jesus' story does not function in order to convey ideas about God nor about how one should or should not behave, nor does it make the listener contemplate himself as if he were looking in a mirror, nor does it direct the listener's attention to the storyteller. He himself remains invisible,[2] keeping silence about how to judge or to evaluate the actions or words of his characters. The story functions in order to disclose the everyday world, stimulating observation of the incongruous and frequently perplexing dimension of the personal. The story functions in order to open up this dimension of reality and by so doing suggests that this is where the real is to be located.

The listener's attention is directed to the man's vulnerability as he prepares to give a dinner for invited guests. This vulnerability is built into every situation in which someone, with all his own hopes and expectations, opens himself for relationship with other people, who have their own attachments and projects. Any invitation offers the possibility of promise and fulfillment or of disappointment and emptiness. The narrative opens all of this up very deftly. First there is the *anticipation* of the approaching dinner party. Then the *expectation* that the invited guests will soon arrive and, of course, the *confidence* that they will come when the servant calls for them. There is an undercurrent of uncertainty, but initially this is totally muted. The successive refusals of the three guests bring *disappointment,* then *bewilderment,* and finally *anger.* And all of this has developed out of the man's *vulnerability.* Without using a single word indicating emotions, the storyteller has succeeded in touching the heart of man's fundamental *uncertainty* in the midst of his concrete entanglements.

Why then did the man order his servant to go outside to the streets and bring back those whom he happened to meet? Is this the culinary version of "Random Samples"? Since Jesus does not attribute motives to the man, we must take his words at face value.

His words show that he intends to have a dinner party even though his invited guests have refused to come. This means that we can exclude certain interpretations. He has not taken their refusals personally because he does not express his anger by directing an action *against* them. At this point, they drop out of the picture. He does not do anything that might suggest deflected anger.

2. Perhaps inevitably, the story was used by the Christian communities to refer to Jesus' own table fellowship, but that is not the original reference of the story, and this host can hardly be understood to be the storyteller's cameo appearance.

The man's directive to his servant shows that in this situation, which appears to determine a *re*-active re-sponse, he instead *acts* to complete his own programme of having a dinner with invited guests; *he* will complete his story, which has the purpose of dining with invited guests.

Given the situation, the evangelists cannot imagine a man behaving purely in the active mode, and so they have attributed various re-active impulses to explain his totally creative idea of having a dinner with people brought in from the streets. The sheer gratuitousness of his inspiration shows that he is a free man. And his transcendence of the conditions that would obtain for most people in this situation (their anger would be very different!) evokes a smile, just as we smile in relief when someone has surprised us by negotiating certain catastrophe—like a circus performer.

J.D. Salinger points to this phenomenon in *Franny and Zooey* when Zooey, unable to overcome the factors in his relationship with Franny that are inhibiting his ability to act on his love for her, has the idea of going to another room in the apartment and phoning Franny, pretending to be their other brother, Buddy. Franny, thinking she is talking to Buddy, complains to him about Zooey. Zooey does not feel injured by Franny's criticisms, and so does not retaliate. Instead, he makes an imaginative leap:

> "The cigars are ballast, sweetheart. Sheer ballast. If he didn't have a cigar to hold on to, his feet would leave the ground. We'd never see our Zooey again."
> There were several experienced verbal stunt pilots in the Glass family, but this last little remark perhaps Zooey alone was coördinated well enough to bring in safely over a telephone.[3]

The man who once gave a dinner is not a *verbal* stunt pilot, but he is a stunt pilot nevertheless, someone whose transcendent *activity* and inspiration in a situation which ordinarily would have produced a mean response evokes sheer delight.

At this point in our inquiry, suffice it to observe that the account about the man who once gave a dinner and invited guests retains the generic markings and dynamics of narrative. In spite of the various forces at work here, it ends as a story rather than, for example, simply a vignette or an episode. The man who once gave a

3. Salinger, *Franny and Zooey*, p. 191.

dinner and invited guests is someone who refuses to abandon living in story.

The rich man's steward lives episodically, thinking only of self-preservation. Those who live in story are oriented to something or someone outside themselves—the rich man to trusting others, and the man who planned to give a dinner to having guests. The difference between the picaresque figure and those who live in story can perhaps be understood better by considering a distinction made by T.S. Eliot:

> There are three conditions which often look alike
> Yet differ completely, flourish in the same hedgerow:
> Attachment to self and to things and to persons, detachment
> From self and from things and from persons; and, growing
>   between them, indifference
> Which resembles the others as death resembles life,
> Being between two lives—unflowering, between
> The live and the dead nettle. This is the use of memory:
> For liberation—not less of love but expanding
> Of love beyond desire, and so liberation
> From the future as well as the past.[4]

If one were not thinking clearly, one might conclude that the steward is someone attached to himself. But that would be to overlook that those who use everyone and everything, treating them as dead matter, also treat themselves as mechanical, and that is why the egoist's mode of being is vitally deficient. His mode is the unflowering one of indifference to self and to things and to persons.

Those who are attached to things and to persons are also attached to their selves—not as ones oriented to self-preservation—but rather as, for example, parents who are attached to their children and to their spouses are also attached to each other and to all the things that make their home. This mode of being is living among the live nettle, which stings. It is a vital and flowering mode.

The third mode is what Eliot calls detachment from persons and things, and hence, from self. Although it looks to the untrained eye like indifference, it resembles indifference as life resembles death. Detachment refers to a mode of love that has been liberated beyond desire—attachment—and is a mode that is active *in spite of*

---

4. T.S. Eliot, "Little Gidding," III, *The Complete Poems and Plays*, p. 142.

the injuries it receives from being oriented in openness to actual others.

It is obvious that the rich man does not exist in the re-active mode, for he did not try to retaliate against his steward for wasting his goods, but rather decisively ended a relationship whose basis the steward had destroyed. So far is he, in fact, from reacting self-protectively that it is his failure to protect himself in the "normal" way that provides the steward with the opportunity to use the situation to ingratiate himself with his master's debtors. The master's vulnerability allows the plot to develop and provides the main narrative interest—it remains *his* story and the steward's actions refer back to him.

Since the rich man lives neither in the mode of indifference, nor in the mode of attachment, it would appear that he might live in the mode of detachment. Someone living in the mode of attachment, if he were strong enough, would have been expected to execute justice on the steward if he had heard that the steward was squandering his goods: "There was a rich man who had a steward, and charges were brought to him that this man was squandering his goods, and he took him to court." A man who was an egoist, living in what Eliot calls the mode of indifference, would be expected to protect himself: "There was . . . and he said to himself, 'How was I supposed to know that my steward was incompetent? Who hired him, anyway?'" That is a re-active response to the situation. The rich man in Jesus' story appears to be detached and hence *transcends* the normal human responses apparently determined by the situation. Similarly, the man who planned to give a dinner appears as someone whose actions and words are not dictated by his circumstances. His novel idea resolves the dilemma caused by the three refusals in a unique way. What an inventive solution to instruct his servant to invite anyone he happens to meet in the street! Both the rich man and the host speak and act in ways that are superior to the situation. This, apparently, is what it means to exist as a free person—it is a mode of transcendence.

The detachment of the transcendent mode must not be confused, as Eliot says, with indifference. It is the opposite of the self-protective shallowness exhibited by the steward, who conducts himself as though there were no point in striving for anything good or true or beautiful, so he might as well live for the moment. All of his experience appears to be governed by the sense that situations threaten him, and so he cultivates indifference to protect himself and to enable him to use people and things.

Both the rich man and the host began their stories by being oriented to other human beings (to the steward and to invited guests), and both had their orientation complicated and challenged by the unexpected. Revenge, retaliation, petulance, self-protectiveness, indifference—all were possible options offered by these situations, and all are "normal" human responses. Yet each of these men transcended the normal, and therefore continued to live out his story! For Jesus as storyteller helplessness, loneliness and thinking oneself victimized are not the only possibilities when a situation appears to throw into doubt one's open engagement with others; instead, the rich man and the host exhibit free creativity and imagination (like stunt pilots?) in order to fashion their activity into the form of a story. And this, apparently, is what it means, for Jesus, to be a person: to live in story.

Why Jesus was unsentimental

Nietzsche believed that Jesus exhibited the psychology of the redeemer, that he was oriented totally to an inner world of blissful feelings that arise from knowing oneself to be a child of God and to be in heaven. Such a feeling, as we have seen, can be achieved only by denying all opposites, by collapsing all otherness.

The evidence of both the photodramatic and phonodramatic parables which we have so far examined shows that Jesus was an unusually keen and detached observer of human actions and words. Since the listener cannot categorize them in terms of already established ideas, the characters appear as unfamiliar, retaining their otherness. Moreover, they remain other in still another, no less important, sense. The listener cannot identify with these individuals, and hence in their specificity they resist the listener's impulse to collapse all distance through an inner feeling of union with these persons. Whatever "love" might mean in connection with Jesus' world-attitude, it certainly does not mean having nice feelings about people, nor does it mean feeling in union with them.

Jesus' attitude toward the subject matter of his parables is analogous to that of Hopkins and to that of Zooey. When Hopkins notices what is beautiful, or when Zooey lets his attention be drawn to the sublime, neither makes a judgment regarding the beautiful or the sublime in terms of how they affect him, that is, in terms of the pleasure he derives from what he perceives. On the contrary, what Hopkins and Zooey notice remains outside the sphere of their own gratification. Both demonstrate a capacity to enjoy things in their otherness, without referring things back to themselves. When Zooey says "there are nice things in the world— and I mean *nice* things," he is *not* saying "there are things in the world that give me pleasure, and therefore I approve of the world." He is observing that there are scenarios which occur in the world without reference to anyone's ego—like the story which the schoolgirl enacted together with her dog, unhampered by writers, producers, or directors.[5]

Zooey's world-attitude differs completely from that of Woody Allen in his film, "Manhattan." Toward the end of the film, Woody Allen is lying on the sofa in his apartment talking into his tape recorder, and is asking himself whether there are things that make life worth living. He proceeds to give a whole list of things that tip the scales in favour of life against death: Groucho Marx, Willie Mays, the second movement of the Jupiter Symphony, Louis Armstrong's recording of "Potato Head Blues," Swedish movies, "Sentimental Education" by Flaubert, Marlon Brando, Frank Sinatra, those incredible apples and pears by Cézanne, the crabs at Sam Woo's, and Tracy's face (Tracy is a seventeen year-old with whom he, a man in his forties, had been having an affair).

Woody Allen's question presupposes that life functions in order to gratify him, and after listing this whole series of films, books, entertainment figures, and so on that please him, he decides that after all life is good. In other words, he judges life in terms of its ability to give him pleasure. His world-attitude is that of a tough, doubting consumer. In Zooey's words, he refers everything that happens right back to his lousy little ego. This hedonistic attitude can only end in hatred of the actual other, and this is evident in Woody Allen's recent film, "Stardust Memories," which is a document of how much he hates all those who have failed to satisfy him (lovers, friends, audiences).

The parables of Jesus exhibit the sensibility of an acute observer of what people do and say, and they describe the everyday realistic activities of persons in the world. Each narrative treats the world

5. Salinger, *Franny and Zooey*, p. 151.

not in its typicalness but in its specificity. Jesus does not collapse reality toward his own ego, nor is his own ego in flight from itself into the world; he is not in flight from others, nor in flight from himself. On the contrary, his ability to allow others to be in their difference shows that he is confident in his own particularity.

It is not difficult to understand why the early Christians remembered Jesus as someone who knew the minds and hearts of men (Mark 2:8 par.; Mark 12:15 par.; Luke 11:17 = Matt 12:25; Luke 6:8; John 1:47-48; John 6:61). Every single one of the photodramatic parables describes the actions of a different individual, and the two phonodramatic parables describe six different individuals. In the nine parables we have examined, Jesus has created thirteen completely different characters!

Zooey said that Jesus was the best, the smartest, the most loving, the least sentimental, the most unimitative master that God could have picked for the job in the New Testament. That these parables reflect an original sensibility, are utterly unsentimental, and are the products of an extremely intelligent observer of human actions and words should be clear. But the parables also urge a reconsideration of the meaning of "love," if one should want to use that word to describe Jesus' world-attitude. These parables suggest that Dostoyevsky recognized rightly that Christ-like love is love of neighbour, meaning an orientation toward the actual other.

CHAPTER TEN 🌿

The householder who went out at dawn to hire labourers

The original story

Matthew is our only source for the parable known traditionally as "The Labourers in the Vineyard" (Matt 20:1-16). At this point in his gospel, Matthew is following his Markan source (Matt 19—20 = Mark 10) and inserts the parable into Mark's framework to illustrate the meaning of the statement that "many that are first will be last, and the last first" (Mark 10:31 = Matt 19:30). Matthew repeats this statement again at the end of the parable (Matt 20:16) to form an inclusion, and then resumes his transmission of the Markan narrative.

Matthew uses the parable to illustrate his idea that those Christians who joined the movement late will receive the same heavenly reward as those who were working from the beginning. In order to make the story refer clearly to the heavenly judgment, Matthew has inserted into the story a command by the owner of the vineyard to his "steward" to "Call the labourers and pay them their wages, beginning with the last, up to the first." The steward, for Matthew, is the Son of Man or Jesus in his role as dispenser of justice at the last judgment. The language of "first" and "last" picks up this motif from Mark 10:31 = Matt 19:30 = Matt 20:16. He has also inserted "the first" in Matt 20:10.

These editorial alterations to the story are easy to spot, as is Matthew's characteristic introduction "For the kingdom of heaven is like . . . ," an introduction which, as we have seen in Chapter Six, Matthew uses in order to represent situations of eschatological judgment. Once these minor editorial additions are removed from the story, we have virtually intact the original parable of Jesus. There is one phrase that must be removed for stylistic reasons: "they thought they would receive more" (Matt 20:10). In his other phonodramatic parables, Jesus communicates the thoughts of his characters only by having them express their thoughts in words. This phrase clearly anticipates the words of the workers, and so must be a secondary, explanatory gloss. The wording of the original story was, then, as follows:

The householder who went out at dawn to hire labourers

(1) There was a householder who went out at dawn[1] to hire labourers for his vineyard.

(2) After agreeing with the labourers for a denarius a day, he sent them into his vineyard. And going out about the third hour he saw others standing idle in the market place; and to them he said, "You go into the vineyard too, and whatever is right I will give you." So they went. Going out again about the sixth hour and the ninth hour, he did the same. And about the eleventh hour he went out and found others standing; and he said to them, "Why do you stand here idle all day?" They said to him, "Because no one has hired us." He said to them, "You go into the vineyard, too."

(3) And when it was evening, those hired about the eleventh hour came, and each of them received a denarius. Now when the others came, each of them also received a denarius.

(4) And on receiving it they grumbled at the householder, saying, "These last worked only one hour, and you have made them equal to us who have borne the burden of the day and the scorching heat."

(5) But he replied to one of them, "Friend, I am doing you no wrong; did you not agree with me for a denarius? Take what belongs to you and go; I choose to give to this last as I give to you. Am I not allowed to do what I choose with what belongs to me? Or is your eye evil because I am good?[2]"

1. R.S.V. "early in the morning." "At dawn" renders the Greek literally.
2. A literal translation of the Greek.

Form, content, and style of the story

Form-critically, we can observe that this parable displays the same structure as the other five phonodramatic parables of Jesus. The story is about a man (the householder) who is speaking at the end of his story. From the point of view of subject matter, this story is also identical to the others. It tells about a man who has a relationship with other persons. The first story we examined told about a rich man who had a steward; the story develops out of the relationship based on trust. The second story we examined told about a man who once gave a dinner and invited guests; the story develops out of the relationship based on an invitation. This story tells about a householder who went out at dawn to hire labourers for his vineyard; the story will, we anticipate, develop out of a relationship based on a contract. Each of the seven *photo*dramatic parables deals with a different kind of relationship between persons and things; so far, each of the *phono*dramatic parables deals with a different basis for inter-personal relationship, and explores the implications of that particular kind of relationship.

From the point of view of style, this parable also is identical to the others. Characters are created through their words and actions, through what they say and what they do. Jesus does not intrude into the story by using adjectives to tell his listener what to think about any of the characters nor to describe them physically. Moreover, there are no references to any system of evaluation (the Law, moral standards, religious doctrines, etc.) by which the actions and words of the characters can be judged. The characters all belong to the everyday world and are utterly realistic; they serve neither as examples nor as types, nor even as ciphers for some external "teaching" or system of ideas. The listener is forced to attend closely to what is said and to what is done.

Listening to the story

"There was a householder who went out at dawn to hire labourers for his vineyard." The storyteller announces the subject matter of his story, namely the householder. It is his story. He went out at dawn, that is, before six o'clock in the morning, and he went out with a purpose, to hire labourers for his vineyard. We learn that he is of sufficient means to own a vineyard. The storyteller does not tell us why the householder went out at dawn, but there are

144

several possibilities. There could be some urgency connected with the cultivation of the vineyard, or with the harvesting of his produce. However, we are not told what season this is, and we do not know whether the vineyard is being prepared at the beginning of the growing season or whether its produce is being harvested. It is also possible that this man is extremely energetic, that he wants to get a jump on things or he wants to hire the best labourers. It could be that he goes out at dawn out of anxiety. All of these are possibilities, but they are possibilities about which Jesus remains silent. The story evokes a whole range of questions, but does not provide answers for them. We must simply listen to the story as it unfolds.

"After agreeing with the labourers for a denarius a day, he sent them into his vineyard." The householder made a verbal contract with the labourers that he would pay them a denarius, that is, a day's wage for a day's work. After reaching an agreement with them, he sent them into his vineyard. This both reminds us that it is *his* vineyard and also connotes that he is in charge of the situation.

"And going out about the third hour . . . ." The first time, the householder went out with the purpose of hiring labourers for his vineyard. But the second time no reason is given for his going out. Why did he go out, and where was he going? Did he go out for a purpose, was there some urgency, or was he just restless? Jesus does not answer these questions which the narrative evokes. The story only says that he went out again about nine o'clock in the morning, thus suggesting once again his energy.

". . . he saw others standing idle in the market place." The information that "he saw" others suggests a certain casualness or fortuitousness about his seeing the others. It does not say that he was looking for more workers. He could have gone to the market place for a variety of reasons, as we have seen. While he was there, he saw others standing idle.

". . . and to them he said, 'You go into the vineyard too, and whatever is right I will give you.' So they went." He decides to put those standing idle in the market place to work. Since Jesus has remained silent about the householder's reason for going out to the market place at nine o'clock in the morning, we cannot assume that he went there to find workers for his vineyard. Moreover, he does not say to them that he needs more workers. He only tells them to go into the vineyard, too. Is he someone who does not like to see people standing around idle, and he wants to put them to work?

Does he need more workers for his vineyard? Does he send them into his vineyard because he wants to provide income for the unemployed, that is, welfare? All of these possibilities are evoked by the narrative, but Jesus remains silent as to which it may be. Jesus does state, however, that the householder did *not* make a verbal contract with these workers. He simply sent them into his vineyard, assuring them that he would *give* them "whatever is right." In other words, he reserves the freedom to decide "what is right." Nevertheless, those standing idle in the market place went as he commanded them.

"Going out about the sixth hour and the ninth hour, he did the same." The householder went out again at noon and at three o'clock in the afternoon. Why does he keep going out? Since Jesus does not say that the man needs workers, nor that he went out to the market place to hire more workers, his actions begin to seem a little odd. Since "he did the same" at noon and at three o'clock in the afternoon, it appears that he went to the market place, for whatever reasons, or maybe for no particular reason at all, and that when he saw others standing idle he told them to go into his vineyard—again without making a verbal contract. He simply ordered them into his vineyard and told them he would pay them whatever he thought was right. There is something a little incongruous about all of this, since Jesus does not offer any practical reasons for the householder's behaviour.

"And about the eleventh hour he went out..." This is five o'clock in the afternoon!

"...and found others standing; and he said to them, 'Why do you stand here idle all day?' They said to him, 'Because no one has hired us.' He said to them, 'You go into the vineyard, too.'" Once again, he seems to come rather accidentally upon these idlers, presumably while he is going about his affairs. This time, he asks the men why they stand in the market place idle all day. This strongly suggests that he has been sending labourers into his vineyard to work because he does not like to see people standing idle. Since Jesus does not say that the householder was compassionate, that he hired workers in order to prevent them from going hungry, we cannot assume that this was his motivation. The story simply pictures the householder as an energetic man. He went out first at dawn, and has gone out to the market place four more times during the day, presumably in the pursuit of his own interests or affairs. Each time when he sees men standing idle he puts them to work. But this time he does not

146

even offer to give them "what is right"; instead, he simply sends this last group into his vineyard. They are totally dependent on his freedom to decide what to give them.

"And when it was evening, those hired about the eleventh hour came, and each of them received a denarius." Evening is the end of the working day; the time is about six o'clock. The workers whom the man sent into his vineyard rather unexpectedly receive wages for a whole day's work even though they have only laboured for a single hour. The story has increasingly communicated the impression that this energetic man does what *he* thinks is right. The only time that he acted with a practical goal, whose purpose anyone could approve of, was when he went out at dawn to hire labourers for his vineyard. All the other times he has gone out to the market place for reasons that are unexpressed, and when he saw men standing idle he told them to work for whatever he himself thought would be right. Now the story tells us that he paid those who had only worked one hour a whole day's wage. This man certainly does act according to his own understanding of things! The narrative raises the question of what he will pay the other labourers, who have worked more or less of a full day.

"Now when the others came, each of them also received a denarius." He gave those who had worked from six o'clock, from nine o'clock, from twelve o'clock and from three o'clock the same pay, a full day's wage. In other words, he paid his workers far more than he had to by any criteria. He had told the workers hired at the third, sixth, and ninth hours that he would give them "whatever is right," and that implies some fraction of a day's wage. He has apparently decided that "what is right" to him is to pay all the labourers the same wage, regardless of how long they worked. He has even paid those who only worked one hour a full day's wage. What could his reasons possibly be? Is he generous, foolish, charitable, or just plain eccentric?

"And on receiving it they grumbled at the householder, saying, 'These last worked only one hour, and you have made them equal to us who have borne the burden of the day and the scorching heat.'" The other workers "grumble" at the householder. The verb indicates a way of talking and a whole attitude, all of which is almost audible to us. The other workers have, they say, (a) worked all day, while those hired at five o'clock only worked an hour and (b) they have had to work in the scorching heat. Their words show that it is the labourers hired at dawn who are grumbling, because they are the ones who have borne the burden of the day. They object because those hired last have received the same pay that they have received.

"But he replied to one of them, 'Friend, I am doing you no wrong; did you not agree with me for a denarius?'" The householder consents to judge his actions from the point of view of the labourers he has hired. He could have said immediately, "Begone!" but instead he takes an attitude that involves looking at himself with some distance. He addresses one of the labourers, singling him out from the crowd, and calls him "Friend," not meaning "my friend" in the sense of intimacy, but rather something like the British form of address, "my good fellow." There is a certain formality about this form of address; it both concedes something to the one addressed, but keeps him at a certain distance. "I am doing you no wrong." Now we see why the householder bothers at all to deal with the labourers' grumbling; he thought that they felt he had done them wrong. He answers the charge which he believes is implied in their grumbling. He is not an arbitrary man who scoffs at the view of his hired labourers; if they believe he has wronged them, then at least he will try to answer the charge. His very willingness to submit his actions to judgment shows something about this man: that he has a conscience. He judges that he has done them no wrong, and, furthermore, he offers for public scrutiny the basis of his judgment: "did you not agree with me for a denarius?" By asking "did you not . . . ?" he involves the labourer in the process of making a judgment. He stands outside his own actions, and invites the labourer to stand beside him while they make a judgment. He reminds the labourer that they had made a verbal contract and since he had kept his word, the labourer should recognize that he has no grounds for believing that the householder has wronged him. He is assuming that the labourer, remembering their verbal contract, will arrive at the same conclusion.

"Take what belongs to you and go." Since he judges that they have no grounds for feeling wronged, he dismisses the labourer, telling him to take what belongs to him, meaning that the householder makes no effort to retaliate in a petty way against the grumbler.

"I choose to give to this last as I give to you." Although he has already dismissed the man, he is still thinking about what the labourers' grumbling means. His second thought is to point out that he *chose* to give to those who laboured only one hour a full day's wage, thus making explicit his conviction that when he is not bound by a contract in his relationship with the labourers, he is *free to give away what he has*. We remember that he had told those he hired at nine, noon, and three o'clock that he would pay them what *he thought was right*, and that he sent those hired at five o'clock into his vineyard without making *any* promises. Acting on his own sense of right is evidently a strong aspect of the householder's self-understanding.

The story pictures him as energetic and self-confident, and yet as someone who scrutinizes his own behaviour. He has a conscience, meaning that he evaluates his actions in the light of standards to which he holds himself.

"Am I not allowed to do what I choose with what belongs to me?" Again, the question indicates that the householder attributes some dignity to the labourer. He is not someone who simply asserts: "I can do whatever I choose with what belongs to me." He expects the labourer to agree that after all he is the owner of the vineyard and therefore he is *free to give more than required* if he so chooses.

His whole line of questioning is searching for some standard for human behaviour on which he and the labourers can agree. He does not want to be arbitrary. He looks at what he has done from a number of different perspectives, and still cannot locate the principle that he has violated, something that might explain why the labourers are grumbling at him. He still believes that the problem might have been caused by his having wronged them in some way.

"Or is your eye evil because I am good?" The householder finally realizes that he has been asking the wrong questions. He is a man of conscience, and so instinctively looks first to his own actions, to see whether he has violated some principle or other of human relationship, thus injuring the labourers he has hired. Having examined his actions, he has decided that he has not acted in order to exploit the labourers, he has honoured his word, and he has in fact given more than required. He has given more because he chose to do so, and there is nothing wrong in giving away what he owns. He has wronged no one, and so can call his actions good.

To look with the "evil eye" means to look with envy or jealousy at others. The labourers hired at dawn are grumbling because they are *jealous of the other workers* who have also received a full day's wage. It is not even the money in itself that troubles them, but rather what bothers them is that the householder's paying them *all* a full day's wage has made the others *equal* to them. Finally, the householder realizes that this is the problem: he has quite unconsciously and contrary to his own best intentions precipitated a drama of conflict in which one group of people resents the good fortune of another group. Their eye is evil because he is good.

The evil eye

The householder's words at the end of his story function as an epiphany. He has shown a determination to learn whether he has wronged the labourers he has hired, and in pursuing the question has come to the realization that the labourers who are grumbling at him do so because in fact they *envy* the other group of labourers. They grumble at him because they believe that his paying them all a full day's wage has made the workers hired last "equal" to those hired at dawn. The issue is not money as such, but dignity. The grumbling labourers have had their sense of self-worth called into question. Jesus makes this quite obvious by the words the labourers speak. They do not grumble at the householder saying, "These last worked only one hour, and you have paid them the same wage as you have paid us." That would still have been a comparative and competitive statement, but it would have left the whole question on the level of money and the appropriate wages to be paid to each group. The labourers state quite clearly that the issue for them has to do with their sense of dignity. They grumbled at the householder saying, "These last worked only one hour, and *you have made them equal to us."* These words show that they blame the householder for what has happened, namely that they feel that their dignity has been challenged. And these words show that they establish their own dignity by comparing themselves with the other workers. The grumbling labourers know themselves and their own value only by comparing the way the householder treats them with the way he treats the other labourers.

There are several components to this situation which need to be unravelled. (1) The grumbling workers envy (their eye is evil) the other workers. (2) Their way of knowing themselves has been called into question. (3) They know themselves by comparing themselves with the other workers. (4) They envy the other workers' good fortune, but they blame the householder for what has happened.

Scheler points out that envy and the urge to compare are closely related to one another, and that these two phenomena can be the origins for the creation of *ressentiment*. Envy is associated with the "tendency to make comparisons between others and oneself."[3] Scheler distinguishes between two different kinds of comparison, one natural and the other leading to the formation of *ressentiment*. The natural and healthy mode of comparison apprehends the nature and value of two terms of a relation separately, as, for example, when a person who is confident of his own value notices that another person has qualities or gifts which he lacks or which are superior to his own. It is quite normal to construct one's own ideals on the basis of those whom one admires when one notices that another possesses certain attributes that one would like to develop in oneself. It is healthy to fashion one's own self-understanding through this mode of comparison.

But there is another kind of comparison. A person who has no independent sense of his own value, whose vitality is blocked and weakened, is capable of perceiving his own value only in and through comparison with others. He has no sense of his self-worth apart from making comparisons. This means that his whole identity is established through comparison, that he knows who he is only by comparing himself with others.

This second way of securing identity is particularly prevalent where the value of people is tied up with their visible success or failure. Where this is the case, people and things lose their inherent value, and all activities are pursued only for their usefulness in making one seem big in the eyes of others. No thing or person is desired for its own inherent value. Any person or thing can be exchanged for any other person or thing of equal or, preferably, greater relative value. This leads to boundless aspiration, because desire is not directed to particular persons or things, but rather to their relative value in the eyes of others. "The objects have become 'commodities,' destined for exchange and defined by their monetary value."[4] In this system, desire is never satisfied. One can never have enough, because one's desire is not oriented to the concrete; one's desires are meta-physical, that is, surpassing the actual. From this perspective, the contemporary system of free competition for commodities (including people) is actually the expression of hostility toward the actual. Materialism is an extreme expression of offence at the actual—an extreme form of world-denial!

Envy and the urge to compare are by themselves not sufficient

3. Scheler, *Ressentiment*, p. 53.
4. Scheler, *Ressentiment*, p. 56.

to produce *ressentiment*. In addition, there must be repression of these impulses. They must be removed from the sphere of consciousness so that one ceases to be aware of them. When these impulses are driven underground, when they can no longer cross the threshold of consciousness, then *ressentiment* is produced. At that stage, *ressentiment* begins to nourish one's intentions and to inform one's experience. "The *ressentiment* attitude even plays a role in the formation of perceptions, expectations, and memories. It automatically selects those aspects of experience which can justify the factual application of this pattern of feeling."[5]

Moreover, *ressentiment* is characterized by value delusion. Such positive values as power, health, beauty, freedom, independence, generosity, spontaneity are no longer perceived as values. *Ressentiment* unconsciously devalues all of these positive expressions of vitality in favor of other values which allow the man of *ressentiment* to feel good in his own eyes. "The systematic perversion and reinterpretation of the values *themselves* is much more effective than the 'slandering' of persons or the falsification of the world view could ever be."[6]

Using this model as a framework for analysis, it is evident that the grumbling labourers are men of *ressentiment*. In the first place, they have selected only those aspects of the situation which permit the factual application of their envy. They could have, for example, rejoiced in the unexpected good fortune of the other labourers who also received a full day's wage. Instead, they have construed their experience in order to allow the factual application of their envy, which is quite unconscious. It is the householder, not the grumbling workers, who recognizes that they in fact envy the other labourers' good fortune.

What is even more telling, however, is the way they have perceived the householder. They could have, for example, viewed him as simply a bit eccentric. They could have responded by saying "Oh, that's the way the householder is. Who can understand him? He just throws his money away." That was a possible response contained in the situation. Another response would have been to view the householder as a generous man. They do not see the householder's actions in themselves, for what they are, but only in terms of how his actions *affect them*. They are, in that sense, egocentric.

5. Scheler, *Ressentiment*, p. 74.
6. Scheler, *Ressentiment*, p. 77.

The labourers are suffering from value delusion, meaning that they quite unconsciously establish the value of things and persons only in terms that allow them to feel good about themselves. They feel absolutely justified in their perception of the situation. The householder's efforts to discover whether he has wronged them point to this; they blame him because they feel right and feel that he has done something that contradicts their mode of valuation. *His* mode of evaluating his own behaviour, as we have seen, proceeds by examining the concrete bonds that he has established with the various groups of workers, and the concrete bond that he has with his own vineyard. Having examined his actions from the perspective of his concrete bonds with persons and things, he concludes that he has done them no wrong. And yet they grumble. Why?

We have seen that the grumbling workers quite unconsciously select from the situation those aspects which permit them to apply their envy. The second factor in the situation is even more important. They do not see the other labourers' good fortune for what it is, nor do they see the householder's activity for what it is. Instead, they unconsciously interpret the whole situation as it affects *them*.

They think it is self-evident that labourers should be paid equal wages for equal work, not because they are concerned with fairness. After all, the other labourers have received *more* than is fair. They raise the principle of equal pay for equal work because they think of money as a symbol which establishes the relative value of people, and understand themselves and their own value in terms of what they earn in comparison with what others earn. Thus they are able to establish their own sense of who they are. They grumble because they feel that the other labourers have been made *equal* to them, and they feel that this is a self-evident case of injustice. They are then in the grip of value delusion, an unconscious inability to see the inherent value of the other labourers' good fortune, an inability to see the inherent value of the householder's actions. They want everything to be controlled by a system that prevents anyone from benefiting unexpectedly from someone else's spontaneous gift.

They are controlled by this system, and they want the householder also to be controlled by it. They say implicitly to him: "You should not allow yourself to act freely, nor to give to others according to what you think is right. You should be controlled by the principle of equal wages for equal work. Then you would be reinforcing the system of valuation through which we know ourselves in relationship to others." It is crucial for their understanding of themselves and their experience to ensure that everyone plays by the same rules. The fact that the householder has acted freely offends them, and they feel justified in grumbling at him. After all, he has broken their rules.

It is important to notice that the comparative system of valuation replaces concrete human bonds between people with an *abstract* system of relationships. They are offended when human actions in personal relations grow out of concrete bonds between people because they want human relationships to be governed only by the monetary value which is assigned to them. According to their viewpoint, no human action has inherent value of its own.

The householder has a very different attitude toward money. He thinks of it as something to use to hire labourers for his vineyard, or he thinks of money as something to give away if he so chooses. Nothing in the story suggests that he thinks of money as a means of establishing his own identity or as a symbol of his social status. It is the grumbling labourers who think that way, and it is a way of thinking that is rooted in *ressentiment*.

The householder has acted spontaneously to give away more than he had to; he feels rich enough to give away what he owns. He has done this without considering whether he is making some workers "equal" to the others, because such considerations are foreign to his mode of being. He knows his own value instinctively. He "goes out" to achieve his purpose at dawn, he "goes out" to the market place when he wants to, and he hires labourers according to his own idea of what is right. He can allow himself to act according to his own instincts because he knows intuitively that his instincts are "good," that is, that his instincts are not oriented to self-preservation, nor to exploiting the labourers he hires. He trusts himself and what he does.

He hires some labourers and makes a verbal agreement with them. He hires other labourers and promises to give them whatever is right. He trusts what he does because he acts out of a sense of personal responsibility to the labourers he hires, and he understands himself in terms of his concrete relationship with his labourers. When some of the labourers grumble, his willingness to examine his own behaviour shows that he holds himself to certain standards. He is concerned that he might have wronged someone.

His is a concern for doing injury to others, and he trusts himself and the human bonds which he forges with other people. They want an abstract system to control everyone because, basically, they *distrust* others. They do not have an instinctive sense of their own value, nor do they have any instinctive trust of the value of others. Their value delusion is the expression of their fundamental distrust of actual living people and the bonds between them. They do not want there to be bonds between people; they want systems to control people. Their mode of selecting from their experience, then, and their mode of valuation, together with their sense that their principles put them "in the right," show that the grumbling workers are rooted in *ressentiment.* Their words reflect the fact that they are offended by the actual.

How the story means

This story opens onto a specific dimension of human relationships. Indeed, this story opens onto the problems that have traditionally but incorrectly been read into the story of "The Man Who Had Two Sons," which we will examine in Chapter Twelve. Jesus does not take sides in the story of "The Householder Who Went Out at Dawn to Hire Labourers," nor does he include in the story any standards by which the listener can categorize one as "right" and the other as "wrong." Rather, the story opens onto the complexities which emerge in a relationship between people, and the divergent points of view of each are built into the story. Both the householder and the labourers hired at dawn will have to live out the consequences of the mode of being in which each one lives. The labourers are filled with *ressentiment,* they insist on knowing themselves through comparison and on treating themselves and others as abstractions. The storyteller shows the listener what this means, without going any further. The householder's mode of being human is completely different. He, too, will have to live out the consequences of his mode, in which he trusts himself and his own instincts, but he has come to an awareness of how his freedom affects men of *ressentiment.*

The only indication we have of the meaning of the story lies in the fact that this is the *householder's* story. Like all other persons about whom Jesus tells a story, his situation has become extremely complicated. However, he transcends the "normal" human responses apparently dictated by the situation, and continues to live in story! He is a free person.

Why did Jesus not tell a story about the labourers, picturing the employer, for example in Marxist fashion, as one who exploits his labourers? Because to live in story entails being oriented to some value outside one's self. The labourers have no relationship with actual people at all. In fact, they do not want bonds between people to be determinative. They want abstractions to govern human relationships. They just move from job to job, living episodically.

The householder lives in story because he trusts himself and his instinctive way of relating to people. This orientation is challenged by what happens, but the householder does not abandon the narrative mode of being. At the end, he is still oriented to persons, to things, and to self; he has not opted for indifference or for self-preservation or for pettiness. But his striving for a better understanding of the human dynamics which he has precipitated shows that these complications have not overwhelmed him. To live in story is to be *detached* (in T.S. Eliot's sense) from the "normal" human responses which are dictated by situations. The only preference Jesus accords him is the preference accorded to those who live in story.

One final observation. Nietzsche is credited by Scheler and by most contemporary philosophers with having discovered the phenomenon of *ressentiment*. We have seen how Nietzsche has employed the concept in his critique of certain forms of Christianity, and particularly in his critique of certain understandings of Christian love. We have also seen that while Nietzsche did not view Jesus as rooted in *ressentiment*, Nietzsche did believe that Jesus was oriented to the inner life and was motivated by an aversion to all otherness. I need hardly point out that this parable shows that Jesus was not only acutely observant of human actions and human words, but that he had a profound grasp of the dynamics of interpersonal relationship. It is frankly difficult for me to think of any storyteller who has more accurately represented the *ressentiment* mentality and the factors that produce it. The story uncovers the unconscious attitudes which govern human words and actions, those instincts and moods which are the basis of altogether different varieties of being human.

Jesus does not present himself as the bearer of a truth which, if believed, will immediately remove all the complications of human existence. Unlike the Grand Inquisitor, Jesus does not tell his listeners what to think, *how* to find meaning in life or how to live in story. Jesus does not feel sorry for the householder, neither does he pity the labourers. He sees each character in terms of what he says and does and describes them as such. This means that implicitly the story grasps the responsibility of each character for his mode of being. Each is responsible in the sense that each must live out the consequences of his own mode of being human, and Jesus neither provides an abstract system for approval or disapproval, nor suggests a transcendental mechanism that will reward some and punish others. Human reality is grasped precisely as human reality, that is, as exceptional and enigmatic. In response to man's deep-felt religious questions for which he so urgently demands answers, Jesus remains silent.

CHAPTER ELEVEN

The man going down the road who fell among robbers

Luke's Interpretation

Both Mark and Q contained a dialogue in which Jesus answers a question concerning the greatest commandment. In Mark 12:28-31, one of the scribes asks Jesus a sincere question: "Which commandment is the first of all?" This question functions as an occasion for Jesus to answer with a pronouncement, quoting from the Law: "The first is, 'Hear, O Israel: The Lord our God, the Lord is one; and you shall love the Lord your God with all your heart, and with all your soul, and with all your mind, and with all your strength.' The second is this, 'You shall love your neighbour as yourself.' There is no other commandment greater than these."

In the Q version of this exchange, instead of a sincere question, a lawyer stands up to put him to the test (Luke 10:25; cf., Matt 22:35). In Q, the lawyer tests Jesus by asking, "Teacher, which is the great commandment in the law?" (Matt 22:36). Jesus responds to this test by quoting the Law, with slightly different wording from Mark's version.

Luke characteristically prefers the Q version of sayings to the Markan version, and in this case he has adapted Q to his own purposes. In the first place, he has altered the lawyer's question so that it will have some meaning for Luke's Hellenistic audience. Instead of a question about the greatest commandment in the Law, which was a question that held not very much interest for Gentiles, Luke has the lawyer ask: "Teacher, what shall I do to inherit eternal life?" (Luke 10:25). This is the kind of question with which Luke had to deal in his own time, more than fifty years after the death of

Jesus, and outside Palestine. Luke then has Jesus ask a counter-question: "He said to him, 'What is written in the law? How do you read?'" (Luke 10:26). After Luke's changes, it is the lawyer, not Jesus as in Mark and Q, who quotes the double command of the Law to love God and love one's neighbour (Luke 10:27). This alteration enables Luke to have the dialogue between Jesus and the lawyer continue. Jesus then says to the lawyer: "You have answered right; do this, and you will live" (Luke 10:28). This statement shows that the issue for Luke has to do with what one should *do* to inherit eternal life. He had altered the lawyer's question to conform with this interpretation, and now he composes a statement for Jesus that will enable a further development of the issue.

Then the lawyer continues the discussion: "But he, desiring to justify himself, said to Jesus, 'And who is my neighbour?'" *This* is the question to which Luke has been leading through his alterations. The parable known traditionally as "The Good Samaritan" (Luke 10:30-35) came to Luke without any narrative context, and so he created a context for the parable which would illustrate his view that the parable is about the Samaritan who, in Luke's view, provides an example of what it means to love one's neighbour. Luke has reworded the Q dialogue between Jesus and the lawyer in order to create a new dialogue between them that will permit Jesus to utter this parable in answer to the question, "And who is my neighbour?" In line with his view that the Samaritan offers a model of what it means to love one's neighbour, Luke has Jesus ask the lawyer, "Which of these three, do you think, proved neighbour to the man who fell among robbers?" (Luke 10:36). Since he has taken a dialogue which leads to the question "Who is my neighbour?" (meaning "Whom should I love?") and a parable which, in his view, illustrates what it means *to be* someone who loves the neighbour, there is some awkwardness in the final product. Nevertheless, it is serviceable for Luke's purposes.

The lawyer's answer to Jesus' final question, "The one who showed mercy on him" (Luke 10:37), indicates that Luke understands the Samaritan as someone who shows mercy. In order to reinforce this view, Luke, or perhaps his source, has inserted into the story the idea that the Samaritan "had compassion" (Luke 10:33). We have seen that Jesus describes in his stories only what is visible and what is audible. The idea that the Samaritan "had compassion" is an interpretation depending on taking the point of view of omniscience and, as a storyteller, Jesus neither interprets the actions of his characters nor assumes the attitude of omniscience. So the "compassion" of the Samaritan not only is external and secondary from a stylistic point of view (the text should read: "and when he saw him, he went to him . . ."), but the idea that the Samaritan "had compassion" reflects Luke's own view that the story is about someone who is an example of what it means to be a neighbour. Being a neighbour means to have compassion on those in need, it means showing mercy on anyone who needs help, even if he or she turns out to be someone from an alien or even hostile group.

When Luke has Jesus say to the lawyer, "Go and do likewise" (Luke 10:37), it is really Luke as the Christian teacher who is saying to his own contemporary audience: in order to inherit eternal life, you must do what the Samaritan did. Luke's interpretation of the story has proved so powerful that it has governed its understanding for nineteen centuries.

This is not the only time that Luke places a parable without context into a setting of controversy as a means of interpreting it. We will see that he does this with the story of "The Man Who Had Two Sons" in Luke 15:1-32, and I have mentioned that Luke also does this with three other parables. He sets the parable of "The Rich Fool" in such a setting in Luke 12:13-21; he sets the parable of "The Fig Tree" in a controversy setting in Luke 13:1-9; and he does the same with the parable of "The Rich Man and Lazarus" in Luke 16:14-31. I am using "parable" here in the loose sense, for of course neither "The Rich Fool" nor "The Fig Tree" nor "The Rich Man and Lazarus" reflects the same stylistic, formal, and functional characteristics as do the five core phonodramatic parables of Jesus.

"The Rich Fool" (Luke 12:16-21) illustrates the kind of behaviour that one should not follow; it is a negative example story. "The Fig Tree" (Luke 13:6-9) is an allegorical story illustrating early Christian teaching about the last judgment. "The Rich Man and Lazarus" (Luke 16:19-31) uses the terminology of Hellenistic Judaism ("Abraham's bosom," "angels," "Hades," "Moses and the prophets," etc.), and was probably adapted by early Christian teachers to illustrate their idea that the poor and not the rich would inherit an eternal reward after death.

All of the example stories which occur in the synoptic tradition, both positive and negative example stories, appear only in Luke's gospel: "The Good Samaritan," "The Rich Fool," "The Rich Man and Lazarus," and "The Pharisee and the Publican" (Luke 18:10-14). Luke had a particular interest in communicating the moral behaviour appropriate to the Christian life through the use of example stories, the most probable explanation being that he wrote for a specifically Gentile audience.

All of the evidence, then, leads to the same conclusion, namely that Luke understood "The Good Samaritan" as an example story of what it means to be a neighbour, and that he composed the context (Luke 10:25-37) in order to communicate his own interpretation of Jesus' story. If we would understand the story, then, we must attempt to disregard completely the context which Luke has provided and consider only the story itself.

The Man Going Down from Jerusalem to Jericho

(1) There was a man who was going down from Jerusalem to Jericho, and he fell among robbers,

(2) who stripped him and beat him, and departed, leaving him half dead.

(3) Now by chance a priest was going down that road; and when he saw him he passed by on the other side.
So likewise a Levite, when he came to the place and saw him, passed by on the other side.
But a Samaritan, as he journeyed, came to where he was; and when he saw him, he went to him

(4) and bound up his wounds, pouring on oil and wine; then he set him on his own beast and brought him to an inn, and took care of him.

(5) And the next day he took out two denarii and gave them to the innkeeper, saying, "Take care of him; and whatever more you spend, I will repay you when I come back."

Form, content, and style of the story

This story displays the same formal structure as the other four core phonodramatic parables of Jesus. The story is about a man, and the story ends with direct discourse, but this story differs from the other phonodramatic parables because it is not the man whose story this is who is speaking at the end of the story; instead, the Samaritan is speaking to the innkeeper. That it is not the man himself who is speaking at the end of his story does not disqualify this parable as being authentic; on the contrary, this represents a significant variation on the fundamental structure of Jesus' parables, which contributes to the meaning of the story, as we shall see.

The story possesses a five part structure, as do the other four core phonodramatic parables. Scenes one and five, and two and four, correlate to one another; in the center is the triadic passing of three men.

There are no internal systems of valuation in this story. No moral, religious, or prudential criteria indicate to the listener how to judge the actions of the characters. No one is rewarded or punished, no one is praised or blamed by the storyteller. This feature of the parable is identical to that of the other four core phonodramatic parables and, indeed, to the seven core photodramatic parables. In none of his parables does Jesus explain to the listener how to understand or how to interpret the story; the listener must listen to the story and understand it only as story, drawing from it what conclusions he may.

There is one aspect of this parable, however, which makes it different from all the core parables of Jesus. This is the only parable which includes place names (Jerusalem, Jericho[1]) or the identification of characters by cultural code (Samaritan, priest, Levite[2]). My

1. Jerusalem is situated in central Judea on a plateau about 2500 feet above sea level. Jericho, also in Judea, was about seventeen miles to the northeast of Jerusalem, at the western edge of the Jordan valley, about 800 feet below sea level. The road from Jerusalem to Jericho is a tortuous mountain road which drops some 3300 feet between the two cities. If the geographical specification for the story is secondary, it is at least a good location for it, since the road was notorious for the frequency of robbery.

2. The priesthood was hereditary, and the priestly families were responsible for the religious institutions connected with the Temple in Jerusalem, which was completely rebuilt by Herod the Great beginning in 20 B.C. The Levites also were a hereditary group, who also carried out their functions at the Temple in Jerusalem, but their duties kept them subordinate to the priests, who alone had authority for carrying out sacrifices in the Temple. The Samaritans claimed to be the descendants of the northern tribes of Israel who were not deported by the Assyrians in 722 B.C., and their beliefs and practices, in so far as they are known to scholars, appear to be a variation of Jewish belief and practice. There was, in any case, long-standing hostility between the northern tribes of Israel and the southern tribes of Judah, a hostility which continued into the time of Jesus between the Samaritans and the Jews. The Samaritans at the time of Jesus had their own

own sense of the stylistic canons governing Jesus' parables is so strong that I believe that all of these features are secondary Christian additions, and that the story told by Jesus was about a man who was going down a road, not specifically the road from Jerusalem to Jericho. I also believe that the story told that "Now by chance a man was going down that road; and when he saw him, he passed by on the other side. So likewise a second man, when he came to the place and saw him, passed by on the other side. But a third man, as he journeyed, came to where he was . . . ." My reasons for believing this are primarily stylistic, but also literary-critical; the story functions in a way that renders these cultural codes irrelevant, as we shall see.

However, in proffering these views to students and colleagues alike, I have encountered such strong resistance to tampering with the familiar and much beloved wording of the story that I do not think it worthwhile to press the point. Since these cultural codes do not carry the meaning of the story, and since they do not interfere with the way the story functions as narrative, I am content to admit that the story can be understood reasonably well in its familiar version.

I might mention here that there are redaction-critical and historical, in addition to stylistic and literary, reasons for viewing these cultural codes as secondary. The reader will note that all of the references to Samaria and Samaritans come from Lukan works (Luke and Acts) and from John. These works both belong to the last decades of the first century—no less than fifty years after the death of Jesus. The only reference in either Mark or Matthew to Samaritans is Matt 10:5: "Go nowhere among the Gentiles, and enter no town of the Samaritans, but go rather to the lost sheep of the house of Israel." As Matt 16:17-19 shows, Matthew is a gospel in the Petrine tradition. Until Peter left Jerusalem, he was one of the three leaders of the Christian community there, together with James (the brother of Jesus) and John.

---

temple, on Mount Gerizim, which is located about thirty miles to the north of Jerusalem. The territory of the Samaritans was between Judea and Galilee. The Samaritan version of the Pentateuch is a quite ancient version, and with some probability can be dated to approximately the second century B.C. It preserves in some of its readings corroboration for a Palestinian text type that is more original than the Masoretic text produced by the rabbis after the destruction of Jerusalem in 70 A.D. by the Romans.

We know from Acts 8:4-25 that the mission to the Samaritans was undertaken by the miracle-working Phillip, one of the Hellenists, and that this mission created discussion among the Jerusalem leaders concerning its validity. This mission was undertaken only after the persecution of the Hellenists in Jerusalem by the Jews, who persecuted only those Christians who did not obey the Law, that is, the Hellenists. These Christians who were observant Jews were left alone (James, the brother of Jesus, and his circle). After the martyrdom of the Hellenist, Stephen, another one of the Hellenists, Phillip, apparently evangelized in Samaria. As Luke tells it, the Samaritan Christians were finally recognized by the Jerusalem authorities after they sent Peter and John to baptize the Samaritan Christians with their own baptism (Acts 8:14-17). The mention of Samaritans in John 4 also shows that the evangelizing of the Samaritans required justification. In this case, the story about Jesus and the Samaritan woman appears to be the product of the Hellenists who had evangelized Samaria, to justify their own activities by suggesting that the Samaritan mission was inaugurated by Jesus himself.

However, Matthew 10:5 preserves a prohibition against evangelizing in Samaria, a prohibition that presumably entered his sources through the Petrine tradition from the Christian community in Jerusalem.

Luke's gospel and Acts, on the other hand, belong to the traditions of the Hellenistic Christian communities. Luke says that Jesus sent messengers to a village of the Samaritans (Luke 9:52), "but the people would not receive him, because his face was set toward Jerusalem" (Luke 9:53). In other words, Luke both claims that Jesus himself authorized missionary activity in Samaria, but also defers to the views of Jerusalem Christians by saying that the reason Jesus himself did not carry out this mission was because he first had to complete his earthly mission by going to Jerusalem. In other words, Luke preserves the primacy of Jerusalem and also confers legitimacy on the Samaritan mission.

Once we have reconstructed a partial picture of the early Christian controversy surrounding the validity of the Samaritan mission, we have the clues for explaining why the cultural codes would have been added to Jesus' story about the man going down the road. The cultural codes must have been added in the context of controversy between the Hellenists who evangelized Samaria and the Christians in Jerusalem who observed Jewish ways. The story as it stands argues that the Samaritan, not the Jews, acts as a good Christian by showing mercy on the man who was beaten and left half dead by the robbers. The same sort of argument is evident in Luke's story of the healing of the ten lepers. According to Luke, the only leper who demonstrates the appropriate gratitude for being healed was a Samaritan (Luke 17:11-19). This story, too, has its provenance in the context of an apologia for the Hellenists' mission to Samaria, because it makes the Samaritan out to be a better Christian than the Jews.

My best judgment, then, regarding the original wording of the story is that Jesus narrated it this way:

The man going down the road who fell among robbers

(1) There was a man who was going down the road, who fell among robbers,

(2) who stripped him and beat him, and departed, leaving him half dead.

(3) Now by chance a man was going down that road; and when he saw him, he passed by on the other side.
So likewise another man, when he came to the place and saw him, passed by on the other side.
But a third man, as he journeyed, came to where he was; and when he saw him, he went to him

(4) and bound up his wounds, pouring on oil and wine; then he set him on his own beast and brought him to an inn, and took care of him.

(5) And the next day he took out two denarii and gave them to the innkeeper, saying, "Take care of him; and whatever more you spend, I will repay you when I come back."

Listening to the story

"There was a man going down the road (or: going down from Jerusalem to Jericho), and he fell among robbers ...." Jesus tells a story about a particular individual, a man, and the story introduces the man in relationship with other people—robbers. Everything in the story focuses on the relationship, for we know nothing else about the man or about the robbers than is mentioned by Jesus. The subject matter of this story is analogous to that of the core phonodramatic parables of Jesus: (1) There was a *man* who once gave a dinner and invited guests; (2) There was a *rich man* who had a *steward*; (3) There was a *householder* who went out at dawn to hire *labourers*; (4) There was *a man* who had *two sons*. Each one of these stories develops out of the relationship between one man and other people, and each one of the stories explores a different kind of human relationship. In each story a different set of issues regarding the meaning of human relationships is explored, and what is characteristic, and ultimately of crucial significance, is that Jesus explores these deeper dimensions of human relationships by means of a story.

The relationship set up by Jesus at the outset opens up a whole set of narrative possibilities ranging from, on the one hand, the possibility that the man will join the robbers as a member of their group, to the possibility, on the other hand, that he will be robbed by them. As so often happens in the stories of Jesus, the storyteller selects a possibility that comes as a surprise.

"... who stripped him and beat him, and departed, leaving him half dead." The storyteller has introduced the group of people with whom the man enters into a set of possible relationships as "robbers," whose activities have the purpose of taking money and/or goods from other people, so we assume that they might possibly rob the man. Instead, Jesus says that they stripped him *and beat him*, and departed, *leaving him half dead*. Jesus does not even mention that they robbed the man. Even if the listener makes the assumption that the robbers' stripping the man includes taking his money and his goods, he must nevertheless notice that the description pictures not robbing, specifically, but stripping.

The story introduces the robbers as a group, in the plural, so they outnumbered the man. The listener is therefore not prepared for the information that they beat him half to death, and their violence demands an explanation. But since their purpose for banding together was robbery, since they outnumbered the man, and since Jesus does not introduce any cultural or social or psychological or political or economic factors which would account for their violence, the story itself *precludes any reason* for their beating him half to death, and describes without modification the occurrence of absolutely naked violence imposed upon the man going down the road.

The man whose story this is has had it abruptly terminated by the robbers' evil. At this point, the narrative evokes quite a different set of possibilities, all of which congregate around the question whether the man's story will resume. The question is, then, will evil dominate the story by ending it, or are there other possibilities?

"Now by chance a man (or: a priest) was going down that road . . . ." The appearance of another man carries with it all potential that the entrance of another human being brings with him into the situation, ranging from the chance that he will pass by without noticing the man lying there half dead, to the various events that might unfold if he sees the man. The man who is lying half dead has had all of his own active opportunities stripped from him by the violent beating of the robbers, and is incapable of resuming his own story. Therefore, the whole burden of responsibility connected with the possibility that the man's story might be resumed rests on the passerby who is vital and active.

". . . and when he saw him . . . ." The man who was by chance going down that road actually saw the man. The storyteller can observe the movement of the passerby's eyes, even the turning of his head, and tells the listener that the passerby *saw* the man who was lying half dead. This information forecloses the set of narrative events that would ensue if the passerby did not notice the man lying there, and opens up all the possibilities that devolve from his seeing the beaten man. These new possibilities range all the way from the one extreme that the man might kill the man lying there and so terminate his story, to the other set of possibilities which attend the extreme response that the man passing by might in some way enable the man's story to resume—by talking to him, by aiding him, by entering into a relationship with him in some way. In any case, the beaten man's story can resume only through the activity of the man passing by.

". . . he passed on the other side." Although the chance appearance of another human being on that road has offered the hope that the man's story would be resumed, whether to be terminated or to be continued, those possibilities come to nothing. The storyteller explicitly describes the man passing by as going to the *other side* of the road in order to continue his own journey, meaning that in order to continue his own journey he *avoided* the beaten man.

Jesus remains silent regarding the reasons for the passerby's avoidance. He might, if indeed he was a priest, have feared ritual defilement. He might have been afraid for his own safety. He might not have wanted to get involved for a whole range of reasons, none of which Jesus mentions. The reasons could be selfish, religious, or personal. He could, for instance, be a married man with a family to support who simply thought it better not to expose himself to danger because others cared for him and were dependent on him. But the important thing is that Jesus does not say anything about the man's (or priest's) reasons for avoiding the man lying beaten on the road. It could even be the case that the man passed by because he was revolted by the sight of the man lying there half dead. All Jesus tells the listener is that the man who by chance was going down that road *avoided* the man whose story this is, and passed by on the other side to continue on his way, wherever that might lead him. In other words, all the possibilities that were created by his chance appearance on that road have come to nothing by the man's own free action of avoidance. For the time being, at least, the man's story remains in a state of suspension, terminated by the violent actions of the robbers, and so evil appears to dominate the story.

"So likewise another man (or: a Levite), when he came to the place and saw him, passed by on the other side." Another man appears on that road, and he, too, carries with him the potential to activate a whole range of possibilities in connection with this man's story. He also saw him, and thus created for a moment all the human possibilities ranging from the destructive to the creative. However, he too saw the man and pased by on the other side, meaning that he also *avoided* the man. For a second time the possibility has been raised that the man's story would be resumed and, a second time, this possibility has been brought to nothing by a passerby's response of avoidance.

On the level of narrative possibilities, it makes no difference, really, whether or not the two men who chose avoidance were a priest and a Levite or not. From the point of view of hypothetical reconstruction of the cultural sanctions at that time in history, it is impossible to know whether the priest and Levite did what they should have done by avoiding the man (that is, that they were observing regulations that prohibited them from coming into contact with what might have been a corpse), or whether they would have been expected to help the man and so violated expectations. The possibilities from the point of view of reconstructing the historically operative cultural codes cancel each other out.

It is only in the context of early Christian debate about the relative merits of observant Jews, on the one hand, and the Samaritans who were avoided by the Jews and to whom the Jews were hostile, on the other hand, that the cultural codes have any force. For the most part, modern Christians, of course, prefer the story in this form because it implies that the priest and Levite, both Jews, act without Christian mercy whereas a non-Jew, a foreigner, does show mercy on the man, thus behaving like a good Christian. This view conforms with the Christian opinion that Jews are legalistic, a view which has its origins in the Christian-Jewish controversy and polemic of the early first century when many Christian communities were still Jewish sects and were establishing their identity in opposition to that of observant Jews.

That Jesus inaugurated a new mode of being human that was perceived as a challenge by those of his generation hardly needs to be stressed. We have seen in the analysis of Jesus' core sayings, in Part One, that Jesus completely reinterpreted the meaning of the traditional symbol "kingdom of God", and that in his own actions and words Jesus lived out of the power that engenders the free being of persons. It is not surprising that this new mode was perceived with hostility and even dealt with violently by those who lived out of a different mode, which conceived of being human as being a member of a specific group of people. But the differences between those who choose to enter into that dimension of human experience sustained by the power that Jesus recognized as "God" and those who choose to continue living in the tribal mode goes much deeper than Jewish-Christian controversy usually realizes.

The real distinction between Judaism and Christianity is not between legalism and love, nor between one religion and another, but rather between differing perceptions of what it means to be human. The shifts and surprises, the fulfillments and deprivations of the personal mode of being human differ in kind from those of the tribal mode, and each mode carries with it differing creative and destructive possibilities. The debate between these modes cannot be resolved at the theoretical level, for that is impossible when it is a question of the fulfillment or deprivation of existance as human.

Jesus, certainly, spoke and acted in terms of the perception that the *personal* mode of being human is the one grounded in the *real*, and he lived out the consequences of his understanding, even unto death. From the point of view of those who take *survival* to be the highest good, Jesus' death demonstrates the deficiency of the personal mode. But, as Dostoyevsky's Grand Inquisitor observes, it is only from the point of view of those who want miracles (viz., who want God to meet their expectations), and *not* God that Jesus' "refusal to come down from the cross" signals the bankruptcy of what he represented.

This was an issue that the early Christians addressed in various ways, but they did face the issue squarely. In the Gospel of Mark, for example, Peter represents those who believe that Jesus should fulfill traditional Jewish Messianic expectation, and that therefore he should avoid death and suffering. Jesus' response to Peter is to point out that such a position, which presupposes that death and suffering drain life of its meaning, is equivalent to worshiping them, and so Jesus tells Peter "Get behind me, Satan! For you are not on the side of God, but of men" (Mark 8:27-33).

Matthew handles the issue in quite a different way. Matthew's Christology, which focuses on his sense of the centrality of the *person* Jesus, reinterprets the meaning of the title "Son of God" in order to show that the being of Jesus as a person remains untouched by death, even though in the crucifixion Jesus' being is altered from an earthly presence to a presence of another kind. The meaning of the person "Jesus" is "God with us" (Matt 1:23), and at the end of Matthew's gospel, Jesus (whose reality is unchanged by biological death) promises to those who observe all his words: "Lo, I am with you always" (Matt 28:20). Matthew's theology, and his Christology, are intelligible only if one recognizes that he functions with a totally new understanding of reality and of what it means to be human[3].

The early Christians were convinced that the reality of Jesus can be neither validated nor invalidated by either his ability or his inability to avoid suffering or to *survive*. They expressed this conviction with various conceptions borrowed from the religious terminology available at the time, but their common conviction was that neither death nor suffering is ultimate; in other words, in the Christian literature, survival and the absence of pain are not the highest goods. This is because where the personal mode of human existence is considered to be the highest possibility, "God" is not conceived of as something that ensures survival.

3. I have developed this interpretation in detail in my Ph.D. dissertation, "Crucifixion as Ordeal: Tradition and Interpretation in Matthew 26—28" (Harvard University: 1976).

For those who do hold survival to be the highest good, and who take being a member of a people to be the primary mode of being human, death will always throw into doubt the existence of a God whose basic role is considered to be that of ensuring the survival of the people.

If the cultural codes "priest," "Levite," and "Samaritan" in the received version of Jesus' parable have any meaning, then it is in connection with these more fundamental issues. If leaving them in the parable aids the reader to grasp its deeper significance, then include them. But if they prove to be distractions, limiting one's understanding to the superficial level having to do with Jewish-Christian polemics, then perhaps it would be best to ignore them and to attend to the story only on the level of narrative.

"But a third man (or: a Samaritan), as he journeyed, came to where he was . . . ." Jesus employs the triadic form in the central section of another parable, "The Man Who Once Gave a Dinner and Invited Guests." In that parable, as we have seen, Jesus employs the form in order to arouse the hope that the third guest will come to the dinner. The narrative structure leads the listener to expect that the third guest will provide relief, but he frustrates that expectation, provoking the host's anger. Based on the analogy of how the other parable functions, the listener to this story cannot assume that the appearance of a third man on the road will bring relief in the form of help. It is still possible that he will pass by without even seeing the man, or that if he does see him, that he also will avoid him. If the third man also avoids the one lying half dead on the road, the parable will cease functioning as story and will change into a transitory episode dominated by the evil of the robbers. The appearance of the third man alerts us to expect that he will bring the man's story to a conclusion, but we do not know what will happen.

"And when he saw him, he went to him." Jesus has not assumed the attitude of omniscience by explaining why the robbers beat the man half to death, nor has he said what the motives were of the men who avoided the man. Similarly, Jesus simply describes what the third man did: when he saw him, he went to him. In other words, his response was not one of avoidance; but we do not yet know what he will do to the man. Anything is possible.

". . . and bound up his wounds, pouring on oil and wine . . . ." The wine is a disinfectant, and the oil soothes the wounds. The description shows that the man was not simply beaten black and blue, but that he had received open wounds from his beating by the robbers —in other words, it was a brutal beating.

The third man enters into a relationship with the man, not one of avoidance, nor of imposing violence on him, but of cleansing and bandaging his wounds. The story is no longer in suspension, because the third man has resumed it in a particular way. *He* is the one who is now active and the beaten traveller is a patient. The narrative raises the question about whether and how the man will himself become active, resume his own story, and get back on the road.

"... then he set him on his own beast and brought him to an inn, and took care of him." This scene corresponds to the scene in which the robbers stripped the man and beat him, and departed, leaving him half dead. In both scenes the man is a passive character in his own story. In the former, violence was imposed on him, thus temporarily terminating his story and raising the very real possibility that his story would end not as a story but as a transitory episode punctuated by death. In this scene, the man is also passive, and it is the third man's actions which enable the story to move forward. This time, however, the man is vulnerable not to human beings who impose violence on him but to a human being who imposes care on him. He is the chief character, because it is his story, yet he is not the actor but someone acted upon, a patient.

"And the next day ...." The narrative has raised the questions as to whether and how the man will resume his story. At this point, the specific narrative possibility in view is that the next day the man recovers and continues on his journey down the road.

"... he took out two denarii and gave them to the innkeeper, saying, 'Take care of him; and whatever more you spend, I will repay you when I come back.'" The third man had left his own story temporarily to come to the man, bind up his wounds, take him to an inn, and care for him. Now he is leaving the story and resuming his own journey. Jesus does not say that the man ever recovered consciousness, nor that he ever will. The beaten traveller is not speaking at the end of his own story; the third man is speaking in his stead.

The story ends with the third man speaking to the innkeeper, giving him the equivalent of two days' wages to defray the expenses incurred in keeping and caring for the man. Jesus does not explain why the third man leaves at this point. We hear that he intends to return, and that he promises the innkeeper that he will reimburse him for any expenses incurred beyond the two days' wages he is giving him now. The third man assumes total financial responsibility for what has happened to the man who was beaten half dead; he does not tell the innkeeper that if he recovers the man himself should pay the innkeeper. On the other hand, the third man does not stay at the inn to care for the man until he recovers or dies. On the contrary, he continues on down the road, leaving the man in the care of the innkeeper, whom he has, by his own initiative, involved as a participant.

The story about the man who was going down the road ends at this point. The third man (or: the Samaritan) is leaving. The innkeeper is being given money to take care of the man. And the man remains someone acted upon, a patient. Nevertheless, the narrative ends as the traveller's story.

The story as commencement

Jesus has told a story about a man who was going down the road (or: going down from Jerusalem to Jericho). The man falls in with robbers who strip him and beat him and depart, leaving him half dead. The man's story is truncated abruptly by the robbers' violent action, and the man never becomes active again in his own story. Jesus inserts no systems into the story by which the listener can evaluate the actions of the various characters. No one is punished, no one is rewarded; no one is praised, no one is condemned. The story functions only on the level of narrative, as story. It describes a particular individual in circumstances that remain totally within everyday human experience. God does not enter the story, nor do any religious or moral systems.

This story directly addresses the problem of evil, in the form of death which threatens to terminate the man's story. The negativity of death enters Jesus' parables in various ways. In the story of "The Rich Man Who Had a Steward," the steward treats people as dead matter by using them. We will also see that death enters into human relationships in the story about "The Man Who Had Two Sons." In "The Householder Who Went Out at Dawn," the grumbling workers make every effort to maintain relationships between people on an abstract level, thus attempting to negate the living bonds between actual human beings. It cannot be said, then, of

Jesus, that he holds the very restricted view that death is simply the termination of biological life. His stories explore and uncover the various ways in which death functions in relationships between human beings.

In this narrative, death is present as a reality potent with the ability to end the story. The robbers beat the man half to death without apparent motive; they are the agents of evil, and impose it on the man who was going down the road. If this group were not a group of robbers, but a group of killers, if Jesus had offered some reason for their violence, then the story would mean something quite different.

In Margaret Atwood's novel, *Surfacing*, Anna reads detective novels constantly. The narrator observes that Anna reads detective novels for the theology: "cold comfort but comfort, death is logical, there's always a motive."[4] What is the theology of detective novels? It is the theology that there is always an explanation, a logical explanation, when human beings murder others. In detective novels, there must always be an opportunity and a motive for murder; in other words, death can be explained. Precisely because Jesus refuses to attribute a motive to the robbers' brutality, their random violence raises the problem of evil in its starkest form. Detective novels proceed on the premise that when human beings commit murder, there is always an explanation that can satisfy the rational mind. In *The Brothers Karamazov*, Smerdyakov has both the opportunity and the motive to kill his father, Fyodor, and so the novel remains within the canons of the detective novel, without confronting the ultimate question raised by Jesus' parable. The detective novel belongs to a rational world. But what happens when there is no motive for murder, when death is not logical? When murder is done in cold blood, without motive, as it is in Jesus' parable, then the whole meaning of human existence and the project of living in story are called into question.

That is what fascinated Truman Capote when he wrote his "True Account of a Multiple Murder and Its Consequences," the novel *In Cold Blood*. On the night of November the 14th, 1959, Dick Hickock and Perry Smith murdered four members of the Clutter family (father, mother, son and daughter) at their farm house in Holcomb, Kansas. There was no apparent motive for their murders. No one hated the Clutters, robbery was not a motive, nor was rape. The

4. Atwood, *Surfacing*, p. 170.

horror of the murders was not only that they were brutal, but more especially that they were done without motive. As one woman, a schoolteacher observed, "Feeling wouldn't run half so high if this had happened to anyone *except* the Clutters. Anyone *less* admired. Prosperous. Secure. But that family represented everything people hereabouts really value and respect, and that such a thing could happen to them—well, it's like being told there is no God. It makes life seem pointless. I don't think people are so much frightened as they are deeply depressed."[5]

Capote's entire novel is geared toward understanding *why* these murders occurred, and his explanations are largely psychological. However, psychological explanations, while they offer some comfort of a cold kind, finally do not explain why the Clutters were murdered, they only suggest that the murderers were both psychopaths. But this does not alleviate the depression of those who feel that random violence makes life seem pointless.

Contemporary cinema is preoccupied with the apparent pointlessness of human life, and film after film ends with meaningless death or catastrophe: "Easy Rider," "Bonnie and Clyde," "The Marriage of Maria Braun," "Stroszek," and "Reds" are all examples of this mode of narration that *ends* with the destruction of human beings, thus calling into question the meaning of everything human. If a Peter Fonda or a Warren Beatty or a Herzog or a Fassbinder had told about the man going down the road, the narrative would have ended with the man's lying on the road half dead. If Luis Buñuel had done a film of this episode, he would have had the scene repeated over and over again, with person after person being obliterated in a gratuitous, accidental, and unexplained way—perhaps shot at random by someone in a tower firing away with a high-powered rifle.

In both "Bonnie and Clyde" and "Easy Rider," the first part of the story, the going-down-the-road part, is developed extensively, and then the rattling of machine guns or the blast of a shotgun provides the *ending* which is, therefore, from the point of view of the narrative's dynamic, *ultimate*. In many contemporary films, there is nothing to tell about other than a transitory, episodic journey terminated by catastrophic *destruction*. The very structure of such films implies that everything human, especially the project of

5. Truman Capote, *In Cold Blood* (New York: Random House, 1965), p. 88.

fashioning one's life into the shape of a story, seems pointless at best because the ultimate reality is obliteration. According to the theology of these films, death is the ultimate reality, and its potency undermines the viability of all human projects.

Jesus structures his story so that the question of the viability of the human is raised in its most acute form. The man who was going down the road was beaten half to death and left lying there. Then by chance another man was also going down that road; his appearance raises the possibility that random violence will not be the termination of the man's story. But the first man sees the one who was beaten and passes by on the other side, avoiding him. A second man by chance comes down the road, but he too sees the man and passes by on the other side, avoiding him. What is the meaning of their avoidance? Their responses show that for them death is something to be avoided, that for them the effects of death are something that they are unwilling or unable to address with their own activity. They implicitly assign absoluteness to the force which has been imposed upon the beaten man. In other words, their avoidance confers sacral power onto death and implicitly recognizes it as the force which is ultimate in human life.

Now we can see why Jesus does not attribute any motives, good or bad, to either of the men who passed by on the other side of the road. To have done so would have been to blur the story's focus. Wondering "why" either man passed by on the other side distracts attention from the phenomenon of avoidance, which must be grasped in its starkness. To speculate about whether they should or should not have stopped to address the man's condition is to shy away from the more fundamental question of whether death makes it impossible to live in story.

Conversely, if Jesus had offered some motivation for the third man's going to the beaten man—that he did it out of religious or moral duty, or that he felt pity on the man—that also would have been to blur the focus. Given the problematic which emerges in the story, the third man's motivations are irrelevant. The very fact that when he sees the man he goes to him, binds up his wounds, sets him on his own beast and brings him to an inn and takes care of him—all of his activity means fundamentally that he acts out of an orientation that is contrary to what has been imposed on the beaten man. Jesus' very manner of telling the story shows that while he recognizes the presence of *evil* in human experience, he does not regard it as the *final* possibility.

176

Now the listener can grasp why Jesus does remain silent about whether or not the man ever recovered. IT IS IRRELEVANT WHETHER OR NOT HE RECOVERED. The narrative meaning of what the third man does is not determined by religious or moral or practical considerations. The story does not say that the third man did what religion or morality dictates, and for that reason the listener should regard him as a good man. The point is not to focus on the question of evaluating the third man's actions. The story does not even say that what the third man did was good because it was successful. When the story concludes, it remains possible that the beaten man never recovered. This ensures that the meaning of the third man's activity will be contained solely within the dynamics of the narrative.

We can see a similar perception in Shakespeare's *King Lear*. Kent, Edgar, and Cordelia all act in the service of Lear and Gloucester, and they act contrary to those who are agents of destruction: Edmund, Regan, and Goneril. The fact that they are "unsuccessful" does not diminish the meaning of their activity in terms of the dynamics of the play. All of these characters recognize the existence of evil, and oppose it, but they do not defeat it, and they certainly neither eliminate nor abrogate its destructive effects. But the fact that they act out of life's creative possibilities makes real and actual the human option of acting contrary to the power of destruction. Avoidance is not the only possibility, nor is becoming an agent of destruction, nor is submission to its force.

But there is a difference between the way *King Lear* and the way "The Man Going Down the Road" function, because the latter retains the coherence of story. Neither Shakespeare nor Jesus ignores man's inhumanity to man or the existence of evil in human experience, nor does either regard evil as the ultimate reality. But each communicates his understanding of reality in terms of a different genre, and the differing genres communicate different meanings. In *King Lear*, Cordelia, Kent, and Edgar all act out of a deep personal relationship to Lear and to Gloucester, respectively. But in Jesus' story, no personal relationships are established. The third man has no conversation with the man, does not become friends with him, nor invite him to his home. Nor does he abandon his own journey in order to stay at the inn to take care of the man until he recovers. Instead, he concludes the story by giving instructions to the innkeeper to take over the activity of caring for the man. In other words, the problem of evil is not resolved in terms of inter-personal relationships, as it is in *King Lear*, where Cordelia's love, Kent's loyalty, and Edgar's love all function to counter-act Regan, Goneril, and Edmund. But this shows then that the question of what it means to be a person is not answered by Jesus' parables by referring to "love" in the sense in which we ordinarily understand the term.

If one wants to characterize the third man's activity as "loving," then one must recognize that this does not refer to a close personal relationship which he establishes with the beaten man. Indeed, the story concludes with the third man going back on the road again to resume his *own* story! The story functions in order to focus attention on the fact that the third man's activity is opposed to the robbers' activity, that it is oriented to enabling the beaten man to continue his story, and that it can be communicated to the innkeeper. The innkeeper is engaged in caring for the man as the story closes because the third man has initiated him into this activity.

But since the story does not say whether or not the man recovers, no resolution is provided to the issues addressed by the story as to the viability of living in story in the face of meaningless destruction. These issues cannot be resolved at the theoretical level. It is possible for someone to affirm that destruction governs human life, and so everything is pointless, and everyone should found his existence on that perception, living episodically from day-to-day—like the steward or the robbers. It is also possible for someone to affirm that there is a creative power that governs all human life, and so the venture of living one's life in story as a person should be the basis for one's existence. But what do these affirmations mean at the human level where each one must make his own decision? After all, it always remains a possibility that someone who lives in story can by chance fall into the hands of men of violence or into the hands of psychopaths. It always remains a distinct possibility for anyone to have his life ended by a meaningless accident or by a motiveless murder. And this is precisely the possibility that Jesus' parable explores, without however offering any simple solution.

Jesus keeps the issues at the human level, and they are dealt with only in terms of story. The third man acts with the purpose of enabling the beaten man to get back on the road to resume his journey. But since we do not learn whether or not the man even regains consciousness, the meaning of the third man's activity is contained in the phenomenon that by so acting the man's story continues rather than being terminated by random violence. The man continues to live in story even though he never again becomes active in it! The third man acts *in his stead* to transcend the apparently determinative factors indicated by the situation (random violence, avoidance of death, and death's apparent ultimacy). The third man transcends the situation in order to continue the man's story for him to a conclusion which therefore is not an ending but, as in all the phonodramatic parables of Jesus, a commencement.

The story directly addresses the destructive possibility inherent in living in story, but does not offer the cold comfort that death is logical, nor offer any reassurance that everything will turn out all right in the end. If the listener allows his attention to shift totally to the third man's activity, forgetting whose story this is, then the central issues are ignored. Luke's view that Jesus told a story *about* a good Samaritan who provides an example of how people should behave is not a misinterpretation of the story exactly, but it is an interpretation that remains at a very superficial level and distracts attention away from the story's true subject matter. And construing the third man as an example to be imitated, thus founding an ethic on his activity, can have negative consequences. We have had occasion to examine Nietzsche's critique of pity and charity as modes of *ressentiment* which can realize themselves only in the presence of suffering. It should by now be obvious that the third man is not motivated by a sense of duty nor does he act out of what Ivan calls "self-laceration." He does not feel sorry for the man, but rather acts in order to communicate to him the ability to resume *his own* story. The third man enters the man's story briefly, and then exits to continue his own journey, but only after he has initiated the innkeeper into caring for the man and thus attempting to enable the traveller to get back on the road.

The third man's actions show him to be quite the opposite of that kind of pity which needs sickness in order to be itself. He is not afraid that he might lose something by going to the man, binding up his wounds, and taking him to the inn and caring for him. His actions are the free expression of his own vitality, and he freely engages with the beaten man in order to restore to him the freedom to live in story. The third man, in Scheler's words, acts out of a profound confidence in life's own vigour.[6] In his actions he is indifferent to the

---

6. Scheler, *Ressentiment*, p. 90.

accidents which might befall him, such as the robbers coming out from behind the rocks and attacking him, too. His actions are the opposite of those who live out of self-preservation, or of those who act only in terms of goals and achievements. In short, he is rich and wants to bestow.[7]

His own fullness of life overcomes the natural reaction of avoidance, and acts *against* the evil that has been imposed upon the beaten man. The very fact that Jesus says he left the next day shows how little interested Jesus is in representing the third man as primarily someone who cares for or who helps others. Helping is not an end in itself, but rather is the direct expression of the third man's vital mode of being, rather than the purpose of his life. The distinction is crucial. When this distiction is not made, when helping is taken as the meaning of the story, and when people begin to fashion their lives with the purpose of caring for and helping others, then the situation is ripe for the development of *ressentiment*, as both Nietzsche and Scheler make clear.

The Grand Inquisitor is someone whose whole purpose in life is to help mankind and, as Dostoyevsky shows, the Grand Inquisitor's programme for saving mankind is founded on a thorough contempt for man and man's higher possibilities. From the Grand Inquisitor's perspective, Jesus did not love man. But then the Grand Inquisitor's secret was that he served "the wise and dread Spirit, the spirit of self-destruction and non-existence."[8]

The superabundance of the actual

The *ultimate* force grasped by Jesus' vision in the parable is not evil, but rather that superabundant power out of which the third man lives, and which he communicates to the innkeeper.

The parable directly addresses the question concerning what is ultimate. Is it the force of evil, out of which the robbers act, and which the first and second man avoid? Some would say so for, according to their perceptions, the important thing to notice is that the traveller is not reported as having survived his brutal beating. Some could focus on this aspect of the situation, and conclude that the man is an innocent victim of meaningless violence, and therefore life is meaningless unless one can avoid suffering and death.

7. See Scheler, *Ressentiment*, p. 89, and Nietzsche, *The Anti-Christ*, p. 126.

8. Dostoyevsky, *The Brothers Karamazov*, p. 261.

Avoidance of suffering and death governs the projects and preferences of the first and second men who pass by, which means that they are survivors, people who hold on to life because they unconsciously apprehend life's vitality to be deficient. Life is real for them only when they are holding on to it. Those who take survival and success as dominant criteria for judging situations are freed by Jesus as storyteller to see things in the light of their underlying attitude toward reality. They are free to pass by. But, in terms of the language of Jesus' core sayings, they are not fit for, nor do they enter, nor do they receive the power of the kingdom.

Nothing of what the third man does is directed back to his own ego. His activity has the character of free giving, without reference to any transcendental rewards or punishments which he might receive. Viewed impartially, the third man's actions seem rather pointless. What does he gain or accomplish? Nothing, absolutely nothing, that is mentioned in the parable. What he does is neither more nor less than to make real a mode of human being which is the free expression of confidence in life's own vigour, quite apart from questions of success or survival. The only preference that Jesus accords the third man is the preference accorded to those who live in story, for at the end the third man is speaking in the traveller's stead, in effect continuing the story on the other man's behalf! Those oriented to success and survival will doubtless ask, "So what?" And, indeed, no one can prevent them from imposing their own patterns of construing experience onto the story. Each one sees what he *is*.

In *The Brothers Karamazov*, for example, Dmitry has been arrested, wrongly, for the murder of his father, and has been exposed to an exhausting, humiliating ordeal of being cross-examined by officials who hold him, and everything he believes in, in contempt. The translator of the Penguin edition of the novel, David Magarshack, believes that the novel is about "the *victim* of a miscarriage of justice."[9] But understanding Dmitry as a victim is the last thing Dostoyevsky would want the reader to do and, indeed, Dmitry refuses to feel victimized, even though Rakitin would like him to do so in order to facilitate Rakitin's literary career. After interrogation, Dmitry falls asleep and while he is sleeping some unknown person slips a pillow under his head. Dmitry selects this gratuitous

9. Fyodor Dostoyevsky, *The Brothers Karamazov*, translated with an introduction by David Magarshack (Harmondsworth: Penguin Books, Ltd., 1958), p. xiii.

kindness from an anonymous stranger—*not* his supposed grounds for feeling victimized—as determinative for understanding the situation. While sleeping, he dreams about the predicament of others, of starving children, and his heart yearns for their suffering to end. One might ask, why did Dmitry select the simple act of someone putting a pillow under his head rather than his being unjustly accused as pivotal for the formation of his world-attitude? The situation seems to dictate that he understand himself as a victim, and yet he does the opposite, instead understanding himself as responsible for all others.

The question of which experiences one unconsciously selects as determinative for one's world-attitude is also addressed by Zossima's account about his older brother, Markel, who was dying of consumption at the age of seventeen—a situation which would seem to dictate that one view oneself as a victim and cry outrage against life. Markel, however, selected not his own unfortunate condition as determinative, but rather the loving care bestowed upon him by his mother and his servants—caring offered even though he was an unbeliever, did not share their piety, and had, in fact, ridiculed it. Nevertheless, this was what his consciousness selected for his understanding of reality:

> " ... life is paradise, and we are all in paradise, but we won't see it; if we would, we should have heaven on earth the next day .... One day is enough for a man to know all happiness. My dear ones, why do we quarrel, try to outshine each other and keep grudges against each other? Let's go straight into the garden, walk and play there, love, appreciate, and kiss each other, and glorify life."[10]

Even though he is dying of consumption, Markel wants to glorify life, exclaiming that life is paradise, because he apprehends as determinative not the disease which consumes him but his mother's care.

There is an analogous situation described in J.D. Salinger's *Franny and Zooey*. Zooey reminds Franny of something their older brother, Buddy, said to him long ago:

> "He said that a man should be able to lie at the bottom of a hill with his throat cut, slowly bleeding to death, and if a pretty girl or an old woman should pass by with a beautiful jug balanced perfectly on the top of her

10. Dostoyevsky, *The Brothers Karamazov* (Random House), pp. 300-01.

head, he should be able to raise himself up on one arm and see the jug safely over the top of the hill." [Zooey] thought this over, then gave a mild snort. "I'd like to see him do it, the bastard."[11]

From the perspective of contemporary thinking, the man whose throat has been cut is a victim, and would be expected to construe his experience in terms of the "injustice" that has befallen him. Buddy theorizes that a man in this situation ought to be able to let his attention be drawn not to what has happened to him but to something beautiful that has no reference whatsoever to himself.

No one can police another to apprehend the superabundance of the actual in such a situation. Each person's perceptions would be an expression of his or her fundamental attitudes and orientation toward existence. Who can see which factor is revelatory of reality: Dmitry's ordeals, Markel's consumption at seventeen, the man's throat having been cut, the robbers' evil? Or the pillow, the jug balanced perfectly on the top of her head, the care of mother and servants, or the third man's activity?

If the power that engenders humans in the mode of being as persons is ultimate, then life in the personal mode is paradise, as Markel exclaimed, and "hell," as Zossima says, "is the suffering of being unable to love [the neighbour, or not living in this dimension]." Jesus' parable of the man going down the road quite clearly construes actuality as charged with superabundant vitality, the power that sustains those who are human in the personal mode of living in story. Jesus can say no more. In answer to all of mankind's perennial religious questions, he can only remain silent.

11. Salinger, *Franny and Zooey*, p. 153.

CHAPTER TWELVE

The man who had two sons

Luke's version

Luke is our only source for the parable known traditionally as "The Prodigal Son" (Luke 15:11-32), and he has used this parable, together with the parables of "The Lost Sheep" and "The Lost Coin," in order to provide an answer by Jesus to the "Pharisees and scribes who murmured, saying, 'This man receives sinners and eats with them'" (Luke 15:2). Luke has composed the setting for these parables (Luke 15:1-2) by paraphrasing the scene which he found in his source, Mark, that showed Jesus eating with tax collectors and sinners (Mark 2:15-17 = Luke 5:29-32). In this scene, "the Pharisees and their scribes murmured against his disciples, saying, 'Why do you eat and drink with tax collectors and sinners?'" (Luke 5:30). Jesus replies with a saying: "Those who are well have no need of a physician, but those who are sick; I have not come to call the righteous, but sinners to repentance" (Luke 5:31-32). Characteristically, Luke had added "to repentance," because he thinks of Jesus as eating only with *repentant* sinners.

It will be remembered that, in the sayings tradition, sayings occurred without context. We know that Luke found the parable of "The Lost Sheep" in Q without a setting, for Matthew has inserted the parable in a completely different context, in his chapter dealing with the proper behaviour of members of the Christian community (Matt 18). We have already seen, in Chapter Six, that Luke has used the parables of "The Lost Sheep" and "The Lost Coin" to illustrate his idea that Jesus eats with tax collectors and sinners who have repented, and that his dining with them is a sign of his joy that they who were "lost" have been "found." Luke has, then, interpreted these two parables, along with "The Prodigal Son," as parables which provide an answer to the charge made against Jesus by his opponents that he "receives sinners and eats with them."

In this section of Luke's gospel, Jesus resolves a controversy provoked by his opponents by responding with three parables, or rather Luke has created the context of controversy as a technique of providing an interpretation for these three parables. This is, in fact, a favourite compositional technique of Luke's. He also inserts parables that apparently were free-floating, without context, in his sources in four other sections of his gospel: Luke 10:25-37 ("The Good Samaritan"); Luke 12:13-21 ("The Rich Fool"); Luke 13:1-9 ("The Unfruitful Fig Tree"); Luke 16:14-31 ("The Rich Man and Lazarus"). (Those scholars who assume that Jesus uttered his parables in situations of controversy have apparently not noted that *in every single case* the controversy has been created by Christian editorial work.)

In line with his interpretation of the parable of "The Prodigal Son" as reflecting Jesus' response to sinners who had repented, Luke has made some minor internal alterations in the story. Most obviously he has inserted twice the expression "he was lost and is found" (Luke 15:24, 32). He has inserted this in order to link this parable with the parables of "The Lost Sheep" and "The Lost Coin." At the end of "The Lost Sheep," Luke has the shepherd say to his neighbours, "Rejoice with me, for I have *found* my sheep which was *lost*" (Luke 15:6). At the end of "The Lost Coin", Luke has the woman say to her neighbours, "Rejoice with me, for I have *found* the coin which I have *lost*" (Luke 15:9). In both cases, Luke interprets the expression to refer to the sinner who repents (Luke 15:7, 10). Obviously, Luke views the younger son as an example of a sinner who repents. Consequently, Luke has added that when his father saw him, he "had compassion" (Luke 15:20). Luke adds "he had compassion" to make the reader think of the father as a figure for God (or Jesus) who rejoices over the sinner who repents, and "has compassion" on him.

There is only one other point in Jesus' core photodramatic and phonodramatic parables where an emotion is attributed to a character from the point of view of an omniscient narrator, an emotion which is not externally observable and which places a value judgment on the character's actions, and that is in the parable of "The Good Samaritan" (Luke 10:30-35). There, too, Luke has added that the Samaritan "had compassion" (Luke 10:33) on the man who had been left half dead by the robbers. In that case, Luke has inserted the indication that the Samaritan had compassion because Luke interprets the parable as an example of what it means to love one's neighbour. In both parables, then, he had redaction-critical motives for inserting this emotion. From the point of view of stylistic criteria, not only are such interior emotions which attribute a value to characters' actions totally absent in Jesus' core parables, but in both of these stories the words are secondary to the sentences in which we find them. Once removed, Luke 10:33-34 reads: "... and when he saw him, he went to him ..." and Luke 15:20 reads: "... his father saw him and ran and embraced him ...." The descriptions in both cases are solely of externally observable actions, which is in keeping with the style of Jesus' core parables.

There is one other slight addition which Luke has made to the parable, in order to make the story illustrate the ideas he wishes to present in this passage. In Luke 15:32, the father says, "It was fitting to make merry *and be glad* ...." Not only is "and be glad" secondary from a grammatical point of view, but the Greek word here is precisely the same one used in Luke 15:6 and 9 which the R.S.V. translates as "rejoice." In other words, Luke has inserted this word here to make explicit his understanding that the celebration which the father ordered for his son is a celebration that represents Jesus' eating with tax collectors and sinners who had repented. Once these secondary additions to the parable have been removed, we have the following story.

The man who had two sons

(1) There was a man who had two sons;

(2) and the younger of them said to his father, "Father, give me the share of property that falls to me." And he divided his living between them. Not many days later, the younger son turned everything into cash[1] and took his journey into a far country, and there he squandered his property in loose living. And when he had spent everything, a great famine arose in that country, and he began to be in want. So he went and joined himself to one of the citizens of that country, who sent him into his fields to

---

1. R.S.V. "gathered all he had." The Greek expression means he "turned everything into cash."

feed swine. And he would gladly have filled his belly with[2] the carob pods that the swine ate; and no one gave him anything. But when he came to himself he said, "How many of my father's hired servants have bread enough and to spare, but I perish here with hunger! I will arise and go to my father, and I will say to him, 'Father, I have sinned against heaven and before you; I am no longer worthy to be called your son; treat me as one of your hired servants.'" And he arose and came to his father.

(3) But while he was yet at a distance, his father saw him and ran and embraced him and kissed him. And the son said to him, "Father, I have sinned against heaven and before you; I am no longer worthy to be called your son." But the father said to his servants, "Bring quickly the best robe, and put it on him; and put a ring on his hand, and shoes on his feet; and bring the fatted calf and kill it, and let us eat and make merry; for this my son was dead, and is alive again." And they began to make merry.

(4) Now his elder son was in the field; and as he came and drew near to the house, he heard music and dancing. And he called one of the servants and asked what this meant. And he said to him, "Your brother has come, and your father has killed the fatted calf, because he has received him safe and sound." But he was angry and would not[3] go in. His father came out and tried to conciliate him,[4] but he answered his father, "Lo, these many years I have served you, and I never disobeyed your command; yet you never gave me a kid, that I might make merry with my friends. But when this son of yours came, who has devoured your living with harlots, you killed for him the fatted calf!"

(5) And he said to him, "Son, you are always with me, and all that is mine is yours. It was fitting to make merry for this your brother was dead, and is alive."

2. R.S.V. "fed on." "Filled his belly with" is the more difficult reading in the manuscripts, which does not necessarily make it preferable, but in this case the more difficult reading coheres with the way Jesus characterizes the younger son.
3. R.S.V. "refused" suggests that someone has invited him to go in, but this is not the case. "Would not" translates the Greek literally.
4. R.S.V. "entreat" suggests that "to go in" is understood, as if the father came out to invite his elder son to come to the celebration. But the party is already over! The R.S.V. consistently translates the Greek to make it appear that the elder son was invited to go in, which was not the case. The Greek here is more accurately translated "try to conciliate," and refers to the father's effort to try to conciliate his elder son's anger.

Form, content, and style of the story

This story reflects the same form precisely as the other core phonodramatic parables of Jesus. The story is about a man, and that man is speaking at the end of his story. The story has the same five-part structure as the others; the beginning correlates with the ending, the second and fourth parts are correlated, and the central section is pivotal.

From the point of view of content, the story is also identical to the others. It tells a story about a man's relationship with others, in this case his two sons. The whole story develops as an exploration of what it means to have two sons, through fictional characters who are nevertheless rooted in the everyday world. The characters are not types or examples, but real individuals.

From the point of view of style, the story coheres with the others as well. Jesus creates his characters through what they say and do. There are no adjectives categorizing them which tell the listener what to think about them. We observe them from the outside, and have access to the inner world only of the younger son; but we have access to what he thinks only through the words which he uses to express his thoughts. Jesus simply observes and listens, and that is what the listeners of this story must do as well. The storyteller does not intrude any systems of valuation into the story which would allow the listener to judge their words or actions; the only modes of valuation are those expressed by the characters themselves. As in the other stories, then, there is a variety of different points of view that contributes in different ways to the emergence of meaning in the narrative. This story, like the others, functions in order to invite the listener to pay attention to the words and actions of particular people in their entanglements with other people. The meaning of the story emerges solely through the way the narrative itself unfolds. And it is to this that we must listen.

Listening to the story

"There was a man who had two sons." The narrator's first words inform the listener of the ground rules for the ensuing oral communication. The speaker is telling a *story*; it is in terms of the canons of storytelling that the listener must hear the narrator's words. The listener also learns *what* the story is *about*—a man.

Furthermore, this story will tell about the individual man in relationship with others—his two sons. No other information is given that would deflect attention from the man and his two sons. We know nothing else about him, although subsequently we learn that he is a landowner with servants.

"And the younger of them said to his father, 'Father, give me the share of property that falls to me.'" The storyteller identifies one of the sons as "the younger," but uses no other descriptive adjectives that might guide the listener's evaluation of this character. The listener must attend only to what the younger son says and does: Jesus will not tell his listener what to think about the younger son. The younger son addresses his father as "Father," thereby indicating that he is placing what he will have to say in the context of the father-son relationship. What he says will reflect his understanding of that relationship. The first words out of his mouth in this context are "Give me." He relates to his father as someone from whom to get things. What he wants, we do not yet know. He could be asking for his father's advice, or for some time with his father. The narrative style of Jesus always functions in order to offer a variety of narrative possibilities before selecting one of them. The *meaning* of the possibility that is selected is controlled by the full range of possibilities that the narrative evokes. What Jesus says must be heard together with what he does not say.

The younger son demands that his father give him "the share of property that falls to me." The property referred to is that which the man would bequeath to his sons in his will, which they would inherit when he died. Until that time, the property would provide the man with his own means of support. The younger son speaks of it in neutral terms, as "the property," avoiding any allusion to the fact that what is in question is the father's very means of supporting himself and his family. The younger son avoids any mention of the man's death although the words "falls to me" implicitly refer to the time of his father's death. The younger son's cleverly chosen words reveal that he views his father as someone to manipulate verbally in order to get what he wants from him.

Because the younger son demands the property now, he is in effect treating his father as already dead—not only dead in the sense of being lifeless matter to manipulate, but virtually dead in the sense of no longer requiring a livelihood, as well as dead in the legal sense that his death provides the occasion for the younger son to inherit his share of the man's property. No reasons are offered for the son's making this extraordinary demand. The listener expects the man, perhaps, to refuse the demand and to discipline his younger son.

"And he divided his living between them." The storyteller calls the property the man's *living;* that is, the storyteller stresses that the property provides the man with his means of livelihood and support. The younger son may mince words, but the storyteller does not. The father has given in to his younger sons's demand, contrary to expectation. To do so, he had to overlook, or to ignore, the fact that the younger son was attempting to manipulate him, and that the younger son was treating him as though already dead. The man inexplicably does even more than is demanded. He divides his entire living between his two sons, giving the part demanded to his younger son and the rest, unasked for, to his elder son. If the man had simply given his younger son what he demanded, the listener could conclude that the man was under the spell of his younger son. The man's action of dividing his living between his sons creates a situation the significance of which must be clearly understood. In the thinking of the ancient world, questions regarding ownership of property and questions regarding father-son relationships were inextricable. What the man does — allowing himself to be treated as though dead and giving away his proprietary rights — is utterly unparalleled in any of the parabolic narratives which survive from antiquity (Jewish, Greek, or Latin). Since the situation is so extraordinary, the narrative raises the question of why the man, by dividing his living between his two sons, totally altered the basis of his relationship with them. Whatever having two sons means to this man, it will no longer mean having two sons who are bound to him by the bonds of property. This means that the narrative will inevitably focus on only the relationships between the man and his two sons, without distracting, extraneous factors.

"Not many days later, the younger son turned everything into cash ...." The younger son acts very quickly, Jesus emphasizes. Almost immediately he sells the property his father has given him for cash. His action shows that he did not intend to acquire his father's living because he wanted to manage it for his father's benefit. That possibility has been excluded by the narrative. Nor did he retain ownership of the property, which should have remained in the family as the basis for its livelihood from generation to generation. By liquidating a portion of the property, he treats any possible future generations of the family as non-existent. The storyteller does not inform us of the man's attitude toward this turn of events, whether he foresaw the implications but did not care, or whether he was surprised and shocked. In any case, the younger son's actions break his bond with his father and with all future generations of the family.

"And took his journey into a far country." Until now, Jesus has not made clear what the younger son's reasons were for demanding a share of his father's living, nor for turning the family property into cash. At this point, the story selects one out of all the narrative possibilities. The younger son had intended all along to break from his father and family. Jesus provides no explanation for the younger son's leaving his father. He does not say that there was a famine in the land which made living there impossible, or that the younger son sought a better life elsewhere, or that the father was an insufferable tyrant with whom the younger son found it impossible to live. No explanation is offered to mitigate the son's actions. Moreover, the younger son has actualized in the narrative the possibility of breaking from the man. This possibility is now quite real for the elder son as well, and throughout the narrative remains as one which the elder son either will or will not actualize. The man who had two sons at the beginning of the story remains throughout the sequel as the man who is in danger of having no sons.

"And there he squandered his property." The Greek word used here for "squander" is the same one used to describe what the steward did to his master's goods in the story of "The Rich Man Who Had a Steward" (Luke 16:1). In both cases, the verb connotes thoughtless waste. Until this point, the narrative allowed for the possibility that the younger son was guided by the purpose of becoming independent and making a life for himself somewhere else, apart.

How then did he squander his property? The narrative permits the possibility that he made unsound business investments, or that he was defrauded by hustlers, or that he gave away all that he owned. This set of possibilities would indicate that the younger son was oriented to some particular goal, but that misfortune prevented him from achieving his purpose. Whenever someone is oriented toward what he wants, as the son has been, there is always the possibility that *what* he wants is some definite purpose. The steward, for example, was oriented toward what he wanted, and he acted decisively to achieve his purpose, which was to ingratiate himself with his master's debtors so that they would receive him into their houses when he was put out of the stewardship. The steward acted in a self-interested way, and acted with specific goals in mind.

"And there he squandered his property in loose living." The Greek word used here, translated as "loose living," refers to the way gluttons, voluptuaries, or transvestites live. The original meaning is "incurably ill."[5] The storyteller does not yet indicate to what particularly unhealthy or profligate activities the younger son was addicted. The important thing is that the younger son was not merely carefree and easy with money, like the proverbial grasshopper, but that Jesus explicitly states that the younger son was acting in so self-indulgent a way that he could be described as someone who is incurably ill. He was oriented to what he wanted, but not to some specific purpose; rather, he was consumed by his *wants*. He did not even act with enlightened self-interest as the steward did. He squandered his property in loose living, meaning that he squandered the very means for financing his self-indulgence.

"And when he had spent everything, a great famine arose in that country, and he began to be in want." Jesus emphasizes that the young man's actions rendered him incapable of indulging himself any longer. Living out of his "wants," he has squandered his means for indulging himself. Now this mode of activity has caused him to be "in want" in another, more desperate sense. The occurrence of a famine exposed him to externally imposed necessity, completely halting his programme of self-indulgence; now, far from being able to have whatever he wanted for himself, he begins to want the means simply to survive. Unless he can overcome this "want," living according to his "wants" would be impossible. The story has shown so far that living out of one's wants not only destroys one's relationship with others, it also destroys one's relationship with oneself. The younger son has not only hardened his heart towards his father, he has now destroyed the very basis he had for his life of *self*-indulgence.

Those who are *self*-destructive cannot help themselves; they can only put their welfare in the hands of someone else. We now see why the younger son's way of life was described as a form of

5. Werner Foerster, "ἄσωτος, ἀσωτία," *Theological Dictionary of the New Testament*, edited by Gerhard Kittel, translator and editor Geoffrey W. Bromiley (Grand Rapids: Wm. B. Eerdmans, 1964) Volume I, p. 506.

"incurable illness." Self-destructiveness is like an illness that the body's resources cannot overcome. The self devours the self. The last possibility for someone who cannot mobilize his own resources to survive is to place himself in the hands of a doctor.

"So he went and joined himself to one of the citizens of that country." The expression "joined himself to" means literally "he glued himself to" or "he cleaved to," an expression indicating the most intimate association of dependence on someone.

The citizen is someone who is independent and has his own property, and so he has the resources to act not only for his own benefit, but also for the benefit of other people. The younger son could not take care of anyone, not even himself. His situation had become so desperate that he had to attach himself to someone else even to survive.

When the younger son abandoned himself to a profligate life, he knew that his father had the resources to make that possible, to enable him to get what he wanted. Now that he is in want again, but in a more profound sense, he finds someone else who has the resources to meet his needs. The structure of the relationship is the same in both cases. When dealing with his father, and when dealing with the citizen, the younger son initiates a programme of action which involves having someone else provide him with the resources to get what he wants for himself.

". . . who sent him into the fields to feed swine." The description indicates that the younger son has sunk to the lowest possible level. He contributes in an absolutely minimal way to his own maintenance, for feeding swine requires no competence. In other words, he is not doing productive work in exchange for pay; he has attached himself to the citizen who supports him, asking only that he feed his swine.

"And he would gladly have filled his belly with the carob pods that the swine ate." The long, fleshy seed pods of the carob, an evergreen tree indigenous to the Mediterranean area, were commonly used as fodder, but were eaten as food. The story makes explicit that even though the younger son was not starving, his belly was not full, and that he longed to fill his belly with the same carob pods that the pigs ate to fill their bellies. It has usually been assumed in the interpretation of this parable that the worst that could be said of the younger son was that he was reduced to an occupation that was abhorred by Jews. Since Jesus was from Nazareth in Galilee, which had a mixed population, and since there is absolutely no evidence that he told stories only to Jews, and since the story itself does not describe the characters as Jews, the listener cannot assume that the story must be understood in a Jewish context. The story represents the younger son as behaving in a manner similar to the swine that the citizen sent him out to the fields to feed. He was concerned with filling himself up. The picture is consistent with what we have learned of the younger son from his previous words and actions.

In the first place, we have seen him speaking and acting to get what he wanted. Then we have seen him acting as though incurably ill, as someone so self-indulgent that he squandered his means of indulging himself. Now the storyteller completes the whole picture with a vivid image of self-indulgence. The picture is of someone with unlimited cravings, with wants devoted only to filling themselves.

"And no one gave him anything." The younger son has been cut off from the nexus of human giving and receiving; he has gone so far in the direction of being governed by his voracious appetites that no one gives him anything. Since he has functioned by living off others, this statement underscores the desperate straits in which he finds himself.

"But when he came to himself . . . ." The expression means "he came to his senses." The narrative conjures up a whole range of possibilities. It is possible that this means he regrets that he had become a certain kind of person and realizes that he would have to change. It is possible that he was sorry for treating his father as dead, as someone to exploit, and that he wanted somehow to rectify the damage he had done. It is possible that he regretted having abandoned his father who had, thereafter, to depend on his elder son for support and maintenance. It is possible that he realized he had done something wrong by turning his family's property into cash. These are only some of the possibilities offered by the narrative. As we have seen, Jesus' stories function by first evoking a range of possibilities, and then selecting one of those possibilities. The "meaning" of the story emerges in purely narrative terms, in terms of the context of narrative possibilities which are presented but left unselected. In this case, the narrative functions in order to raise the question as to the kind of *self* to which the younger son "returned" when he came to his senses. It is at this point that the story will make clear what his mode of being human actually is, because everything until now has led up to this crucial juncture.

194

The younger son is about to reveal himself for what his *self* is.

"How many of my father's hired servants have bread enough and to spare, but I perish here with hunger!" Here, the younger son is speaking alone, without an audience. He expresses his thoughts in words, and these words are the key to knowing him. What he thinks of when he "comes to himself" is food. He remembers that his father's hired servants had bread enough; and not only enough, but they had bread to spare. They can fill their bellies and still have bread left over. He thinks of not being full as "perishing with hunger." He is not starving, but his belly is not full, a condition which he finds intolerable and which brings him to himself.

His father is alive for him now that he wants something. He comes to himself in the sense that his "self" is always on the lookout for better ways of satisfying its cravings. He realizes that he would be better off as one of his father's servants.

There is nothing Jesus says that would suggest the usual view that the younger son "repented," at least certainly not in the sense of feeling remorse for any injuries he had done others, his father or his elder brother, or the family into which he was born. When he comes to himself, he thinks of himself. Period.

"I will arise and go to my father, and I will say to him, 'Father, I have sinned against heaven and before you; I am no longer worthy to be called your son; treat me as one of your hired servants.'" The younger son has assessed the situation in terms of what he expects will be required of him in order to get food from the man. He believes that the man will judge what he has done as a sin against heaven and against himself. He believes that the man thinks of being a father as living by certain standards, and that he will have to come to terms with these standards in order to fill his belly. He will call him "Father," using the word for the relationship that he *believes* best describes the man's understanding of himself, even though to the young man the word "Father" only means someone from whom to get what he wants.

He has been thinking of a way to fill his belly, but he believes that he will have to deal with his father's disapproval. Therefore, he will present himself as someone who has repented.

The first time that the younger son used clever words to manipulate his father, the listener was not in a position to know the precise meaning of his words, because Jesus had not told the listener what the younger son's thoughts were. This time, however, Jesus has given the listener access to the younger son's thoughts. The listener knows that what brought the younger son to "himself" was the estimation that he could get more of what he wanted from his father than from the citizen or from strangers.

Many listeners probably believe that the younger son *has* sinned against heaven and against his father, and that he *is* no longer worthy to be called a son. The younger son himself admits this possible judgment on himself. Even though for him this judgment is merely a perspective to get around, the judgment has now been expressed within the story. The judgment, once stated and made explicit, presupposes a model of what it means to be a father or a son. For the first time someone expresses the view within the story that being a father or a son entails adherence to standards. But the younger son's attitude toward this model shows that it is impotent to affect him. He is not someone who would feel remorse, even in the face of the severest and truest judgment. So indifferent is he to such a perspective that he can try it on himself while still remaining impervious to what it implies about him. Nevertheless, he has stated one possible understanding of what it means to be a father.

"And he arose and came to his father." We approach the critical turning point of the story. The narrative has suggested series after series of options, but now points to a specific set of possible outcomes. The narrative provokes the question of how the man will respond. The younger son believes that the man understands the father-son relationship in terms of a specific system of valuation that would necessitate viewing what the younger son has done as a sin against heaven and against himself. But the narrative raises the question of how the man who had two sons really understands the father-son relationship. The narrative also makes one wonder whether the man will be gulled by the cunning duplicity of his younger son. What will happen when the two meet again?

"But while he was still at a distance, his father saw him, and ran and embraced him and kissed him." Something quite unexpected occurs in the narrative. The story has led the listener to expect a scene in which the younger son gives his rehearsed speech to the man. But the older man's actions pre-empt the listener's as well as the younger son's expectations.

Before the younger son could do or say anything, while he was still at a distance, the man ran to him. It is often pointed out that it is considered extremely undignified for an Oriental man to run, and the cultural context could contribute something to the significance of the father's action. We have already come to suspect that he is not a man who behaves in a dignified way. But quite apart from the possible cultural factor at work here, his running to his younger son shows that *he* is the *active* party. His actions pre-empt all of the younger son's expectations and calculations. The man's energy dominates, an energy of spontaneous affection. How will the younger son respond?

"And the son said to him, 'Father, I have sinned against heaven and before you; I am no longer worthy to be called your son.'" The structure of the narrative controls the meaning of the younger son's words to his father. He repeats the speech that the listener heard him rehearse while he was still in a far country. If the narrative had developed as the listener and the younger son had expected, his uttering this speech to his father would have pointed to one set of meanings, and the question would have been whether or not the man would be taken in by his younger son's words. But the narrative did not develop in the expected way, and the younger son's repetition of his rehearsed speech serves to underscore the fact that he has not been touched in any way by his father's spontaneous display of affection. He even repeats the speech but leaving out something important, the part asking his father to treat him as one of his hired servants. His words show indifference to his father, and they show that he is still calculating, and doing so very quickly, about how to get the best for himself out of the situation!

If the listener had not heard him rehearse this speech in the context of calculating how to get something from his father, the listener might have believed that the younger son's words were sincere, that he actually did believe that he had sinned before heaven and against his father, and believed that he was no longer worthy to be called a son. But Jesus has structured the narrative so that the listener knows these are only empty words, designed to meet an expected objection of his father's. When the younger son nevertheless utters them after his father has shown how happy he is to see his son, the words sound even more cold, wooden, and inappropriate.

"But the father said to his servants, 'Bring quickly the best robe, and put it on him; and put a ring on his hand, and shoes on his feet.'" The man orders his servants to bestow on him all the outward signs of sonship. Instead of dealing with the one who left him as someone who has demonstrated that he is unworthy to be called a son, the man bestows filial prerogatives on him without holding him to any filial standards.

197

"And bring the fatted calf and kill it, and let us eat and make merry . . . ." A fatted calf would feed dozens of people. The man, in other words, commands the servants to prepare a feast. The younger son will not only have bread enough and to spare, but beef enough and to spare! The father's impulsive response to his son's return has pre-empted the younger son's programme of using his father. He is rendered passive in the face of his father's energy. What occurs is that the younger son can no longer live as the one who indulges himself; instead, the man becomes the one who indulges him. By indulging his younger son, the man has incorporated him into *his own* programme of having a son. To be able to do this, however, as we shall see, the man must be a father with property to give his son. And that, as we shall see, depends on his elder son's maintaining him in the role of father with paternal prerogatives. The man says, "let us eat and make merry." He now has a son whom he can honour and whom he can feed.

". . . for this my son was dead, and is alive again." Death figures prominently in this story. No one, of course, dies in the sense of having his biological existence terminated. But the story explores the ways in which death can be a factor in human relationships. The younger son treated his father as one does dead matter, and nothing in the present situation suggests that the younger son sees the man as anything other than a provider for his wants. The man announces that from his perspective, his son was *dead* when he was not with him. Obviously, the man does not mean that he regarded his son as dead because he had violated the standards of father-son relationships. Everything in the story prohibits that understanding. Rather, the story discloses that when the son was independent of him, not wanting things from him, he was non-existent. In other words, the son is alive to the man only when he uses his father. What counts for the man is having a son, but having a son has nothing to do with any human bond that might be said to exist between them, in the sense that human bonds as *human* suggest some higher level of existence than indulgence of the self's wants.

"And they began to make merry." Being the one who can indulge the younger son's wanting self puts the man in a festive mood. It would have taken some time to kill the fatted calf and to prepare for the eating, which means that several hours have passed before they began to make merry. Jesus composes the narrative in order to evoke, once again, a whole range of possibilities. Since dozens of people will be able to eat from the fatted calf, one wonders who will be present to eat it. Inevitably, the listener wonders whether the man will send for his elder son, who has been absent from the narrative since the second sentence.

"Now his elder son was in the field." Jesus identifies the elder son as the man's son ("his"). This sentence begins the fourth part of the story, a story structured to illustrate, in the second part, how the younger son views the father-son relationship. In the third part of the story, the listener learned that the man does not, as the younger son believed, think of the father-son relationship as involving mutual obligations and responsibilities. In all of what has happened, the usual basis for father-son relationships, namely that of property and inheritance, has been removed. The story has explored the relationship in the absence of proprietary necessity, thus allowing the characters to behave without external constraint or financial motive toward one another. But how does the elder son behave toward the man, and what is the man's view of his relationship with his elder son?

Jesus re-introduces the elder son into the story by describing him as being "in the field." This tells the listener two things. In the first place, we learn that the elder son was working on the family property at the time of his brother's return. Secondly, it informs us that the man who had two sons has not sent for his elder son to include him in the eating and merry-making. Apparently, he has forgotten about his elder son's existence.

"And as he came and drew near to the house, he heard music and dancing." There is a structural contrast here between this scene and the younger son's homecoming. The man has not come for his elder son, nor has he sent for him. The elder son comes and draws near to the house where the man and his younger son are making merry. The music and dancing indicate that the father has taken the time to send for musicians and for other guests. It is a large, well-organized party, and it does not include the elder son. The banquet itself is *already over* when the elder son returns from the field, since the dancing takes place after dinner.

Ever since his father abdicated ownership of the family property, the elder son has been the master, since he owns the portion not liquidated by the younger son. In other words, the elder son has not selected or acted upon the possibility of selling his portion for cash. This option, which he has not exercised, determines the significance of his being in the field and of his returning to his house. One son turned his share of his father's living into cash,

199

liquidated it, and squandered it, while the other has maintained the property in order to support his father.

"And he called one of the servants and asked what this meant. And the servant said to him, 'Your brother has come, and your father has killed the fatted calf, because he has received him safe and sound.'" The elder son must call for and ask one of his servants what this means because his father has not informed him about his brother's return, nor has his father sent for him to join in the eating and merrymaking. The servant reports that "your brother has come," a prefectly neutral description. There is no mention of the brother's reasons for coming, such as repentance or love. He does not say, "Your brother has repented and asked for forgiveness" or anything of the sort. From the servant's point of view, the brother has simply "come." The servant's report, then, serves as a disinterested observer's assessment of what transpired when the brother returned home.

The servant reports that the elder brother's father has ordered a banquet to be prepared "because he has received his younger son safe and sound." This disinterested observer reports that the father has killed the fatted calf because he has received back what he did not have for some time. The fact that he once again has his second son makes him happy. This also means that the father understands the situation from his own perspective. He is not happy and ordering a feast and celebration because the family has been reconstituted; for if that had been the case, he would have sent for his elder son. No, he thinks solely in terms of what he did not have but now has once again. He has won back a son, safe and sound. That son is alive for him; he forgets the other son.

"But he was angry and would not go in." The R.S.V. translation of this sentence, "But he was angry and *refused* to go in," has been influenced by Luke's understanding of the story. According to Luke, the elder son represents the scribes and Pharisees who "refuse" to share in table fellowship with Jesus, even though his invitation to follow him is one made to everyone. The Greek only says, however, that the elder son was angry and "would not" go in, and in this description there is no suggestion that he was "invited" to go in, nor is there anything in the story to suggest that he was. He is master of the house in any case, and he could certainly have gone in if he wished. The R.S.V. treats the elder son like a pouting adolescent, but that view is not in the story as narrated by Jesus.

In the five core phonodramatic parables, the only emotion which Jesus ascribes to any of his characters is anger. The other character who displays anger is the man who once gave a dinner and invited visitors. He displayed anger when he heard his servant's report of how his three invited guests refused to come to the dinner which he had organized. We have seen how Jesus' use of the triadic form makes the man's anger emerge almost inevitably from the narrative.

Since anger is an attitude that manifests itself visibly, the observation that the elder son was angry does not violate the stylistic canons of Jesus' parables. He never *attributes* motives or intentions to his characters, nor does he afford the listener access to the inner, private springs of action, that is, unless a character himself expresses his own purposes, as do the steward and the younger son. Only then does the listener know what the character intends to do, because the character says explicitly what his purposes are.

Anger is a polymorphous emotion. It takes many forms and can express itself in a variety of ways. Anger in itself does not determine how one will act, nor even that one will act at all. Thus, although anger's energy can vitalize action, it is not a motive cause for this or that particular action. How one acts, if one acts at all, is determined by other factors.

Anger can be caused by a variety of circumstances. Frustration can cause anger. An injury done to oneself can cause anger. One can, if one is sufficiently developed morally, feel angry outrage at an injustice or an injury done to another. One can also become angry when someone for whom one cares acts in a foolish, thoughtless, or self-destructive way. In other words, anger is not only caused by something done to oneself; it can be caused by something done to another, or by something another does to himself.

The narrative raises the question of *why* the elder son is angry. Certainly the situation points in a certain direction; it *appears* that the elder son is angry because he returns to his house to find a party going on and then learns *from a servant* what he could reasonably have expected to have been informed of by his father. But the listener still does not know *for certain* why the elder son is angry. What Jesus does say is that in his anger the elder son would not go into his house.

"His father came out and tried to conciliate him. . . ." This is the meaning of the Greek. The R.S.V. has translated the Greek as "entreated him" because the R.S.V. understands the parable as Luke does, namely that the elder son represents the Pharisees who "refuse" to participate in Jesus' table fellowship even though they are invited. The story shows, however, that the father came out *to try to conciliate* his elder son's *anger*. The narrative raises the question of what form the father's attempts to conciliate his elder son's anger will take. Depending on what the father says, his words should reveal his understanding of his relationship with his elder son. In any case, it is clear that now that the elder son has come to the house and stays outside, angry, the man is once again aware of his existence.

"But he answered his father, 'Lo, these many years I have served you, and I never disobeyed your command; yet you never gave me a kid, that I might make merry with my friends.'" The elder son replies to his father's conciliatory efforts. His words inform the listener that the younger son has been gone for many years. During these many years, then, the elder son has managed the family property and has supported his father with the income from the share of the property remaining after the younger son has liquidated his portion. He continued to administer the family property for his father's benefit and for the benefit of his family's posterity. Although his position was one of authority, he continued to treat his father as a *father*. He not only served, but he also deferred to the man's authority *as father* and never disobeyed his command. In other words, it was solely in virtue of the decisions made by the elder son that the man who had two sons was enabled to continue in his role *as father*.

The whole situation throws into sharp relief the elder son's understanding of his relationship with his father. The elder son understood his relationship with his father in terms of a human bond that was not dependent on external circumstances. Jesus has ensured that all the factors were stripped away which could have *necessitated* that the elder son treat his father as a father. The fact that he continued to serve his father and that he continued to recognize his father's authority was the result of a completely free decision on his part; he was acting under no compulsion.

We have seen repeatedly how the narrative context determines the meaning of the characters' words, and in this case the narrative context is particularly crucial for understanding the elder son. When the elder son says to his father, "yet you never gave me a kid," he is not telling his father that he wanted a kid; he did not want things. His words to his father, *in the context*, show that what he wanted was a spontaneous gift from his father, some sign that his father reciprocated his filial devotion. He now realizes that his father has taken him for granted all these years. What his father's behaviour shows him is that his father did not value the human bond the elder son *thought* he had with his father. He freely treated the man as a father, and thought that his father freely considered him to be a son. What the father has done now has thrown into question their relationship and everything the son had based his life on for many years.

Two different understandings of the father-son relationship have emerged in the course of the story, and both have been shattered. The younger son believed that his father was a man of principle, that his father thought of the father-son relationship as involving certain mutual obligations. Although he did not himself share his father's views, the younger son reckoned that in order to get what he wanted from his father he would have to deal with those views. The elder son had a quite different understanding of his relationship with his father. He thought of himself as freely serving and obeying his father, and believed that his father shared that understanding of their relationship. He did not think of their relationship as involving certain obligations based on property and norms, but as one of free exchange and freely recognized human bonds. He now realizes that he has been mistaken.

"But when this son of yours came, who has devoured your living with harlots, you killed for him the fatted calf!" The elder son's words inform the listener of the precise nature of the younger son's "loose living." (How the elder son knew this, or whether the father also had access to this information previously, the story does not say. In any case, the father now does know *how* his younger son squandered his living.) The younger son had been addicted to fornicating with prostitutes; he was a voluptuary. The whole picture of the younger son is of someone who lives out of his bodily wants.

But the elder son does not condemn the younger son on moral grounds. What angers him is that the younger son "devoured your living." The elder son's words show that he does not think of the property that was squandered in terms of his own self-interest, but rather in terms of his father's interest. He is angry because the younger son has devoured (note the image of voracious wanting) the property the income of which should have provided support for his father. In other words, the elder son is someone who experiences outrage not at the injury done to himself, but at the injury done to someone for whom he cares. This is "righteous indignation," and it is completely different from the kind of anger caused by an injury done to oneself or caused by someone's having broken rules.

The elder son does not express indignation at not being informed of his brother's return, nor indignation at having been left out of the celebration. The narrative had led the listener to expect that one of these was the cause of his anger. The listener's expectation is, however, not fulfilled by what the elder son says, because he states that he is angry *because the father does not care about himself*. To care for someone who does not care about himself *is* exasperating.

"And he said to him, 'Son, you are always with me, and all that is mine is yours. It was fitting to make merry, for this your brother was dead, and is alive.'" The man's words provide information that is crucial for understanding the story—that all the man's property *does* belong to the elder son ("all that is mine is yours") and that the feast is over ("it was fitting to make merry" so the father's words cannot be construed as an invitation to join the celebration).

At the end of each of the other three phonodramatic parables to which we have listened, the man about whom Jesus tells the story exhibits a surprising degree of freedom from the "normal" human response apparently dictated by the situation. We have seen that he responds spontaneously to indulge the son whose existence is characterized by voracious wanting. Having that son with him excites him, and he behaves in accordance with the excitement he feels. He prefers the excitement to maintaining any standards as a father. Indeed, from this perspective he cannot be said to live as a "father." Everything in the first three parts of the narrative has driven home this point. But the man has another son. In what sense is he a "father" to his elder son? What stimulates him to respond to his elder son? It is his elder son's anger. The exchange between the man and his elder son in the concluding section of the narrative has the quality of an absurdist drama in which people talk but do not communicate with one another. The man is concerned to conciliate his elder son's anger but does not hear what the elder son is saying about why he is angry. On the contrary, his words only serve to confirm that he takes the elder son for granted ("Son, you are always with me"). He attempts to *explain* his behaviour to his elder son ("It was fitting . . ."), as if what concerns him is not the effect his behaviour has had on one who is attached to him, but rather what concerns him is the possibility of being judged by his elder son. His explanation is thus *self*-protective. The man has an elder son, but reveals through his words that he is not a "father" to him, either. The whole narrative provides Jesus' most complex variation on the theme of living in story.

What has happened in the story?

Not only is this parable the longest, but it is also undoubtedly the most complex one which Jesus composed and narrated, and certainly the most difficult to interpret. If one simply tells the story word for word as Jesus composed it, the story speaks for itself. However, difficulties arise as soon as one attempts to use secondary language to explain the story's meaning. The reason, I would suggest, lies in the degree to which Luke's interpretation of the story has governed all subsequent readings and, perhaps even more important, the degree to which Luke's view of love as unconditional, uncritical acceptance of others has permeated Western attitudes. Luke's interpretation of this story as exemplifying "compassion" has had an enormous impact on the Christian (and non-Christian!) understanding of forgiveness, which has come to be identified with an unwillingness to make judgments about people. That such an attitude is totally at odds with that of the Jesus who uttered the sayings and parables we have been studying should by now be patently clear. Nevertheless, this story is commonly cited in support of the view that one should not judge others — meaning that one *should* not discriminate, *should* have no standards, and *should* "accept" people "as themselves" regardless of what their behaviour reveals about them. This is the modern ideal of tolerance, an ideal which springs from an unwillingness to see things as they are, as Nietzsche has so clearly stated:

> Love is the state in which man sees things most of all as they are *not*. The illusion-creating force is there at its height, likewise the sweetening and *transforming* force. One endures more when in love than one otherwise would, one tolerates everything. The point was to devise a religion in which love is possible: with that one is beyond the worst that life can offer —one no longer even sees it.[6]

6. Nietzsche, *The Anti-Christ*, p. 133.

This view of love which tolerates everything and which does not see things as they are is rooted in the contemporary hatred of actuality, in *ressentiment*. As an illusion-creating force, this type of so-called "love" does not want vital things to be. It needs decadence in order to become operative. The words and actions of the younger son have revealed that he is a decadent. To hold up the man's attitude toward him as a paradigm of love and forgiveness would involve understanding "love" as primarily indulging the parasitical and the decadent.

This does not mean that Christian theology should abandon the concept of forgiveness; this concept has other, sounder, bases.[7] But it does mean that Luke's notion that forgiveness is identical with non-discriminating awareness requires critical re-examination. It is especially important to divorce the theological concept of forgiveness from this parable (viewed as an example-story). I would suggest that the theological effort to reconsider the meaning of forgiveness should begin with reflection on the attitude of the storyteller to his characters. He sees each one, through his words and actions, as he is, without sentimentality about any one of them being "merely human" or any comparably Satanic attitudes. The fundamental question, it seems to me, is whether discriminating awareness is compatible with love. In our culture, the overwhelming view has been that love and discriminating awareness are mutually exclusive. However, if love can be understood as voluntary engagement with the freedom of an*other* (Part One), then the narrator of the core parables manifests this complex attitude. For it is only when one sees others as they are that one grasps their otherness.

Another difficulty for the modern listener hearing this parable stems from the value our culture gives to such attitudes as being "spontaneous," "unguarded," "unconditionally accepting," and "affectionate." As we listened to this story, we used such descriptions to characterize the man's behaviour. Had I been able to use descriptive terminology that is free from contemporary values, I would have done so. But perhaps it is just as well that we are forced to address the issues head on. Notice that in themselves these types of behaviour have no inherent value; it is the listener or the reader who attributes value to such behaviour. Spontaneity can be the *modus vivendi* of an extremely selfish person. Unguarded behaviour can be a sign that someone *wants* something so much that he or she

7. See Scheler, *Ressentiment*, pp. 99-100.

206

does not count the cost to himself or herself. Setting no conditions on one's relationships with others *can* be an indication of fundamental weakness in one's character. The meaning of the man's affection, spontaneity, and unguardedness, of his lack of standards, can be determined only by the overall structure of the narrative which Jesus has composed about him.

The interpretive issues can be clarified somewhat by comparing Jesus' story with Shakespeare's *King Lear*. Both begin with a situation created by the father's decision to divide his property between his children. Lear decides to divest himself of his territory because he wants to "shake all cares and business" from his old age, so that he can "unburdened crawl toward death" (I, i, 39, 41), retaining only "The name, and all th'addition to a king" (I, i, 136). He believes that he can continue to enjoy the prerogatives of being a king and father without having the cares and responsibilities of one.

In exchange for giving the ownership of his territory to his three daughters, Lear demands an expression of their affection for him, and both Goneril and Regan respond by telling Lear what he wanted to hear. Each replies in extravagant terms. Goneril professes to love Lear . . .

> . . . more than word can wield the matter;
> Dearer than eyesight, space, and liberty;
> Beyond what can be valued, rich or rare;
> No less than life, with grace, health, beauty, honor;
> As much as child e'er loved, or father found;
> A love that makes breath poor, and speech unable. (I, i, 55-60)

Regan asserts that she loves Lear just as much and in the same ways as Goneril, except that in addition she professes herself . . .

> . . . an enemy to all other joys
> Which the most precious square of sense possesses,
> And find I am alone felicitate
> In your dear Highness' love. (I, i, 73-76)

Both Goneril and Regan are willing to tell Lear what he wants to hear because they want something from him. As soon as they have achieved their purpose, they reveal what they really think of him. Goneril says:

> The best and soundest of his time hath been but rash; then must we look from his age to receive not alone the imperfections of long-ingraffed condition, but therewithal the unruly waywardness that infirm and choleric years bring with them. (I, i, 294-98)

What Cordelia calls their "plighted cunning" (I, i, 280) differs not at all from the younger son's cunning plan to profess to his father "Father, I have sinned against heaven and before you; I am no longer worthy to be called your son; treat me as one of your hired servants."

Having divested himself of his kingly authority, and having divided his kingdom between Goneril and Regan, Lear expected them to support him and to honour him as a father. But Goneril has no respect for Lear. To her, he is just an . . .

> Idle old man,
> That still would manage those authorities
> That he hath given away. Now, by my life,
> Old fools are babes again, and must be used
> With checks as flatteries, when they are seen abused.
> (I, iii, 16-20)

Naturally, Lear is stung by this treatment by a daughter from whom he expected devotion and gratitude for his paternal generosity:

> Ingratitude! thou marble-hearted fiend,
> More hideous when thou show'st thee in a child
> Than the sea-monster. (I, iv, 250-52)

In a fury, Lear goes to his other daughter, Regan, expecting that she, at least, will treat him with dignity, but she instead chides him as someone infirm:

> O, sir, you are old;
> Nature in you stands on the very verge
> Of his confine. You should be ruled, and led
> By some discretion that discerns your state
> Better than you yourself. (II, iv, 141-45)

Lear's heart begins to break with grief because his daughters act neither out of the natural bond of childhood, nor out of gratitude, and runs outside into a raging storm. Regan coldly claims that he has brought this on himself:

> . . . to willful men
> The injuries that they themselves procure
> Must be their schoolmasters. Shut up your doors.
> (II, iv, 297-99)

On the heath, Lear asks the central question of the play: "Is there any cause in nature that makes these hard hearts?" (II, vi, 75-76). As the play unfolds, it becomes quite clear that hard-heartedness remains just as enigmatic and inexplicable as the loving hearts of a Cordelia or an Edgar. Ultimately, there is no explanation to account for the heart of man.

In Jesus' story, the younger son treats his father in very much the same way that Regan and Goneril treat Lear. In Shakespeare, however, we know that Lear is deceived by Regan and Goneril. Jesus' story, on the other hand, shows no interest in the question of the man's subjective apprehension of the situation. What we do know is that the man finds his relationship with his younger son stimulating, for it is this relationship which makes him come alive, makes him affectionate, stimulates his desire to give presents and his urge to celebrate. Quite apart from the man's subjective apprehensions of the situation, we can deduce from his behaviour that he enjoys being used. In Nietzsche's terms, the father is a dependent man: " he can be only a means, he has to be *used*, he needs someone who will use him."[8] That being used stimulated him and evokes his spontaneous delight is made absolutely obvious by the first three parts of the narrative.

The elder son's position and behaviour, on the other hand, are analogous to Cordelia's. He does not use his father, does not take from him, but gives freely of his service and his obedience, and would like his father to give freely in return. Once Lear was dependent on them, Goneril and Regan mistreated Lear. The elder son freely gives precisely what Lear demanded, but did not receive, from Goneril and Regan; he conferred on him the authority appropriate to a father—served and obeyed him "for many years" and allowed him to dispense with the property as if it were still his (for example, the father felt free to give gifts to the younger son and to order a banquet prepared). In the same way, Cordelia maintained her affection and loyalty to her father even after he had disowned her. Of course, the test of the elder son's loyalty and affection is not so severe as Cordelia's—Regan and Goneril, on the one hand, and Cordelia, on the other, represent more extreme opposites than do the younger and elder sons. But the parallels are instructive.

What makes the elder son different from Cordelia is that he gets

8. Nietzsche, *The Anti-Christ*, p. 172.

angry. Our culturally determined assumptions about anger make it difficult for us to see that the elder son's anger was caused because his father has responded affectionately and generously to a son who had devoured *the man's* living. He is angry because his father, for whom he cares and whom he respects as a father, is indifferent to the way his younger son has treated him. The story does not deal with sibling rivalry. Rather, the elder son's anger is caused by his *attachment* to his father. In T.S. Eliot's words, he is caught in the living, flowering nettle that stings.

It is true that through his actions and words, the man has revealed a preference for his younger son. He finds his relationship with the one who uses him stimulating. But he has a second son who cares for him. The *man's* dilemma is that his spontaneous display of excitement at having his younger son dependent on him once again has thrown into question the basis of his elder son's relationship with him. In attempting to conciliate his elder son's anger, his self-protective explanations serve only to confirm that he takes his elder son for granted, that he does not understand being a father at all as the elder son does, and that indeed he feels no spontaneous affection for his elder son. So the man who had two sons at the beginning of the story does not really have two "sons" at the end, nor is he a "father" to them.

What does it mean, then, for this man to have *two* sons? A similar question can be asked of the other phonodramatic parables of Jesus. How can the rich man simultaneously have a steward and also value trust? How can the host both give a dinner party and invite guests who make excuses for not coming? How can the householder both act freely with his vineyard and his money and yet have hired labourers? In each of these parables, the problem has to do with the irreconcilability of the human relationship with some other factor. In the story about the man, the problem has to do with the man's inability to reconcile having a relationship with two *sons* simultaneously. In other words, the story explores the basic problem of triangular human relationships. How can this man have two sons at the same time, given the kind of human being he is and given the differing kinds of human beings that his sons are?

The story is not about the younger son because he lives only for himself; he is a picaresque figure, like the rich man's steward. On the other hand, the elder son lives only for the man he treats as father. The elder son has not developed the kind of detachment from his father that would enable him to live his own story. Only

the man has a sufficient degree of detachment from the manipula-
tiveness of his younger son, on the one hand, and from the caring
attachment of his elder son, on the other, even to attempt a double
relationship. Each of his sons is totally single-minded. The man acts
solely in order to carry out his programme of having two sons at
the same time. He refuses to be controlled by the manipulative
indifference of his younger son. Instead, he dominates the younger
son and incorporates him into his own programme by indulging
him. At the same time, he is not controlled by the caring attachment of his elder son. The ending of the story leaves a situation of
such Gordian knottiness that it would be tempting to employ a
simplifying sword to cut through it rather than to ponder the
human complexities which the story uncovers.

The man's concluding words to his elder son show just how
unstable is his programme of having two sons. Subsequent to his
decision to divest himself of his property, the man has had the
possibility of being the man who has two sons only by virtue of his
elder son's continuing maintenance of the property. He is aware of
this ("all that is mine is yours"), at least partly. For if the elder son
had turned his share of his father's living into cash, the man would
have had no means of support. And, more importantly, his
younger son would have had no incentive to return to him. Quite
simply, his story would have terminated. But the elder son continued to support him and to honour him as a father in the belief
that his father's story was *to be a father*, and that his own role was *to
be a son*.

The elder son's situation is similar to what the third man's would
have been in the story of the man going down the road if the third
man had abandoned his own story in order to become a nurse
forever. Just as the third man enabled the man going down the road
to continue living in his story, the elder son empowered his father
to continue being the man who had two sons. Both the third man
and the elder son enable *another* to live in story. The difference
between them is that the third man apparently has his own story
whereas the elder son does not. He completely subordinates his
own possibilities to those of the one whom he believes lives in story
as a father. He does not even feel free to make merry with his
friends on his own initiative. In other words, the elder son's situation is similar to that of all those who, out of a sense of filial
attachment to their parents, do not develop their own stories.
Indeed, the elder son's predicament is analogous to that of anyone

who exists in the role of "helper," enabling others to live in story. Now that the elder son has seen that the man is not a "father," will he continue to enable him to be the man who has two sons? This, it seems to me, is the human predicament onto which Jesus' parable opens.

Obviously, it is virtually impossible to listen to this parable without importing one's own sense of values. At the least, we can guard against expecting that the storyteller provide narratives which exemplify and reinforce our own ideas about, say, fatherly love. This is especially important to guard against since our Western ideas of fatherhood and of familial love have been so influenced by Luke's reading of the parable. The result has been the development of ideas of love and forgiveness which are suffused with *ressentiment*, and this applies not only to ideas of virtue but also to concepts of God as well. I would argue that the more appropriate starting point for theological reflection on the meaning of the fatherhood of God would be the Lord's Prayer (Chapter Five, above). Moreover, I do not believe that the man who had two sons should serve as a model for human fathers. For one thing, Jesus' parables do not function in order to provide such models. This story shows how one *particular* man reveals what he is as he attempts to carry out his programme of having two sons without being a father, either in the sense that the younger son expects or in the sense that his elder son expects.

The core parables of Jesus invite the listener to see things as they are, to ponder the complex dynamics of human relationships. At this level of human reality, no one can tell another *how* to live, and the parables make no such attempt. In this parable, one becomes conscious that each character must live out the consequences of his own mode of being human. That the storyteller himself did so, we know from historical evidence. What the listener does, depends on what he or she hears. What he or she *does* now is an open question.

CONCLUSION

The teller of stories

Why did Jesus compose and narrate all of these parables? I have been suggesting all along, and will now state explicitly, that what is important in the *final* analysis is not the content or the formal features of the stories themselves—not the characters in them, not the style of the stories, not their structure. Nor are the stories *ultimately* important for what they tell us about the storyteller. I say this even though it is presumably an interest in Jesus that provokes one to read a book such as this. Once one has cornered the historical, earthly, human Jesus, however, one discovers that one can learn about *him* only indirectly (the storyteller *is* implicit in his stories). What is the meaning of this phenomenon? I do not believe that this is an accident.

It appears to me that Jesus composed these narratives about particular human beings in order to *communicate to his listeners his own perception of, and attitude toward, human reality.* These stories disclose what it means to exist as a particular person, rooted in the power which, in his core sayings, Jesus referred to using the traditional symbol "kingdom of God." This mode of being human, the personal mode, was inaugurated by Jesus himself. It can be contrasted with, on the one hand, existing as a member of a group, and on the other with existing as a solitary individual. It is not the case that all human life has the character of a story, but only the lives of those who exist in the personal mode—this is the assumption communicated through Jesus' parables. And, after almost two thousand years, his words still have the power to reveal these dimensions of reality. One can agree with what Peter says in the Gospel of John, although in a different sense than the one intended by John, that Jesus has the words of life (John 6:68).

The Silence of Jesus

The Silence of Jesus

In the contemporary world, to be "human" usually means to share certain qualities and characteristics in common with others. Political and religious leaders are thought to be "human" to the extent that they do not hold themselves apart from others. Those once believed to be paragons, men such as Martin Luther King or John F. Kennedy, are discovered to be "only *human*" once unsavoury characteristics and behaviour come to light. There is an enormous resistance nowadays to anything that sets people apart from others or distinguishes them in any way. This manifests itself in the impulse to detract, as well as in an insatiable appetite for gossip. I would argue, in agreement with Scheler, that this urge to locate "humanity" in the lowest common denominator is symptomatic of offence at the actual. The issue, of course, is *what is real*—the typical, or that which is "fickle, freckled ... counter, spare, original, strange"?

But the issue that concerns us most nearly here has to do with the quest for the historical Jesus. Historical research, since it adheres to the canons of scientific truth, proceeds on the basis of discovering analogies; it is oriented to the discovery of the typical. Historiographical method is an important intellectual tool, and it has been employed extensively throughout this book—not only in order to reconstruct critically the authentic words of the historical Jesus, but also in order to confirm those features of his historical activity which can be known with a high degree of certainty (that he came from Nazareth; that he was associated with John the

Baptist; that he probably borrowed John's kingdom language, at least initially, even though he completely reinterpreted that language; that he ate with men and women who were excluded by observant Jews; and that his mode of being human evoked a violent response, even unto death on the cross).

Nonetheless, historiography, by its very nature, cannot recover a human being in his particularity—not that every human being achieves particularity; indeed, the bulk of mankind, as Dostoyevsky clearly saw, prefers other modes of being human. We made no prior assumptions regarding the uniqueness of Jesus. Nevertheless, our analysis of the parables permits us to conclude that when we do listen to them carefully, we are hearing the voice of a human being who was an original. My thesis is that the historical Jesus is discovered in his sayings and parables.

One of the most striking characteristics of Jesus' core sayings and parables is that he remained basically silent about himself. Only two of the core sayings make any reference to Jesus, the saying that states he came eating and drinking, and the one that indicates he liberated persons from the demonic. Nor did Jesus tell stories about himself. In that respect, he is the opposite of most contemporary storytellers who say, "An interesting thing *happened to me* on the way to . . . ." Jesus does not organize his experience in the re-active mode, in terms of what happens *to* him. Rather, the perspective that comes through in all of his parables is that of someone who is intensely observant of what happens in human life, quite apart from any reference to his own ego.

It is not surprising, however, that the early Christians expressed their understanding of Jesus' significance by telling stories *about him* —pronouncement stories and miracle stories at the earliest stages; biographical legends, the narrative of his suffering and death; and finally, the gospel stories, which were created using all of these traditional elements. As we have seen, the earliest Christian teachers also composed parable-like narratives in imitation of Jesus, many of which they composed in order to have Jesus say what they imagined he would have said. There are many such stories in the synoptic tradition which refer obliquely to Jesus, a..d all of them are early Christian compositions, for example "The Parable of the Ten Maidens" (Matt 25:1-13); "The Unmerciful Servant" (Matt 18: 23-35); "The Wicked Tenants" (Mark 12:1-12); "The Parable of the Talents" (Matt 25:14-30=Luke 19:11-27).

Furthermore, Jesus does not attribute any messianic or divine titles to himself in the core sayings. All those sayings in the synoptic tradition which show Jesus talking about himself and defining himself with Christological titles are the products of early Christian reflection on the meaning of Jesus. It is understandable that the early Christians utilized the terminology available to them from their religious and cultural heritage in order to express their understanding of Jesus. The process of transferring their own understanding to the mouth of the Jesus about whom they told stories culminated in the Gospel of John which represents Jesus as speaking about himself in long discourses beginning with "I am . . . ."

Judging from the core sayings and parables, there is absolutely no basis for assuming that Jesus shared the cosmological, mythological, or religious ideas of his contemporaries. The core sayings and parables are absolutely silent about such concepts as heaven and hell, resurrection of the dead, the end of the world, the last judgment, angels, and the like. Thus, we cannot approach Jesus as a "historical personage," assuming that his world-attitudes are totally circumscribed by the language and assumptions of a first-century Galilean, whose "past" meaning we must therefore seek to translate into "modern" terms.

Far from *proclaiming* the kingdom of God, or from urging his contemporaries to reaffirm their commitment to a God who acts in history on behalf of his people Israel, Jesus totally reinterprets the meaning and significance of the traditional symbol "kingdom of God." None of his sayings or parables points to history as the *locus* for its activity. He does not tell stories which deal with political events, social issues, class struggle, or the concerns of the Jewish people as a people. The one saying we do have which comments on Jesus' contemporaries distinguishes both him and John as persons who stand forth in freedom from the tribalized children. Not one of Jesus' parables deals with the question of what it means to be human in the context of the question about what it means to be a member of a people.

Jesus' parables do not teach or illustrate ideas, they do not recommend this or that mode of behaviour over any other, they do not admonish or offer principles by which the listener can lead a meaningful life. In answer to all such questions about what to think, or whom to worship, or how to live, Jesus remains silent. Neither his sayings nor his parables reflect any relationship with either traditional Jewish canons of conduct (the Law) nor of Graeco-Roman ideals of man or the moral personality.

The parables do not contain any supernatural beings; they do not deal with religious institutions, practices, or beliefs; they do not refer to supernatural events. Instead, each story focuses on specific, individual human beings. Each one is described in his or her own particularity, and no effort is made to see them as types or examples. The characters are not described in terms of categories; rather, each one achieves his or her own reality through what he or she does and says. None of the characters is dealt with as a member of a people or of a group (unless he understands himself that way, as does the grumbling worker to whom the householder speaks). None of the characters is dealt with as a member of a religious party or sect, nor as representative of a certain social class.

There is nothing in these sayings or parables to suggest that Jesus adopted the position of critic. With the exception of the saying that states "The kingdom of God is not coming with signs to be observed, nor will they say 'Lo, here it is!' or 'There!' ..." none of his sayings or parables attempts to correct the defective concepts of his contemporaries. All of the stories in the synoptic tradition which picture Jesus as being in conflict with others are products of the early Christian communities. This means that Jesus did not think in the *re-active* mode, against Judaism or any other particular orientation. The mere fact that he stood forth free from the other modes of being current at his time was sufficient to arouse hostility from his contemporaries.

This combination of characteristics, of not being ego-oriented, and of not being re-active, explains why Jesus' sayings and parables reflect nothing of what Baudelaire points out as both profoundly human and yet Satanic in man, that attitude arising from the miserable condition of feeling oneself superior and thinking oneself inferior. The parables show that Jesus was totally oriented to directing consciousness to those human beings who, in their own particularity, lived in story. That Jesus was in his own mode of being human, as Zooey observed, the most unimitative and original master, should also by now be clear; not only was his behaviour that of a free person grounded in the kingdom of God, but through his parables he communicated to others the possibility of perceiving that which is "counter, original, spare, and strange."

Both Jesus' sayings and parables show that he did not understand the personal mode of being human as a matter of cultivating the inner life, as life in flight from concrete actuality. Whatever "being dwells indoors" his characters is known only through what they deal out, in actions and words, in their transcendent relationships with things (the photodramatic parables) and with other people (the phonodramatic parables).

It should be clear that although Jesus did not comment on the social or political issues of his day, and although he did not presume to instruct others how to find meaning in their own lives, there are social, ethical and political implications to his sayings and parables. It is, I think, not too much to assert that the ethical, social, and political thinking grounded in the realities disclosed in Jesus' core sayings and parables would be guided by the question about what structures stunt and inhibit, and what structures enhance, the emergence of persons who live in story. That there are no absolutes from this perspective should be obvious.

There is no indication whatsoever in Jesus' sayings or parables of any one of the familiar modes of offence at the actual. Jesus, on the contrary, directs attention specifically to actual people in the world as they are, and he sees them clearly. He does not attempt to undermine the reality of man's everyday, earthly, human existence by claiming the superior reality of some transcendental sphere. He does not treat living beings as dead matter to be used, either as examples or as vehicles for ideas. Nor does he attempt to collapse all otherness into an inner world—he is not hedonistic. Instead, his parables display an extremely concentrated focus on the *otherness* of actual persons.

That to which someone lets his attention be drawn is the object-ive correlative of his fundamental, usually unconscious world-attitude and hence reveals his implicit understanding of what is real, of which phenomena manifest the nature of reality. In this connection, it is important to observe that Jesus does not focus on the grotesque, the maimed, the insane, or the enslaved. Jesus' parables do reflect a profound awareness of death as a factor in human relationships, and of evil as a potent force in human life. But if anyone could have lain at the bottom of a hill with his throat cut, slowly bleeding to death, and if a pretty girl or an old woman had passed by with a beautiful jug balanced perfectly on the top of her head, and could have raised himself up on one arm to see the jug safely over the top of the hill, it was Jesus.

On the other hand, it was not specifically to a pretty girl or an old woman balancing a beautiful jug perfectly on top of her head that Jesus let his attention be drawn—not, in other words, to specifically aesthetic experiences. Rather, his own attention was drawn to that dimension of reality where those persons exist who live in story. And by composing and narrating his parables he also directed his listeners' awareness to that same dimension of reality.

This dimension of reality is revealed in the context of silence—Jesus' silence about himself, his silence in answer to mankind's perennial religious, moral, social and political questions. (We have also seen that silence functions internally in every one of Jesus' core parables, for their meaning emerges in terms of what is said against the background of *what is not said*; in other words, silence plays an important role in the creation of meaning *within* each narrative.)

In the course of our analysis and interpretation of the core material, we have repeatedly had occasion to note how Jesus' attention is drawn to the particular. I believe that this points to something crucial in Jesus' world-attitude. The human mind habitually notices what is patterned in its experience—that which can be compared, that which is repetitious. As we know, critical and scientific thought has elevated this mode of consciousness to the principle criterion for determining truth. That is held to be true which is in principle available to the scrutiny of anyone, that is, truth is that which is in principle repeatable (this is the basis for experimental science and also for the use of analogy in historiography). But this means that the *rational* mind is most amenable to the *destructive* factors at work in human experience. In medical science, for example, *disease* almost always follows the same pattern. In psychology mental *illness* almost always manifests the same behaviour. Technology is, by definition, oriented to that which can be manipulated, in other words, to that which is *dead*. Our habitual modes of thinking are oriented to those aspects of human experience which are basically dead or destructive.

How does one develop the ability to be conscious of what is alive, what is new in every moment? I would suggest that Jesus' parables function, in part, precisely to break the grip of *ressentiment* on the human mind, and so to free consciousness and intelligence for voluntary engagement with that which is *alive*. In short, they function to invite the listener to enter the personal mode of being human.

The word "love" does not appear in any of Jesus' core sayings or parables. But if the concept love refers to a mode of being which is grounded in the superabundant power which engenders or fathers-forth all that is counter, original, spare, strange; and if love is a concept that refers to the capacity to engage voluntarily with the freedom of the actual other, then it can be said that Jesus was not only "the smartest and the best," not only himself the most original master, but that he was also the most loving and least sentimental man one could imagine.

APPENDICES

The core material

Eight core sayings

(1) But to what shall I compare this generation?
It is like children sitting in the market places
and calling to their playmates,
"We piped to you, and you did not dance;
we wailed, and you did not mourn."
For John came neither eating nor drinking,
and they say, "He has a demon";
I came eating and drinking,
and they say, "Behold, a glutton and a drunkard,
a friend of tax collectors and sinners!"

(2) From the days of John the Baptist until now
the kingdom of God has suffered violence,
and men of violence take it by force.

(3) The kingdom of God is not coming with signs to be observed;
nor will they say, "Lo, here it is!" or "There!"
for behold, the kingdom of God is in the midst of you.

(4) If it is by the finger of God that I cast out demons,
then the kingdom of God has come upon you.

(5) Truly, I say to you, whoever does not receive the kingdom of
God like a child shall not enter it.

(6) No one who puts his hand to the plow and looks back is fit for
the kingdom of God.

(7) It is easier for a camel to go through the eye of a needle than for a rich man to enter the kingdom of God.

(8) Father,
Hallowed be thy name.
Thy kingdom come.
Give us this day our daily bread,
And forgive us what we owe those whom we have injured,
As we ourselves forgive what is owing from those who have injured us.
And put us not to the test.

Seven photodramatic parables

(1) There was a man who found treasure hidden in a field, which he covered up; then he went and sold all that he had and bought that field.

(2) There was a merchant who, on finding one pearl of great value, went and sold all that he had and bought it.

(3) There was a man who took a grain of mustard seed and sowed it in his garden, and it became a shrub, and the birds made nests in its shade.

(4) There was a shepherd who had a hundred sheep, and one of them went astray. He left the ninety-nine on the hills and looked for that one.

(5) There was a woman who took leaven, and hid it in three measures of meal, till it was all leavened.

(6) There was a man who went out to sow, and as he sowed, some seed fell on the road, other seed fell on rocky ground, other seed fell on thorns, and other seed fell on good soil.

(7) There was a woman who had ten silver coins, and she lost one. She lit a lamp and swept diligently looking for that one.

Five phonodramatic parables

The rich man who had a steward

There was a rich man who had a steward.

And charges were brought to him that this man was squandering his goods. And he called him and said to him, "What is this that I hear about you? Turn in the account of your stewardship, for you are no longer able to be steward."

And the steward said to himself, "What shall I do, since my master is taking the stewardship away from me? I am not strong enough to dig, and I am ashamed to beg. I have decided what to do, so that people may receive me into their houses when I am put out of the stewardship."

So, summoning his master's debtors one by one, he said to the first, "How much do you owe my master?" He said, "A hundred measures of oil." And he said to him, "Take you bill, and sit down quickly and write fifty." Then he said to another, "And how much do you owe?" He said, "A hundred measures of wheat." He said to him, "Take your bill, and write eighty."

[The rich man's final words to the steward have been lost.]

The man who once gave a dinner and invited guests

There was a man who once gave a dinner, and invited guests.

And at the time for the dinner, he sent his servant to call those who had been invited.

The first said to him, "I have bought a farm, and I must go out to see it; I pray you, have me excused." And the second said, "I have bought five yoke of oxen, and I go to examine them; I pray you, have me excused." And the third said, "I have married a wife, and therefore I cannot come."

So the servant came and reported this to his master.

Then the man in anger said to his servant, "Go outside to the streets and bring back those whom you happen to meet."

The householder who went out at dawn to hire labourers

There was a householder who went out at dawn to hire labourers for his vineyard.

After agreeing with the labourers for a denarius a day, he sent them into his vineyard. And going out about the third hour he saw others standing idle in the market place; and to them he said, "You go into the vineyard too, and whatever is right I will give you." So they went. Going out again about the sixth hour and the ninth hour, he did the same. And about the eleventh hour he went out and found others standing; and he said to them, "Why do you stand here idle all day?" They said to him, "Because no one has hired us." He said to them, "You go into the vineyard, too."

And when it was evening, those hired about the eleventh hour came, and each of them received a denarius. Now when the others came, each of them also received a denarius.

And on receiving it they grumbled at the householder, saying, "These last worked only one hour, and you have made them equal to us who have borne the burden of the day and the scorching heat."

But he replied to one of them, "Friend, I am doing you no wrong; did you not agree with me for a denarius? Take what belongs to you and go; I choose to give to this last as I give to you. Am I not allowed to do what I choose with what belongs to me? Or is your eye evil because I am good?"

The man going down the road who fell among robbers

There was a man going down the road, who fell among robbers,
who stripped him and beat him, and departed, leaving him half
dead.

Now by chance a man was going down that road; and when he
saw him, he passed by on the other side. So likewise another man,
when he came to the place and saw him, passed by on the other
side. But a third man, as he journeyed, came to where he was; and
when he saw him, he went to him

and bound up his wounds, pouring on oil and wine; then he set
him on his own beast and brought him to an inn, and took care of
him.

And the next day he took out two denarii and gave them to the
innkeeper, saying, "Take care of him; and whatever more you
spend, I will repay you when I come back."

The man who had two sons

There was a man who had two sons;

and the younger of them said to his father, "Father, give me the share of property that falls to me." And he divided his living between them. Not many days later, the younger son turned everything into cash and took his journey into a far country, and there he squandered his property in loose living. And when he had spent everything, a great famine arose in that country, and he began to be in want. So he went and joined himself to one of the citizens of that country, who sent him into his fields to feed swine. And he would gladly have filled his belly with the carob pods that the swine ate; and no one gave him anything. But when he came to himself he said, "How many of my father's hired servants have bread enough and to spare, but I perish here with hunger! I will arise and go to my father, and I will say to him, "Father, I have sinned against heaven and before you; I am no longer worthy to be called your son; treat me as one of your hired servants." And he arose and came to his father.

But while he was yet at a distance, his father saw him and ran and embraced him and kissed him. And the son said to him, "Father, I have sinned against heaven and before you; I am no longer worthy to be called your son." But the father said to his servants, "Bring quickly the best robe, and put it on him; and put a ring on his hand, and shoes on his feet; and bring the fatted calf and kill it, and let us eat and make merry; for this my son was dead, and is alive again." And they began to make merry.

Now his elder son was in the field; and as he came and drew near to the house, he heard music and dancing. And he called one of the servants and asked what this meant. And he said to him, "Your brother has come, and your father has killed the fatted calf, because he has received him safe and sound." But he was angry and would not go in. His father came out and tried to conciliate him, but he answered his father, "Lo, these many years I have served you, and I never disobeyed your command; yet you never gave me a kid, that I might make merry with my friends. But when this son of yours came, who has devoured your living with harlots, you killed for him the fatted calf!"

And he said to him, "Son, you are always with me, and all that is mine is yours. It was fitting to make merry, for this your brother was dead, and is alive."

Index of names and titles

Index of references to early Christian writings